SHREEMAD BHAGA

CHAPTER I & II

ORIGINAL SANSKRIT TEXT WITH ROMAN TRANSLITERATION, WORD-FOR-WORD MEANING, TRANSLATION AND COMMENTARY

By

SWAMI CHINMAYANANDA

CENTRAL CHINMAYA MISSION TRUST
MUMBAI-400 072

Reprint		1989	-	3000 copies
Reprint		1991	-	3000 copies
Reprint	July	1995	-	3000 copies
Reprint	July	1999	-	1000 copies
Reprint	December		-	1000 copies
Reprint	November	2000	-	1000 copies
Reprint	December	2001	-	2000 copies
Reprint	April	2003	-	2000 copies
Reprint	April	2005	-	2000 copies
Reprint	July	2006	-	2000 copies

Published by:

CENTRAL CHINMAYA MISSION TRUST
Sandeepany Sadhanalaya
Saki Vihar Road,
Mumbai - 400 072, INDIA.
Tel: 91-22-28572367 / 28575806
Fax: 91-22-28573065
Email: ccmt@vsnl.com
Website: www.chinmayamission.com

Distribution Centre in USA:

CHINMAYA MISSION WEST
Publications Division,
560 Bridgetown Pike,
Langhorne, PA 19053, USA.
Tel: (215) 396-0390
Fax: (215) 396-9710
Email: publications@chinmaya.org
Website: www.chinmayapublications.org

Printed by

SAGAR UNLIMITED
28-B, Nand-Deep Industrial Estate,
Kondivita Lane, Andheri Kurla Road,
Mumbai-400 059.
Tel.: 28362777 / 28227699

Price: Rs. 65=00

ISBN 81-7597-084-7

CONTENTS

TRANSLITERATION AND PRONNUCIATION GUIDE

ॐ	oṁ	home	ॐ	oṁ	Rome
अ	a	fun	ट	ṭa	touch
आ	ā	car	ठ	ṭha	ant-hill
इ	i	pin	ड	ḍa	duck
ई	ī	feen	ढ	ḍha	godhood
उ	u	put	ण	ṇa	thunder
ऊ	ū	pool	त	ta	(close to) think
ऋ	ṛ	rig	थ	tha	(close to) pathetc
ॠ	ṝ	(long ṛ)	द	da	(close to) father
ऌ	ḷ	*	ध	dha	(close to) breathe hard
ए	e	play	न	na	numb
ऐ	ai	high	प	pa	purse
ओ	o	over	फ	pha	sapphire
औ	au	cow	ब	ba	but
अं	aṁ	**	भ	bha	abhor
अः	aḥ	***	म	ma	mother
क	ka	kind	य	ya	young
ख	kha	blockhead	र	ra	run
ग	ga	gate	ल	la	luck
घ	gha	log-hut	व	va	virtue
ङ	ṅa	sing	श	śa	shove
च	ca	chunk	ष	ṣa	bushel
छ	cha	match	स	sa	sir
ज	ja	jug	ह	ha	house
झ	jha	hedgehog	ळ	(Note 1)	(close to) wiorld
ञ	ña	bunch	क्ष	kṣa	worksheet
त्र	tra	three	ज्ञ	jña	*
ऽ		unpronounced (a)	ऽऽ	"	Unpronounced (ā)

Note 1: "ḷ" itself is sometimes used. * No English Equivalent.
** Nasaḷisation of the preceding vowel. *** Aspiration of preceding vowel

Shreemad Bhagawad Geeta

Chapter – I

Preface to the Revised Edition

As detailed------ under "*Mahābhārata* in Brief," on return from their long sojourn of 13 years in forest and incognito *Pāṇḍavā*-s claimed their kingdom back, as assured by *Dhṛtarāṣṭra* at the time of their departure. *Duryodhana* who enjoyed the empire without a rival all these years refused to surrender even "enough land which can be carried on the tip of a needle, without war."

War, thus, became inevitable and *Pāṇḍavā*-s approached their mother *Kuntī* for permission. *Kuntī* had a unique personality with exemplary forbearance. She desired no worldly pleasures nor kingdom. She even implored upon Lord *Kṛṣṇ*a to grant her the boon of adversity, which retains one on the path of righteousness, and she may have Lord's rare vision always enabling her to be out of the cycle of rebirth-----*Saṁsāra Cakra* (*Śrīmad Bhāgavat* I-viii-25). But two incidents had hurt her too deeply to be cured even after a lapse of time—One was the sadistically vain effort by *Duryodhana* to disrobe her beloved daughter-in-law *Draupadī* in the presence of all the courtiers in the assembly and—two the vainglorious effort by *Duryodhana*, *Duḥśāsana, Karṇa* and *Śakunī* etc., to arrest Lord *Kṛṣṇa,* when he went to *Hastināpura* as a *Rāja-dūta* (royal emissary) of *Pāṇḍavā*-s with a proposal of reconçiliation, against all cannons of righteous behaviour on the part of a king worth his salt. *Kuntī* thought that such villians need to be put to death before they perpetrate further sinful felonies on the society. She, therefore, granted permission.

In the entire *Gītā, Dhṛtarāṣṭra* the blind king speaks only once i.e., the first verse in Chapter I with which the Song Divine begins and the first words *"Dharma-kṣetre, Kuru-kṣetre"* have special significance. *Kuru-kṣetra* means the land of the *Kurū*-s, because King *Kuru* ruled over it. It is called *Dharma-kṣetra* because gods are said to have performed holy sacrifice, and king *Kuru, too,* did lot of *tapaścarya,* there.

Another significant and noteworthy point here is that both groups of cousins had King *Kuru* as one common ancestor and as such both should be known as *kauravā*-s having common lineage; but the blind King *Dhṛtarāṣṭra* uses the term *"Māmakāḥ"* for his own sons, while *Pāṇḍavā*-s for his brother *Pāṇḍava*'s sons. By considering them *Pāṇḍavā-s* and differentiating them from *Kauravā-s* (the epithet reserved for his own sons), he is subtly trying to eliminate their claim to *Kuru* Kingdom and thus betraying his partial attitude right from first verse in the *Gītā*. Ironically in the entire Song Divine, the sons of *Pāṇḍu* are dubbed as *Pāṇḍavā*-s, whereas sons of *Dhṛtarāṣṭra,* instead of being called *Dhārtarāṣṭrā*-s are analogued as *Kauravā*-s.

The significance of the first chapter depicting Arjuna's grief is meant to show the conditions under which a man generally listens to the "Voice of the Spirit" within. Often it is a mighty crisis or a grave tragedy which opens our eyes to the Spiritual Reality within us.

In this revised Edition diacritical marks are used for Transliteration of *Saṁskṛta* words in the verses as well as commentary. Non-English words have been italicised. Transliteration as well as word meanings have been added to *Gītā Dhyāna Ślokā*-s too. In the 'free translation' section where the entire text is italicised, to distinguish *Saṁskṛta* words, 'normal' fonts are used. In the 'word-for-word meaning' section, for the benefit of readers not knowing *Devanāgarī,* transliteration of *Saṁskṛta* words is added. This will help readers to identify and pronounce the words correctly.

The English plural sign 's' has been added to untranslated *Saṁskṛta* words after a hyphen (-) to show that it is not elemental to the words e.g., *mantrā-s, Vedā-s, Ṛṣī-s* etc.

Macrons are used on the last letter e.g., *'ā, ī'* of such words as *mantrā-s*, *Vedā-s*, *Ṛṣī-s* etc., to lengthen the quantity of sound to keep up with the prolonged sound in pronunciation, although grammer rules do not require so.

The commentary on *Gītā* (chapter-wise) has been reprinted repeatedly to meet continuous demand resulting in numerous inaccuracies, rendering some concepts almost unintelligible. Besides its readability was poor in small print. Both these aspects are taken care of in the revised layout, the credit for which is due to Shri Vishwamitra Puri who with consistent perseverance and devotion scrutinised the entire book very minutely to identify misprints, missing words and lines; added diacritical marks and word meanings, improved the get up; and pursued steadfastly, the suggested changes improvements, with the *Ācārya* of *Sāndīpany* Mumbai for approval.

An "Alphabetical Index" in *Devanāgrī* of the first line of verses, and "Glossary of Terms used," "Index to Topics," "the Essence of *Gītā*," "Appellations of *Arjuna*" and "Names of *Śrī Kṛṣṇa*" are added to the volume containing Chapter-I of the present series. An "Alphabetical Index" in Roman letters, the beginning of first line in case of verses with two lines, and of first and third lines of verses having four lines is being appended at the end Chapter XVIII of the series. *Gītā* (chapter-wise) is being printed afresh in the revised format.

To be true to the *Saṁskṛta* text in transliteration, we have used "*brāhmaṇa*" for the first *Varṇa* instead of the commonly used word "*brahmin.*" It need not be confused with the term "*Brahman*" of the *Vedāntin*-s.

A key to the transliteration and pronunciation is added in the beginning of the book.

We are pleased to bring out the present revised Edition of the original commentary given by *H. H. Svāmī Chinmayānanda* whom we all reverentially refer as *Pūjya*

Gurudeva. This is our humble offering at His holy feet with a prayer that may His words and guidance inspire us to carry on His work in all spheres of activities such as this---publication of scriptural thoughts for the benefit of the society.

Mahā Śivarātrī Day,
25th February, 1998. **Publishers**

INDEX TO TOPICS

The Esssence of *Gītā*

Direct Guidance for Your Problems

Topic	Chapter	Verses
1. What is God?	IV	6, 7, 8, 24.
	V	14, 15, 29.
	VIII	3, 11.
	X	12, 15.
	XI	5, 6, 7, 10, 11, 12, 13, 15 to 20, 23, 37 to 40, 43, 46.
	XIV	27.
	XVII	23 to 27.
2&3. How our Mental Confusion, Delusion, Desires, Passions. destroy our Inner Peace, and how to control them?	I	28 to 31, 35, 45.
	II	3, 6, 11.
	III	27, 36 to 43.
	IV	25 to 30.
	V	33 to 36.
	VII	24 to 30.
	IX	12.
	XI	24, 25, 31.
4. Consolation for :	II	11 to 16, 17, 18, 21, 22, 25 to 30.
a. Bereaved		
b. Disillusioned	III	16, 18.
c. Disappointed	IV	40.
d. Morally slipped	VI	37, 38, 40 to 45.
e. Spiritually fallen	VIII	14, 15, 16.
	XI	32, 33.

Topic	Chapter	Verses
	XII	9, 10, 11.
	XIII	8.
5. Guidance to :	II	26, 33, 34, 47, 48.
a. Politicians		50.
b. Business-men	III	8, 12, 13, 17, 21, 35.
c. Teenagers	IV	15, 16, 17, 31, 33, 34, 35 to 39, 42.
	VI	9.
	XIV	25.
	XVI	1, 2, 3.
	XVII	3.
	XVIII	47, 60.
6. The Grand Vision of the Universe :	XV	1, 2, 3.
7. God is everywhere, in all :	II	12, 17, 19, 20, 24.
	VIII	3, 4.
	IX	16 to 19, 24.
	X	4, 5, 6, 20 to 39.
	XIII	13 to 17.
	XV	6, 12 to 19.
	XVIII	46, 61.
8. The Secret of Action :	II	39 to 53.
	III	4 to 9, 11, 14, 15, 19, 20, 21, 29.
	IV	12, 18, 41.
	VII	4 to 11, 21.
	XVIII	11, 18, 56, 57, 60.

Topic	Chapter	Verses
9. How man can step up :	II	14, 71.
a. Efficiency	III	22 to 25, 33, 34, 35.
b. Inner Peace	IV	42.
c. Concentration	VI	6, 15.
d. Usefulness to others	IX	18.
and Joy to Himself	XI	55.
	XII	12.
	XIII	8.
	XV	5, 8, 10, 11.
	XVIII	62, 66.
10. Tips for Meditation :	II	17, 20, 21, 23, 24, 25, 28, 29, 45, 55, 61, 69.
	III	17, 28, 30, 43.
	IV	6 to 11, 13, 14, 24 to 27, 35.
	V	7, 8, 9, 13, 17,19, 20, 21, 24, 27, 28, 29.
	VI	7, 8, 10 to 14, 16, 17, 18, 20, 21, 22, 24, 25 to 32, 47.
	VII	7, 12, 14, 19, 30.
	VIII	5, 7 to 10, 12, 13, 14, 20, 21, 22.
	IX	4, 5, 6, 13, 14, 15, 18, 22, 29, 34.
	X	3, 8, 9, 10, 12, 20, 39, 41, 42.
	XI	7, 17, 18, 37, 38, 46, 55.

	Topic	Chapter	Vers
		XII	2, 3, 6, 7, 8, 14.
		XIII	10 to 17, 22, 24, 27, 28 to 32.
		XIV	19, 23, 26, 27.
		XV	4, 5, 15, 17, 19.
		XVI	1.
		XVIII	20, 46, 54, 55, 57, 61, 62, 65, 66, 77.
11.	The Nature of a Perfect Man—Spiritually evolved in full :	II	21, 54 to 72.
		III	26, 28.
		IV	9, 10, 18 to 23.
		V	3, 5, 7 to 11, 13, 18, 20, 22 to 26.
		VI	7 to 10.
		VIII	24, 28.
		XII	13 to 19.
		XIV	22 to 25.
		XVI	1, 2, 3.
		XVIII	10, 11, 12, 17, 49, 50 to 54.
12.	Signs of :		
	a. Spiritual Growth	XIV	5 to 18, 20, 26.
	b. Spiritual Fall	XVII	8 to 22.
	c. Impotent Stagnation	XVIII	5 to 9, 17, 20 to 28, 33 to 35, 37 to 39.
13.	The Distict Nature of "Matter" :	IX	8.
		XIII	19, 20, 21.
		XIV	3, 4.

Topic	Chapter	Verses
14. The Beauties of the "Spirit" :	IV	11, 13, 14.
	XIII	22 to 33.
15. Some effective Techniques of Meditation :	VI	1 to 6.
	VII	1, 3, 12 to 19.
	IX	5, 6, 13, 14, 15, 22, 23, 25 to 34.
16. The ways of reaching the Divine Goal :	II	17, 20, 21, 24, 25, 38, 45, 47 to 51, 55 to 58, 61, 64, 68, 71.
	III	7, 9, 17, 19, 25, 28, 30, 34.
	IV	6, 8 to 11, 14, 18 to 28, 34, 38, 39, 41, 42.
	V	2 to 8, 10 to 13, 17 to 21, 24, 25, 26, 28, 29.
	VI	1, 3, 4, 7 to 10, 14, 18, 20, 25, 26, 29 to 32, 35, 47.
	VII	1, 7, 12, 14, 16, 19, 23, 28, 29, 30.
	VIII	5, 7, 8, 9, 13, 14, 22, 24, 27.
	IX	4, 5, 6, 9, 13, 14, 15, 17, 18, 19, 22.
	X	25, 26, 27, 29 to 34.
	XI	7, 11, 13, 15 to 20, 36, 38, 39 40, 43, 46, 54, 55.
	XII	2, 3, 6, 7 to 19.

Topic	Chapter	Verses
	XIII	2, 7 to 17, 22, 24, 25, 27 to 32.
	XIV	19, 20, 22 to 27.
	XV	1, 4, 5, 15, 19.
	XVI	1, 2, 3.
	XVII	11,16, 20, 23, 25, 27.
	XVIII	2, 9, 10, 11, 17, 20, 23, 33, 42, 46, 49, 55, 56, 57, 62, 65, 66, 68, 70.
17. The Glory of the *Gītā* :	VIII	28.
	XVIII	67 to 71, 75 to 78.

The Appellations of Arjuna as defined in the Gītā.

Anagha	—	The sinless one.
Arjuna	—	The pure in nature.
	—	One who is not crooked.
Bharatarṣabha	—	The best among the descendant of *Bharata.*
Bhārata	—	The descendant of King *Bharata.*
	—	One who is revelling in Truth (Light)
Bhārata-sattama	—	The best of the *Bhāratā-s.*
Bhārata-śreṣṭha	—	The noblest amongst the *Bhāratā-s.*
Dhanañjaya	—	The conqueror of wealth. (During the *Rājasūya Yajña, Arjuna* defeated numerous kings and appropriated the hidden and stagnant wealth of the inactive rulers, which he utilised for public welfare.)
Guḍākeśa	—	The conqueror of sleep. (*Guḍākā* means sleep and *Īśa* is Lord).
Kapidhvaja	—	He whose ensign is a monkey.
Kaunteya	—	The son of *Kuntī.*
Kirīṭī	—	He who wears a diadem (given by *Indra)* in his crown.
Kurunandana	—	The joy of the *Kurū-s.*
Kuruśreṣṭha	—	The best of the *Kurū-s.*
Mahābāhu	—	The mighty-armed (brave).
Narottama	—	The best among men.

Pāṇḍava	—	The son of *Paṇḍu* (being the chief of all *Pāṇḍvā-s*—it is used for *Arjuna*).
Pārtha	—	The son of *Pṛthā* (which is another name of *Kuntī*).
Parantapa	—	The scorcher of foes.
Puruṣa-śarabha	—	The best among men.
Puruṣa-vyāghra	—	The tiger among the men.
Savyasācin	—	One who could shoot arrows with his left hand.

The Names of Śrī Kṛṣṇa employed in the Gītā.

Acyuta — He who does not fall from His divine nature.

Arisūdana — He who destroys the enemies.

Bhagavān — He who is endowed with *Bhâga* (wealth). [The six-fold wealth comprises of power, virtue, fame, glory, detachment and freedom.]

Devam — The Supreme Lord.
— The Effulgent One.

Deveśa — The Lord of Gods.

Deva — The Bestower of light.

Govinda — The knower of the *Jīvātman.*
— The Rulers of senses.
— The Saviour of cows.
— An epithet of *Indra*—in the sense of "the finder of the cows."
[According to the legend in *Sant Parva*, he got this name on "winning back the earth."]

Hariḥ — The destroyer of all sins.
— The Looter of Ego.

Hṛṣikeśa — The Lord of the senses.
(*Hṛṣīka* = senses and *Īśa* = Lord)
— The One with Curly Hair.
— The One with Short (standing upright) Hair.
[*Hṛṣ* = standing on end (in delight), (also curly) and *Keśa* = hair.]

Jagannivāsa — The abode of the Universe (in one of His limbs, Cosmic form).

Janārdana — He who is adored by devotees for the fulfilment of their desires.
— Killer of the demon *Jana.*

Keśava — He who has beautiful hair.

-- He who removes all our sufferings and sorrows. [*Keśava* is a term spoilt from *Kleśva* meaning who removes all *Kleśā-s.*]

— The Lord of the Trinity:

'K' stands for Lord *Brahmā*, the Creator;

'A' stands for Lord *Viṣṇu*, the Preserver;

'*Īśa*' stands for Lord *Śaṅkara*, the Destroyer;

'Va' stands for *Vapu* i.e., body or *Svarūpa.*

Keśinīsūdana— He who slaughtered the demon called *Keśin.*

Kṛṣṇa — The dark one.

— The remover of sins.

— He who is *Brahman.*

— He who attracts.

Mādhava — The Lord of *Lakṣmī.*

(*Mā* means *Lakṣmī* and *Dhava* is Controller.)

Madhusūdana— He who destroyed the demon named *Madhu.*

— He who destroys *vāsanā-s.*

[*Madhu* in *Vedik* symbolism, is *Karma-phala*—Impression of the past actions.]

Narottama — The best among men.

Nārāyaṇa — Lord *Viṣṇu.*

Puruṣottama— The Supreme Person.

Vārṣṇeya — He who belongs to the *Vṛṣṇi* clan.

Vāsudeva — The son of *Vasudeva.*

— The Immanent in all.

Viṣṇu — The all pervading One.

Yādava — He who comes of the *Yadu* clan.

Yogeśvara — The Lord of *Yoga.*

Glossary of the Terms used in the *Gītā*

(A) Terms along with their meanings arranged in *Devanāgarī* alphabetical order

Terms	Meanings	Ch. & Verse
Adhidaiva	*Brahmā*, the Creator	VIII-1.
Adhibhūta	perishable world	VIII-1, 4.
Adhiyajñaḥ	Lord *Viṣṇu*	VIII-2, 4.
Ananyāḥ (cetaḥ)	exclusively (mind)	IX-22.
Aparā (prakṛti)	lower (Nature)	VII-5.
Avyakta	unmanifest	II-25; VIII-18, 20, 21; XII-5.
Avyabhicāriṇī	unswerving	XIII-10; XVIII-33; XIV-26.
Aśraddadhānaḥ	faithless	IV-40.
Asaktaṁ	unattached	IX-9; XIII-14.
Asat	unreal	IX-19; XI-37; XIII-12; XVII-28.
Asaṁmuḍhaḥ	undeluded	V-20; X-3, XV-19.
Asvargyam	excluding-heaven	II-2.
Ahaṅkāra	egoism	III-27; XVI-18; XVIII-53, 59.
Ātmā, *Ātmānaṁ*	Self (soul)	VI-5, 6; VII-18; IX-5; X-20; XIII-32.
Ādidevaḥ	Primal Deity	XI-38.
Ābrahma-bhuvanāt	Upto the world of *Brahmā*, the Creator	VIII-16.
Āsurī	demoniac	XVI-5.

Terms	Meanings	Chapter & Verse
Āstikyam	belief in God	XVIII-42.
Icchā	desire	XIII-6.
Indriyasya	sense	III-34.
Iṣṭaḥ	beloved, worshipped	XVIII-64, XVIII-70.
Īśvaraḥ	the Lord	IV-6.
Uccaiḥśravasam	Indra's vehicle, the king of horses	X-27.
Ucciṣṭam	refuse	XVII-10.
Udāsīnaḥ	unconcerned, indifferent, neutral.	VI-9; XII-16.
Uparamate	quietude	VI-20.
Uśanā	*Śukrācārya,* the learned preceptor of the demons	X-37.
Ṛk	One of the four *Vedā-s.*	IX-11.
Ṛddham	affluent rich,	II-28.
Ṛṣayaḥ	sages, holy men	V-25; X-13.
Ekākṣaram	One syllabled—*Oṁ*	VIII-13.
Airāvatam	Indra's elephant, born at the time of churning the ocean.	X-27.
Oṁ	sacred one syllabled *Auṁ, Brahma* (the Absolute)	VIII-13; XVII-23,24.
Oṁkāra	sacred one syllabled *Auṁ, Brahma* (the Absolute)	IX-17.

Terms	Meanings	Chapter & Verse
Karmaṇaḥ	action	III-1, 9; IV-17; XIV-16; XVIII-7, 12.
Karmaphale	fruits of action	IV-14.
Karmabandhanaḥ	bound by action	III-9.
Karmayogam	Discipline (path) of action	III-7.
Karmasaṅgena	attachment to action	XIV-7.
Karmasaṅgrahaḥ	constituents (basis) of action	XVIII-18.
Kāma-krodha	desire (lust)-anger	XVI-12.
Kārya-kāraṇa-kartṛtve	effect, instrument and agent	XIII-20.
Kuntībhojaḥ	*Kunti's* brother	I-5.
Kuntīputraḥ	*Kuntī's* sons (*Arjuna, Bhīma* & *Yudhiṣṭhira*)	I-16.
Kurukṣetre	land of the *Kurū-s* (*Kuru* family)	I-1.
Kṣatriyāḥ	a warrior (a member of the warrior class)	II-32.
Kṣaram	perishable	XV-18.
Kṣetra	field (body) (Nature)	XIII-1.
Kṣetrajña (*Kṣetrī*)	knower of the field (Soul) (Spirit)	XIII-1.
Gatiṁ	end	VI-37.
Gatiḥ	path (Nature)	IV-17.
Gatī	path	VIII-26.
Gandharva	*Gandharvā-s* are celestial singers & musicians	XI-22.

Terms	Meanings	Chapter & Verse
Gāṇḍīvaṁ	*Arjuna's* bow	I-30.
Gāyatrī	most important of all the metres contained in the *Vedā-s*.	X-35.
Guṇa	modes (attributes) of *Prakṛti* (Nature)	III-28, 29.
Guṇasaṅgaḥ	attachment to the modes	XIII-21.
Guṇātītaḥ	risen above (transcend) the modes of nature	XIV-25.
Guruḥ	teacher (preceptor)	XI-43.
Gṛhastha	householder (Inference)	III-13.
Cāturvarṇyaṁ	fourfold caste (order)	IV-13.
Citraratha	the most prominent celestial singer	X-26.
Cekitānaḥ	A *Yādava* (a member of the *Yādava* family who fought on the side of the *Pāṇḍavā-s*)	I-5.
Chandasāmaham	of the metres (*Vedik* verses)	X-35.
Jātidharmāḥ	caste/religious rites (traditions)	I-43.
Jitasaṅgadoṣā	victorious over the evil of attachment	XV-5.
Jitātmā	subdued the self (body etc.)	XVIII-49
Jitendriyaḥ	subdued the senses	V-7.
Jīvabhūtaḥ	having become a soul	XV-7.
Jīvaloke	in the world of life	XV-7.

Terms	Meanings	Chapter & Verse
Jñāna	knowledge (through the study of scriptures)	VI-8.
Jñānacakṣuṣaḥ	eye of wisdom (knowledge)	XV-10; XIII-34.
Jñānatapasā	penance of wisdom (knowledge)	IV-10.
Jñānadīpena	lamp of wisdom (knowledge)	X-11.
Jñānayajñena	by knowledge sacrifice (wisdom-sacrifice)	IX-15.
Jñānayogena	by the Path (Discipline) of Knowledge	III-3.
Jñānī	man of wisdom (wise)	VII-16, 17, 18.
Jyotiṣāṁ	among lights (luminaries)	X-21.
Tattvadarśinaḥ	the wise (seers of Truth)	IV-34.
Tattvavittu	knower of Truth	III-28.
Tattvam	true nature (Truth or essence)	XVIII-1.
Tapasā (tapaḥ)	penance (austerity)	VII-9.
Tapasviṣu	ascetics	VII-9.
Tamasaḥ	darkness of ignorance	VIII-9; XIII-17; XIV-16, 17.
Tamasā	darkness	XVIII-32.
Daivī	divine	VII-14; XVI-5.
Daivīm	divine	IX-13; XVI-3, 5.
Dravyayajñāḥ	wealth-sacrifice	IV-28.
Drupadaputreṇa	*Dhṛṣṭadyumna*, the son of *Drupada*	I-3.

Terms	Meanings	Chapter & Verse
Droṇam	name of the teacher of the *Pāṇḍavā-s*	II-4; XI-34.
Dvandavaḥ	duality	X-33.
Dvandvātītaḥ	who is free from pairs of opposites	IV-22.
Dvijottama	best of the twice-born	I-7.
Dhanurdharaḥ	wielder of the bow	XVIII -78.
Dharmakṣetre	holy field (field of righteousness)	I-1.
Dharme	pious traditions (pious conduct)	I-40.
Dharmam	duty	II-33.
Dharmyāmṛtam	immortal wisdom	XII-20.
Dhātā	supporter	IX-17.
Dhārtarāṣṭrasya	(*Duryodhana*) the son of *Dhṛtarāṣṭra*	I-33.
dhyānaṁ	Meditation	XII-12.
Namaskuru (namaḥ)	bow down, prostrate	IX-34; XVIII-65.
Narake	in the hell	I-44; XVI-16.
(Narakasya)	of the hell	XVI-21.
Navadvāre	nine gates (two ears, two eyes, two nostrils, mouth, genital organ, anus)	V-13.
Naṣṭātmānaḥ	ruined soul	XVI-9.
Nāmayajñaiḥ	sacrifice in name	XVI-17.
Nityayuktasya	always absorbed (ever steadfast)	VIII-14.
Nityasaṁnyāsī	perpetual renouncer (ascetic)	V-3.

Terms	Meanings	Chapter & Verse
Nidrālasya pramādottham	sleep, indolence, heedlessness	XVIII-39.
Nidhānaṁ	store house	IX-18.
Nibaddhaḥ	bound	XVIII-60.
Nimittamātraṁ	merely an instrument	XI-33.
Niyatamānasaḥ	subdued (controlled mind)	VI-15.
Niyatātmabhiḥ	person of steadfast mind	VIII-2.
Tāmasī	mode (nature) of ignorance	XVII-2; XVIII-32, 35.
Tejaḥ	glory (splendour)	VII-10; X-36; XV-12.
Tejaḥ	vigour	XVI-3; XVIII-43.
Tyaktasarva parigahaḥ	giving up all possessions	IV-21.
Tyāgaḥ	renunciation (relinquishment)	XVI-2; XVIII-49.
Tyāgī	relinquisher	XVIII-11.
Traiguṇya	three modes (attributes)	II-45.
Traividyā	knowers of the three *Vedā-s*	IX-20.
Dakṣiṇāyanam	six month of the southern passage (path) of the Sun	VIII-25.
Dambho	hypocrisy (ostentation)	XVI-4.
Dayā	compassion	XVI-2.
Darpaḥ	arrogance	XVI-4.

Terms	Meanings	Chapter & Verse
Dānaṁ (dāna)	charity (gift)	X-5; XVI-1; XVII-7, 20, 22, 25; XVIII-5, 43.
Divyāḥ	divine	X-16, 19.
Dīrghasūtrī	procrastinating	XVIII-28.
Durbuddheḥ	evil minded	I-23.
Durmatiḥ	man of perverse mind	XVIII-16.
Duḥkhayonayaḥ	sources of pain	V-22.
Duḥkhālayam	abode of pain	VIII-15.
Dṛḍhaniścayaḥ	unshakable in determination	XII-14.
Dṛḍhavratāḥ	firm resolve	VII-28.
Devadeva	God of gods	X-15.
Devayajāḥ	worshippers of gods	VII-23.
Devarṣiḥ	celestial sage	X-13
Dehabhṛtā	embodied being	XVIII-11.
Dehavadbhiḥ	by the embodied	XII-5.
Dehī	the embodied	II-22, 30; V-13; XIV-20.
Daityānām	among demons	X-30.
Daivaḥ	the divine	XVI-6.
Niṣṭhā	path	III-3.
Nistraiguṇyo	free from the three attributes (modes)	II-45.
Niḥśreyasakarau	lead to salvation	V-2.
Niḥspṛhaḥ	free from thirst for enjoyment	II-71.
Nīti	righteousness (firm or wise policy)	X-38; XVIII-78.

Terms	Meanings	Chapter & Verse
Naiṣkarmyasiddhiṁ	the Supreme State consisting in freedom from action	XVIII-49.
Naiṣkarmyaṁ	actionlessness	III-4.
Naiṣkṛtikaḥ	malicious	XVIII-28.
Naiṣṭhikīṁ	everlasting (final)	V-12.
Nyāyyaṁ	right	XVIII-15.
Nyāsaṁ	renunciation	XVIII-2.
Paṇavānaka-gomukhāḥ	tabors, drums, cowhorns	I-13.
Paradharmaḥ	duty of another	III-35.
Paramātmā	the Supreme Spirit (God)	VI-7; XIII-22, 31; XV-17.
Parameśvara	Lord Supreme	XIII-27.
Pitaraḥ	manes, fore-fathers	I-34, 42.
Purāṇaḥ	ancient (primeval)	II-20; XI-38.
Puruṣaḥ	Self (soul)	XV-17.
Prakṛtiḥ (mūlā)	Nature (Basic—Primordial Matter)	VII-4; IX-10; XIII-20; XVIII-59
Prajāpatiḥ	the creator (*Brahmā*)	III-10.
Praṇipātena	prostration (humble reverence)	IV-34.
Prapadye	refuge	XV-4.
Prabhuḥ	Lord	V-14; IX-18, 24.
Pramādaḥ	heedlessness (negligence)	XIV-13.
Prayāṇakāle	at the hour of death	VII-30; VIII-2, 10
Pralaya	dissolution, annihilation	VII-6; IX-18; XIV-14, 15.

Terms	Meanings	Chapter & Verse
Pravṛttiḥ	activity	XIV-12; XV-4; XVIII-46.
Prasaktāḥ	addicted	XVI-16.
Prasāda	placidity (serenity or purity) of mind	II-64, 65.
Prāṇāpāna	ingoing and outgoing life-breaths	IV-29; XV-14.
Prāṇāyāma	breath restraint	
Pretān	ghosts, spirits	XVII-4.
Phala (hetavaḥ)	(seeker after) fruit (reward)	II-49.
Badhyate	bound	IV-14.
Bahu-daṁṣṭrā-karālaṁ	many terrible tusks	XI-23.
Buddhiḥ	mind, intellect (intelligence)	II-39, 41, 44, 52, 53, 65, 66.
Brahma	the Absolute (God)	IV-24.
Brahmacaryam	celibacy	VIII-11; XVII-14.
Brahmanirvāṇam	beatitude of God (*Brāhmik* bliss)	II-72; V-24, 25, 26
Brahmabhūtaḥ	identified with *Brahma* (the Absolute)	V-24; XVIII-54.
Brahmabhūyāya	for becoming *Brahma* (the Absolute)	XIV-26; XVIII-53.
Brāhmaṇa-kṣatriya-viśāṁ	the three *Varṇā-s* (castes) known as *Brāhmaṇa, Kṣatriya* and *Vaiśya*.	XVIII-41.
Brāhmī	*Brāhmik* state (eternal state of beautitude of God)	II-72.

Terms	Meanings	Chapter & Vers
Bhaktaḥ	devotee	IV-3; VII-21; IX-31.
Bhakti	devotion	XIII-10.
Bhagavan	the blessed Lord	X-14, 17.
Bhajatāṁ	worshipping	X-10.
Bhāvaiḥ	nature	VII-13.
Bhūtānām	beings	IV-6; X-5, 20, 22; XI-2; XIII-15; XVIII-46.
Bhoktā	enjoyer, experiencer	IX-24; XIII-22.
Bhogaiśvarya-prasaktānāṁ	attached to pleasures and prosperity [man (embodied soul) is a fragment of God]	II-44.
Manaḥ (manasā)	mind	I-30; II-60; (III-6, 7; V-11, 13).
Madhyastha	mediator	VI-9.
Manaḥ prasādaḥ	cheerfulness of mind	XVII-16.
Manīṣiṇām	the wise (philosophers)	XVIII-5, 3; II-51.
Mantraḥ	hymns	IX-16; XVII-13.
Maharṣayaḥ	sages	X-2, 6.
Mahātmā	great soul	VII-19; XI-50.
Mahābhūtāni	the five great (subtle) elements	XIII-5.
Mātrāsparśaḥ	contact of senses with their objects	II-14.
Māyā	divine illusion	VII-14.
Mārgaśīrṣaḥ	a month of *Hindū* calender	X-35.

Terms	Meanings	Chapter & Verse
Muktam (muktaḥ)	liberated	V-28; XII-15; XVIII-40;XVIII-71.
Muniḥ	sage	II-56; V-6, 28; X-26.
Mumukṣubhiḥ	seekers of liberation	IV-15.
Mūḍhaḥ (mūḍhāḥ)	deluded (ignorant)	VII-25; VII-15; IX-11; XVI-20.
Mṛtyu-saṁsāra-sāgarāt	ocean of death bound existence	XII-7.
Mokṣam	liberation (salvation)	XVIII-30.
Mohaḥ	delusion	XI-1; XIV-13; XVIII-73.
Maunī	(silent) he who thinks of God only	XII-19.
Yakṣa-rākṣasām	genies and demons	X-23; XVII-4.
Yajur	one of the four *Vedā-s*	IX-17.
Yajñadānatapaḥ	sacrfice, gift, penance	XVIII-3, XVII-25.
Yatacittasya	disciplined (controlled) mind	VI-19.
Yatacetasām	those who have subdued (controlled) their minds.	V-26.
Yatavākkāya-mānasaḥ	speech, body, mind subdued (controlled)	XVIII-52.
Yatātmavān (yatātmā)	self-controlled	XII-11, 14.
Yantrārūḍhāni	mounted on a machine	XVIII-61.
Yamaḥ	god of death	X-29; XI-39.

Terms	Meanings	Chapter & Verse
Yuktacetasaḥ	steadfast mind	VII-30.
Yuktatamaḥ	most devout	VI-47.
Yuktatamāḥ	most perfect (best versed) in *Yoga*	XII-2.
Yuktaḥ	a *Karmayogī* (a *Sāṅkhya-yogī*)	V-12, (V-8).
Yuktātmā	steadfast in mind	VII-18.
Yogakṣemaṁ	gain and security	IX-22.
Yogabhraṣṭaḥ	He who has fallen (deviated from *Yoga*)	VI-41.
Yogaḥ	equanimity (even-mindedness)	II-48.
Vijñāna	wisdom (Self-Realisation)	VI-8.
Vyaktayaḥ	manifest	VIII-18.
Vyavasāyātmikā	determinate (resolute, single pointed)	II-41, 44.
Vyāsaprasādāt	by the grace of *Vyāsa*	XVIII-75.
Vaiśya	trading class	XVIII-44.
Vānaprastha	retired order	
Śaṅkhaṁ	conch	I-12, 13, 14.
Śabdha brahma	rules laid down in the *Vedā-s*	VI-44.
Śaraṇam	refuge	II-49; IX-18; XVIII-62, 66.
Śarīravāṅmanobhiḥ	body, speech, mind	XVIII-15.
Śarīrasthaṁ	dwelling (seated) in the body	XVII-6.

Terms	Meanings	Chapter & Verse
Śāntiḥ (śāntim)	peace (tranquillity)	II-66, (II-70, 71 etc.) XII-12; XVI-2.
Śāstravidhānoktam	said in the ordinance of the scriptures	XVI-24.
Śāstravidhi	ordinance of the scriptures	XVI-23.
Śuklakṛṣṇe	the bright and dark	VIII-26.
Śūdrasya	one of the four *Varṇā-s* (castes) (service class)	XVIII-44.
Śraddhā	faith	XVII-2, 3.
Śradhāvān	man of faith	IV-39.
Śreyaḥ	good (better)	I-31; II-5, 7; III-2.
Ṣaṇmāsā (śūklaḥ)	six months of the northern path of the sun	VIII-24.
Ṣaṇmāsā (kṛṣṇaḥ)	six months of the southern path of the sun	VIII-25.
Saṅgaḥ	attachment	II-47, 62.
Sataḥ	real	II-16.
Samatā (samattvam)	equanimity (even-mindedness)	X-5; II-48.
Samabuddhayaḥ (samabuddhiḥ)	alike, even-minded	XII-4; VI-9.
Sarvagataḥ	all-pervading	II-24.
Sarvaguhyatamaṁ	most secret	XVIII-64.
Sarvadehinām	all embodied beings	XIV-8
Sarvadharmān	all duties	XVIII-66.

Terms	Meanings	Chapter & Verse
Sarvabhūtahite	doing good (welfare) of all beings	V-25, XII-4.
Sarva-loka-maheśvaram	Great Lord of all the worlds.	V-29.
Sarva-saṅkalpa-saṁnyāsī	renouncer of all thoughts of the world.	VI-4.
Sarvārambha-pari-tyāgī	who has renounce all initiative (in action).	XII-16; XIV-25.
Savijñānam	with real knowledge of manifest Divinity i.e., in the world there is nothing else besides the manifestation of God.	VII-2.
Savyasācin	Arjuna, who could shoot arrows with his left hand also	XI-33.
Sahajam (karma)	innate (duty)	XVIII-48.
Saṅkarasya	confusion of castes	III-24.
Saṁnyāsaḥ	renunciation	V-2, 6; XVIII-7.
Saṁnyāsī	renouncer	VI-1.
Sampadaṁ	nature, state.	XVI-3, 4, 5.
Sādhaka	striver (aspirant)	
Sādhanā	spiritual practice or spiritual discipline.	
Sammohaṁ	delusion	VII-27.
Saṁśuddhakilbiṣaḥ	purified from sins	VI-45.
Saṁsiddhim	highest perfection (God-Realisation)	III-20; VIII-15; XVIII-45.
Saṁsparśajā	born of contact (with objects)	V-22.

Terms	Meanings	Chapter & Verse
Sāttvika	nature (mode) of goodness	XVII-11; XVIII-9, 26 etc.
Sādhuḥ	Saint	IX-30.
sādhūnām	good	IV-8.
Sāṅkhyayogam (saṁnyāsa)	the Discipline (path) of Knowledge	V-4.
Sāma	one of the four *Vedā-s*	IX-17.
Siddhānām	Those who have attained perfection	VII-3; X-26.
Siddhiḥ (asiddhiḥ)	success (failure)	IV-12; (II-48; XVIII-26).
Sukṛta-duṣkṛte	good (virtue) and evil (vice)	II-50.
Sukha-duḥkhe	pleasure and pain	II-38.
Sudurācāraḥ	vilest sinner	IX-30.
Suvirūḍhamūlam	firm rooted	XV-3.
Suhṛdam	dis-interested friend (well-wisher)	V-29, (I-27).
Suhṛn-mitrāry-udāsīna-madhya-sthas-dveṣya	well wishers, friends, neutrals, mediators, hateful	VI-9.
Sūkṣmatvāt	because of its subtlety	XIII-15.
Sūta-putraḥ	*Karṇa* (*Karṇa* was brought up by a charioteer)	XI-26.
Saumadattiḥ	*Bhūriśravā,* the son of *Somadatta*	I-8.

Terms	Meanings	Chapter & Verse
Sthita-prajñasya	a man of steadfast (stable) wisdom	II-54, 55.
Sthitadhīḥ	firm in wisdom	II-54, 56.
spṛhā	craving	IV-14; XIV-12.
Smṛti-vibhramaḥ (Smṛti-bhraṁśād)	loss of memory	II-63.
Svargaṁ	heaven	II-37.
Svādhyāya-jñāna-yajñāḥ	study of the scriptures and Knowledge as sacrifice	IV-28.
Harṣa-śokānvitaḥ	moved by joy and sorrow	XVIII-27.
Hita-kāmayayā	wishing welfare	X-1.
Hṛddeśe	in the hearts	XVIII-61.

******

B:—Terms Denoting Multifarious Meaning.

S.No.	Terms & Different Meanings	Ch. & Verse
1.	***Akṣara* (अक्षर)**	
i.	Supreme Being with form and attributes. (सगुण साकार *Saguṇa Sākāra*)	III-15.
ii.	Supreme being without form and attributes. (निर्गुण निराकार *Nirguṇa Nirākāra*)	VIII-3, 11; XI-18, 37 XII-1, 3;
iii.	Supreme Being with & without form as well as attributes (i) + (ii)	VIII-21.
iv.	*Praṇava—Oṁ* (प्रणव—ॐ)	VIII-13
v.	Alphabets (वर्णमाला *Varṇamālā*)	X-33.
vi.	*Jīvātmā* (जीवात्मा)	XV-16, 18.
2.	***Adhyātma* (अध्यात्म)**	
i.	*Paramātmā* (परमात्मा)	X-32; XI-1; XII-11; XV-5.
ii.	*Jīvātmā* (जीवात्मा)	VII-29; VIII-1, 3.
iii.	Discrimination (विवेक *Viveka*)	III-30.
3.	***Apara* (अपर)**	
i.	Otherness (अन्य *anya*)	II-22; IV-25, 27 to 30; VI-22; XIII-24; XVI-14; XVIII-3.
ii.	Lower nature (जड प्रकृति *Jaḍa prakṛti*)	VII-5.
iii.	Later period (आधुनिक काल *ādhunika kāla*)	IV-4.

S.No.	Terms & Different Meanings	Ch. & Verse
4.	***Amṛta* (अमृत)**	
i.	*Parmātma-tattva* (परमात्म तत्त्व)	II-15; IV-31; XIII-12; XIV-20, 27.
ii.	Nactar (सुधा *Sudhā*)	X-18,27;XVIII-37,38.
iii.	Immortality	IX-19.
5.	***Avyakta* (अव्यक्त)**	
i.	*Jīvātmā* (जीवात्मा)	II-25.
ii.	Unmanifest	II-28.
iii.	*Saguṇa Sākāra* (सगुण साकार)	VII-24.
iv.	*Brahmājī's* subtle body	VIII-18, 20.
v.	Nature Root matter (प्रकृति *Prakṛti*)	XIII-5.
vi.	*Saguṇa Nirākāra* (सगुण निराकार)	VIII-20; IX-4.
vii.	*Nirguṇa Nirākāra* (निर्गुण निराकार)	XII-1, 3, 5.
viii.	Both (vi) & (vii) as also *Saguṇa sākāra* (सगुण साकार)	VIII-21
6.	***Avyaya* (अव्यय)**	
i.	*Jīvātmā* (जीवात्मा)	II-17, 21; XIII-31; XIV-5.
ii.	*Bhagavat-svarūpa* (भगवत् स्वरूप)	IV-6, 13; VII-13, 24, 25; IX-13, 18; XI-4, 18; XIV-27; XV-17.
iii.	Unmodifiable	XVIII-20.
iv.	For long time	II-34.
v.	Eternal	IV-1; IX-2; XI-2; XV-1, 5; XVIII-56.
7.	***Ātmā* (आत्मा)**	
i.	Lord with attributes and form	IV-6, 7; VII-18; X-15, 16, 18, 19 XI-3, 4, 47.
ii.	Lord without attributes and form.	VI-25, 26; XVIII-37.

S.No.	Terms & Different Meanings	Ch. & Verse
iii.	Lord with attributes but without form.	II-45; IX-5; XIII-24.
iv.	Self (*Jīvātmā*)	II-55; III-17, 43; IV-35, 36, 41, 42; V-7, 21, 26; VI-5, 6, 7, 8, 18, 20, 28, 29, VII-18; IX-28, 34; X-11; XIII-24, 28, 29; XV-11; XVI-9, 21, 22; XVIII-16, 39.
v.	Man (मनुष्य *Manuṣya)*	II-34; III-13; VI-11; VIII-12; XIV-24; XVI-17, 18; XVII-19.
vi.	Body (शरीर *Śarīra)*	IV-21; V-7; VI-10, 32; XVIII-49.
vii.	Inner equipment (अन्त:करण *Antaḥ karaṇa*)	II-64; III-27; IV-27, 40; V-7, 11, 21; VI-12, 14, 29; VIII-2; IX-26; XI-24; XV-11.
viii.	Mind (मन *Mana)*	VI-10, 15, 19, 36, 47; XIII-7, 16, 54.
ix.	Sense Organs (इन्द्रिय *Indriya)*	XVIII-51.
x.	Mind, intellect and sense organs	XII-11, 14.
xi.	Expression of a peculiar shape, form or thought (तदाकार *Tadākāra*)	II-43; XIV-7; XVIII-27, 44.
8.	***Ātmanaḥ***	
i.	Manifested Lord Himself	X-18
ii.	*Jivātmā*	IV-42; XV-21, 22; XVIII-49
iii.	Human beings	VI-11; VIII-12; XVII-19.
iv.	related to mind	VI-19.

S.No.	Terms & Different Meanings	Ch. & Verse
9.	***Karma* (कर्म)**	
i.	(mere) Action, deed (कर्म मात्र *Karma mātra*)	II-39; III-1, 9, 28, 29, 31; IV-16, 17, 19, 33, 37, 41; V-13, 14; XV-2; XVIII-3, 10, 11, 12, 13, 15, 18, 19, 23, 24, 25.
ii.	The act of manifestation or creation (सृष्टी रचना रूप *Sṛṣṭi-racanā rūpa*)	VII-29; VIII-1; VIII-3.
iii.	Desire-prompted actions (सकाम कर्म *Skāma karma*)	II-43, 49, 51; III-25, *26;* XVIII-2.
iv.	Actions prescribed by *Śāstrā-s* (शास्त्र विहित (शुभ) कर्म *Śāstra vihita (śubha) karma*)	II-47, 48, 50; III-4, 7, 8, 9, 14, 15, 19, 22, 23, 24, 26, 30; IV-12, 14, 15, 18, 20, 23, 24, 32; V-1,2, 10, 11, 12; VI-1, 3, 4, 17; VII-28;IX-12; XI-55; XII-6, 10, 11, 12; XIII-24; XIV-7, 9, 12, 15; XVI-24; XVII-26, 27; XVIII-2, 3, 5, 6, 8, 9, 11, 27, 41 to 48, 56, 57, 60, 71.
v.	Divine & dedicated action (*Kriyā* क्रिया)	III-7, 27; IV-9, 14; IX-9; XIII-29.
10.	***Kāma* (काम)**	
i.	Desire, wish (कामना *Kāmanā*)	II-5, 43, 55, 62, 71; III-37, 39, 43; IV-19; V-12, 23, 26; IV-24; VII-11, 20, 21; XV-5;

S.No.	Terms & Different Meanings	Ch. & Verse
		XVI-10, 12, 18, 21; XVIII-53.
ii.	Lust (कामदेव *Kāmadeva*)	VII-11; XVI-8.
iii.	Longing for objects (पदार्थ *Padārtha*)	II-70; III-10; VI-18; VII-22; IX-21; X-28; XVI-11, 12, 16; XVII-5; XVIII-24.
iv.	Self-interest prompted action (स्वेच्छाचारिता *Svecchācāritā*)	XVI-23.
v.	Desire-ridden (सकाम पुरुष *Sakāma puruṣa*)	IX-21.
10.	***Kāla* (काल)**	
i.	Time (समय *Samaya*)	II-72; IV-2,38; VII-30; VIII-2, 5, 7, 10, 27; X-30; XVII-20, 22.
ii.	Path (मार्ग *Mārga*)	VIII--23
iii.	Cosmic destruction or the Great Deluge (महाप्रलय *Mahāpralaya*)	XI-25.
iv.	*Bhagavān* (भगवान्)	X-33; XI-32.
11.	***Gati, Gatiḥ, Gatim* (गति, गतिः, गतिम्)**	
i.	*Paramātmā* (परमात्मा)	VI-45; VII-18; VIII-13, 21; IX-18, 32; XII-5; XIII-28; XVI-22, 23.
ii.	State (स्थान *Sthāna*)	VI-37; XVI-20.
iii.	Way (जानना *Jānanā*)	V-17.
iv.	Attainment (प्राप्ति *Prāpti*)	II-43.

S.No.	Terms & Different Meanings	Ch. & Verse
12.	**Guṇa (गुण)**	
i.	*Sattva, rajas* and *tamas* (सत्त्व, रजस्, तमस्)	III-27, 29; IV-13; VII-13, 14; XIII-19, 21, 23; XIV-5, 19, 20, 21, 23, 25, 26; XV-2, 10; XVIII-19, 29, 40, 41.
ii.	Objects, instrument (विषय पदार्थ *Viṣaya Padārtha*)	III-28, 29, XIII-14, XIV-23.
iii.	Organs (इन्द्रिय *Indriya*)	III-28.
iv.	Evil tendency (तमोगुण *Tamoguṇa*)	XIV-18.
13.	***Jñāna* (ज्ञान)**	
i.	*Sat-asat viveka* (सत्-असत् विवेक)	III-3, IV-27, 33; V-16; VII-20; IX-15; X-4; XIII-2, 34; XIV-9, 11, 17; XV-10, 15; XVIII-50.
ii.	*Kartavya-akartavya viveka* (कर्तव्य-अकर्तव्य विवेक)	III-39, 40, 41; IV-41, 42; VI-8.
iii.	*Tattva jñāna* (तत्त्व ज्ञान)	IV-19, 23, 33, 34, 36, 37, 38, 39; V-17; X-11; XIII-17; XIV-1, 2; XVI-1.
iv.	*sādhana-samudāya* (साधन समुदाय)	XIII-11, 17, 18.
v.	*Śaraṇagati* (शरणगति)	XVIII-63.
vi.	*Gītādhyānan* (गीताध्यनन्)	XVIII-70.
vii.	*Śāstra-jñāna* (शास्त्र-ज्ञान)	IV-28; XII-12; XVIII-42.
viii.	*Sāmanya-jñāna* (सामान्य-ज्ञान)	III-32; IX-12; X-38; XIV-1, 6; XVIII-18, 19, 20, 21.

S.No.	Terms & Different Meanings	Ch. & Verse
ix.	Profound special knowledge (दृढता पूर्वक मानना *Dṛḍhatā pūrvaka mānanā*)	IV-10; VII-2; IX-1.
14.	***Jñānī* (ज्ञानी)**	
i.	*Tattvajña Mahāpuruṣa* (तत्त्वज्ञ महापुरुष)	III-33.
ii.	*Vivekī sādhaka* (विवेकी साधक)	III-39.
iii.	Wise men—Knower of Truth	IV-34.
iv.	*Śāstrī jñāna* (शास्त्री ज्ञान)	VI-46.
v.	Loving Devotee (प्रेमी भक्त *Premī Bhakta*)	VII-16, 17, 18.
15.	***Deva* (देव)**	
i.	Gods *Indra* etc., Gods (इन्द्रिदि देवता *Indrādi devatā*)	III-11, 12; VII-23; IX-20, 25; X-2, 14. 15. 22; ; XI-15, 52; XVII-4, 14; XVIII-40.
ii.	*Bhagavān Śrī Kṛṣṇa* (भगवान् श्रीकृष्ण)	XI-11, 14, 15, 25, 31, 37, 44, 45.
iii.	*Bhagavāna Viṣṇu* (भगवान् विष्णु)	XI-45.
16.	***Dharma* (धर्म)**	
i.	Moral Duty *Puṇyakarma* (पुण्यकर्म)	I-1; XVIII-31, 32, 34.
ii.	Traditions of the Clan (कुलमर्यादा *Kula-maryādā*)	I-40, 43, 44.
iii.	Practices and duties (कर्तव्य–कर्म *Kartavya-karma*)	I-43; II-7; III-35; XVIII-47, 66.
iv.	Equipoise of the intellect (सम बुद्धि *Sama buddhi*)	II-40.

S.No.	Terms & Different Meanings	Ch. & Verse
v.	Virtue (सद्गुण सदाचार *Sadguṇa-sadācāra*)	IV-7, 8; VII-11; XI-18; XIV-27.
vi.	Sacred doctrine (ज्ञान-विज्ञान *Jñāna-vijñāna*)	IX-3.
vii.	*Vedik* sacrificial duties (सकाम अनुष्ठान *Sakāma-Anuṣṭhāna*)	IX-21.
17.	***Para, parā, param, parām* (पर, परा, परम्, पराम्)**	
i.	Extreme devotion (परायणता *Parāyaṇatā*)	II-43, 61; IV-39; VI-14; XII-6; XVIII-52, 57.
ii.	*Paramātmā* (परमात्मा)	II-59; III-19; V-16; XI-37; XIII-34.
iii.	Superior (सूक्ष्म *Sūkṣma*)	III-42, 43.
iv.	Highest, Supreme (सर्वोत्कृष्ट *Sarvotkṛṣṭa*)	III-11; IV-39; VI-45; VII-13, 24; VIII-10, 20, 22, 26; IX-11, 32; X-12; XI-38, 47; XIII-12, 22, 28; XIV-1; XVI-22, 23; XVIII-50, 54, 62, 68, 75.
v.	After (भविष्य काल *Bhaviṣya kāla*)	II-12.
vi.	Earlier (भूत काल *Bhūta kāla*)	IV-4.
vii.	World beyond (परलोक *Paraloka*)	IV-40.
viii.	Another (अन्य *Anya*)	III-35; XVIII-47.
ix.	Higher (पराम् *Parām*)	VII-5.
x.	Beyond (निर्लिप्तता *Nirliptatā*)	VIII-9; XIII-17; XIV-19.

S.No.	Terms & Different Meanings	Ch. & Verse
18.	***Paramātmā* (परमात्मा)**	
i.	*Nirguṇa-nirākāra* (निर्गुण निराकार)	VI-7.
ii.	*Saguṇa-sākāra* (सगुण साकार)	XV-17.
iii.	*Jīvātmā* (जीवात्मा)	XIII-12, 39.
19.	***Puruṣa* (पुरुष)**	
i.	Man (साधारण पुरुष *Sādhāraṇa puruṣa*)	III-36; IX-3; XVII-3.
ii.	Man (कर्मयोगी साधक *Karma yogī sādhaka*)	II-60; III-4, 19.
iii.	Man (सांख्य योगी साधक *Sāṅkhya yogī sādhaka*)	II-15, 21.
iv.	*Jīvātmā* (जीवात्मा)	XIII-19, 20, 21, 22, 23.
v.	Perishable & Imperishable (क्षर-अक्षर, नाशवान्-अविनाशी *Kṣara-akṣara—nāśavān-avināśī*)	XV-16.
vi.	Cosmic soul (ब्रह्माजी *Brahmājī*)	VIII-4.
vii.	Supreme Being (सगुण निराकार *Saguṇa-nirākāra*)	VIII-8, 10, 22; XV-4.
viii.	Supreme Being (सगुण साकार *Saguṇa-sākāra*)	X-12; XI-18, 38; XV-17.
20.	***Prakṛti* (प्रकृति)**	
i.	Lower Nature (समष्टि-जड-प्रकृति *Samaṣṭi-Jaḍa-prakṛti*)	III-5, 27, 29; VII-4; IX-7, 8, 10; XIII-19, 20, 21, 23, 29, 34; XIV-5; XV-7; XVIII-40.
ii.	Nature (स्वभाव *Svabhāva*)	III-33; VII-20; IX-8, 12, 13; XVIII-59.

S.No.	Terms & Different Meanings	Ch. & Verse
iii.	Mysterious power or *Māyā śakti* (दिव्य चिन्मय शक्ति *divya cinmaya śakti*)	IV-6.
iv.	*Jīvātmā* (जीवात्मा)	VII-5.
v.	Natural state (स्वाभाविक स्थिति *Svābhāvik sthiti*)	XI-51.
vi.	Bodies (शरीर *Śarīra*)	XIII-21.
21.	***Priya* (प्रिय)**	
i.	Pleasing (अनुकूलता *Anukūlatā*)	V-20
ii.	Dear (प्रेमी *Premī*)	VII-17; XII-14, 15, 16, 17, 19, 20; XVIII-65, 69.
iii.	Attachment (राग *Rāga*)	IX-29.
iv.	Agreeable (रुचि *Ruci*)	XVII-7, 8, 10.
v.	Pleasant (मधुरता *Madhuratā*)	XVII-15.
vi.	Lover (पति *Pati*)	XI-44.
vii.	Beloved (पत्नि *Patni*)	XI-44.
viii.	Favour (हित *Hita*)	I-23.
ix.	Pleasing deed (प्रिय कार्य *Priya kārya*)	XVIII-69.
22.	***Buddhi* (बुद्धि)**	
i.	Unperturbed sameness of mind (अन्त: करण समता *Antaḥ karaṇa ṣsamatā*)	II-39, 49, 50, 51.
ii.	Conviction (अटल निश्चय *Aṭala niścaya*)	II-52, 65, 66; XVIII-17.
iii.	Discriminative faculty (सामान्य बुद्धि *Sāmānya buddhi*)	II-41, 44, 53; III-2, 26, 40, 42, 43; V-11, 28;

S.No.	Terms & Different Meanings	Ch. & Verse
		VI-25; VIII-7; X-4; XII-8, 14; XVIII-16, 29, 30, 31, 32, 49, 51.
iv.	Discriminative insight (विवेक *Viveka*)	II-63, III-1, VII-10.
v.	Purified Intellect (सात्त्विक बुद्धि *Sāttvika buddhi*)	VI-21.
vi.	Macrocosmic Intellect (समष्टि बुद्धि—महत् तत्त्व *Samaṣṭi buddhi—mahat tattva)*	VII-4, XIII-5.
23.	**Brahma (ब्रह्म)**	
i.	*Nirguṇa nirākāra* (निर्गुण निराकार)	II-72; IV-25, 31; V-6, 19, 20, 21, 24, 25, 26, 27, 28; VII-29; VIII-1, 3, 24; XIII-12, 30; XIV-26, 27; XVIII-50, 53, 54.
ii.	*Saguṇa nirākāra* (सगुण निराकार)	III-15; IV-24; VI-38; XVII-23.
iii.	*Saguṇa sākāra* (सगुण साकार)	V-10; X-12.
iv.	*Veda* (वेद)	III-15; IV-32; VI-44; XVII-24.
v.	*Oṁkāra* (प्रणव *Praṇava*)	VIII-13.
vi.	*Brahmājī* (ब्रह्माजी)	VIII-16, 17; XI-15, 37.
vii.	Great Nature (मूला प्रकृति *Mūlā Prakṛti*)	XIV-3, 4.
viii.	*Brāhmaṇa* (ब्राह्मण)	XVIII-42.
24.	***Bhūta* (भूत)**	
i.	Human being (मनुष्य मात्र *Manuṣya Mātra*)	II-69; VII-11; X-5.

S.No.	Terms & Different Meanings	Ch. & Verse
ii.	To become, identify (बनना-होना *Bananā-honā*)	V-7, 24; VI -27; VII- 5; XV-7; XVIII-54.
iii.	Objects (मात्र सृष्टि *Mātra sṛṣṭi*)	VIII-22; IX-4, 5, 6.
iv.	Embodiment (प्राणी-शरीर *Prāṇī śarīra*)	VIII-20; XV-16; XVII-6.
v.	Spirits (भूत प्रेत *Bhūta Preta*)	IX-25; XVII-4.
vi.	Five Great Elements (पञ्च-महाभूत. *Pañca-mahābhūta*)	XIII-5, 34.
vii.	All beings (मनुष्य, देवता, असुर, यक्ष, राक्षस आदि. *Manuṣya, devatā, asura, yakṣa, rākṣasa ādi*)	II-34.
viii.	Living Beings (प्राणिमात्र *Prāṇi mātra*)	II-28, 30; III-14, 18, 33; IV-6, 35; V-7, 25, 29; VI-29, 31; VII-6, 9, 10, 26, 27; VIII-3, 19; IX-7, 8, 11, 13, 29; X-15, 20, 22, 39; XI-2, 15, 55; XII-4, 13; XIII-15, 16, 27, 30; XIV-3; XV-13; XVI-2, 6; XVIII-20, 21, 46, 54, 61.
25.	***Mana* (मन)**	
i.	Inner Equipment (अन्त:करण *Antaḥkaraṇa*)	I-30, V-13, 19.
ii.	Total Mind (समष्टि मन *Samaṣṭi mana*)	VII-4.
iii.	Attitude of the inner Equipment (अन्त: करण की मनोवृत्ति	II-60, 67; III-6, 7, 40, 42; V-11, 28; VI-12,

S.No.	Terms & Different Meanings	Ch. & Verse
	Antaḥkaraṇa kī manovṛtti)	14, 24, 25, 26, 27, 34, 35; VIII-7, 10, 12; IX-34; X-22; XI-45; XII-2, 8, 14; XV-7, 9; XVII-11, 16; XVIII-33, 65.
26.	***Yajña*** **(यज्ञ)**	
i.	Selfless work dedicated to God (कर्तव्य कर्म *Kartavya karma*)	III-9, 10, 12, 13, 14, 15; IV-23, 28, 31; XVI-1.
ii.	Oblations (अर्पण *Arpaṇa*)	IV-25 (first half)
iii.	*Jīvātmā* (जीवात्मा)	IV-25 (Second half)
iv.	*Brahma Yajña* (विवेक *Viveka*)	IV-25.
v.	Material sacrifice—offering wealth etc. (दान आदि *Dāna ādi*) (द्रव्य यज्ञा:)	IV-28, 33.
vi.	Self-study sacrifice (स्वाध्याय ज्ञान *Svādhyāya jñāna*)	IV-28; XVIII-70.
vii.	Perseverance (सहनशीलता तपोयज्ञा: *Sahanaśīlatā tapoyajñāḥ*)	IV-28.
viii.	Sacrifice of means i.e. vital energy, *japa* etc. (साधन *Sādhana*)	IV-30, 32; X-25.
ix.	Sacrifice of meritorious rewards (होम आदि *Homa ādi*)	V-29; VIII-28; IX-16, 20; XI-48; XVII-7, 11, 12, 13, 23, 24, 25, 27; XVIII-3, 5;
x.	*Japa* Sacrifice (नामजप *Nāmajapa*)	X-25.
xi.	Sacrifice for show (दिखावटी कार्य *Dikhāvaṭi kārya*)	XVI-17.

S.No.	Terms & Different Meanings	Ch. & Verse
27.	***Yoga* (योग)**	
	***A—Declined from* (युजिर् योगे)**	
i.	Selfless action (कर्म योग *Karma Yoga*)	II-39; IV-1, 2, 38; V-1, 4, 5; VI-2.
ii.	Procurement and preserving assets (अप्राप्ति की प्राप्ति *Aprāpti kī prāpti*)	II-45; IX-22.
iii.	Evenness of mind (अन्त:करण समता *Antaḥkaraṇa samatā*)	II -48, 50; IV-28, 41, 42; V-6, 7; VI-3, 4, 44; VIII-8, 27; XII-9, 11; XVI -1 XVIII-33.
iv.	*Sādhyarūpa samatā* (साध्यरूप समता)	II-53; VI-23.
v.	*Bhakti yoga* (भक्तियोग)	VII-1; X-7; XII-6; XIII-10.
vi.	*Karma yogī* (कर्म योगी)	V-5.
vii.	*Gītā Grantha* (गीता ग्रन्थ)	XVIII-75
viii.	*Sambandha* (सम्बन्ध)	IX-28.
ix.	*Sāṁkhya-yogī* and *bhakti-yogī* (सांख्ययोगी और भक्तियोगी)	XII-1.
27-B.	***Declined from* (युज् समाधौ)**	
i.	*Citta vṛtti nirodha* (चित् वृत्ति निरोध)	IV-27; VIII-12.
ii.	*Dhyāna yoga* (ध्यान योग)	VI-12, 16, 17, 19, 20, 23, 29, 33, 36, 37.
iii.	*Sādhana* (साधन)	VI-41.
iv.	*Prāṇāyāma* (प्राणायाम)	VIII-10.
27-C.	***Declined from* (युज् संयमने)**	
i.	Mysterious power (भगवान् की सामर्थ्यता *Bhagavān kī sāmarthyatā*)	IX-5; X-7, 18; XI-8, 47.

S.No.	Terms & Different Meanings	Ch. & Verse
28.	***Yogī* (योगी)**	
i.	*Karma yogī sādhaka* (कर्मयोगी साधक)	III-3; V-11; VI-1.
ii.	*Siddha karma yogī* (सिद्ध कर्म योगी)	VI-8
iii.	*Sāṁkhya yogī sādhaka* (सांख्य योगी साधक)	V-24; XV-11.
iv.	*Siddha sāṁkhya yogī* (सिद्ध सांख्य योगी)	VI-32, 42.
v.	*Bhakti yogī sādhaka* (भक्ति योगी साधक)	VIII-14.
vi.	*Siddha bhakti yogī* (सिद्ध भक्ति योगी)	VI-31; XII-14.
vii.	*Dhyāna yogī sādhaka* (ध्यान योगी साधक)	VI-10, 15, 19, 27, 28.
viii.	*All yogī-s* (योगी)	VI-2, 47; VIII-27.
ix.	A fallen *Yogī* (Back slider) (योग भ्रष्ट *Yoga bhraṣṭa*)	VI-45.
x.	*Niṣkāma sādhaka* (निष्काम साधक)	VI-46; VIII-28.
xi.	*Sakāma manuṣya* (सकाम मनुष्य)	VIII-25
xii.	*Niṣkāma* and *sakāma manuṣya* (निष्काम और सकाम मनुष्य)	VIII-23
xiii.	*Bhagavān* (भगवान्)	X-17.
29.	***Loka* (लोक)**	
i.	This world (मनुष्य लोक *Manuṣya Loka*)	II-5; III-3, 9; IV-12, 31, 40, 42.
ii.	Ordinary men (मनुष्य *Manuṣya*)	III-20, 21, 24, 25; V-14; VII-25.
iii.	Human body (मनुष्य शरीर *Manuṣya śarīra*)	IX-33.

S.No.	Terms & Different Meanings	Ch. & Verse
iv.	All the worlds (सम्पूर्ण प्राणी *Sampūrṇa prāṇī*)	XI-23, 30; XII-15; XVIII-17.
v.	Standing army men in the theatre of war. (युद्ध क्षेत्र में खड़े सैनिक— *Yuddha-kṣetra meṅ khaḍe sainika*)	XI-29, 32
vi.	All these worlds (संसार *Saṁsāra*)	V-29; X-3, 6, 16; XI-32, 43; XIII-13, 33; XV-7, 16; XVI-6.
vii.	The three world (त्रिलोकी*Trilokī*)	III-22; XI-20, 43; XV-17.
viii.	Heavenly regions (वैकुण्ठ आदि लोक *Vaikuṇṭha ādi loka*)	XVIII-71.
ix.	Higher religions of enjoyment (स्वर्ग आदि भोग भूमि *Svarga ādi bhoga-bhūmi*)	VI-41; VIII-16; XIV-14
x.	*Vedik* and Secular literature (शास्त्र *Śāstra*)	XV-18.
30.	**Śānti (शान्ति)**	
i.	Peace of mind (अन्त:करण की शान्ति *Antaḥ karaṇa kī śānti*)	II-66; XVI-2.
ii.	Peace Supreme (परमात्मा प्राप्ति *Paramātmā Prāpti*)	II-70, 71; IV-39; V-12, 29; VI-15; IX-31; XII-12.
iii.	Ever-lasting peace on complete withdrawal (संसार से सर्वथा उपरति *Saṁsāra se sarvathā uparati*)	XVIII-62.
31.	***Śreya* (श्रेय)**	
i.	Gain or good (लाभ *Labha*)	I-31.

S.No.	Terms & Different Meanings	Ch. & Verse
ii.	Leading to one's good (श्रेष्ठता *Śreṣṭhatā*)	II-5; III-35; IV-33; XII-12; XVI-22; XVIII-47.
iii.	Highest good (मुक्ति *Mukti*)	II-7, 31; III-2, 11, 35; V-1.
32.	***Sat*** **(सत्)**	
i.	Being (सत्ता *Sattā*)	II -16; IX-19; XI-37; XIII-12; XVII-23, 26, 27.
ii.	Action oriented (क्रिया *Kriyā*)	III-13; IV-6; XVIII-16.
iii.	Exalted womb (births) (देव आदि योनी *Deva ādi yonī*)	XIII-21.
33.	***Sama*** **(सम)**	
i.	*Paramātmā* (परमात्मा)	V-18, 19
ii.	*Sama-darśanaḥ*—Everywhere (आत्म स्वरूप *Ātma svarūpa*)	VI-29.
iii.	Ever mindedness (अन्त:करण समता *Antaḥkaraṇa samata*)	II-48; X-5; XVIII-54.
iv.	Alike-ness, Evenness (समानता *Samānatā*)	II-15, 38, 48; IV-22 VI-8, 9, 32; IX-29; XII-4, 13, 18; XIII-9, 27, 28; XIV-24.
v.	Erect, Straight (सीधा *Sīdhā*)	VI-13.
34.	***Sukha*** **(सुख)**	
i.	Pleasure, Enjoyment (सामान्य सुख *Sāmānya sukha*)	I-32, 33; II-14, 15, 38; VI-32; X-4; XIII-6, 20; XIV-24; XV-5; XVIII-36, 37, 38, 39.

S.No.	Terms & Different Meanings	Ch. & Verse
ii.	Favourable circumstances (अनुकूल परिस्थिति *Anukūla paristhiti*)	II-56; VI-7; XII-18.
iii.	Virtuous goodnes—Bliss (सात्त्विक सुख *Sāttvika sukha*)	II-66; V-21 (1st Line), 24; VI-27; XIV-6, 9; XVI-23; XVII-8.
iv.	Easily set free from bondage (सुगमता *Sugamatā*)	V-3; VI-28; IX-2.
v.	In one's own natural being (स्वभाविकता *Svabhāvikatā*)	V-13.
vi.	Most sublime Bliss (परमार्थिक सुख *Paramārthika sukha*)	V-21 (2nd line); VI-21, 28; XIV-27.
35.	***Saṁnyāsa* (संन्यास)**	
i.	Renunciation of action (सांख्य योग *Sāṁkhya yoga*)	V-1, 2, 6; VI-2; XVIII-1, 2, 49
ii.	Surrender (समर्पण *Samarpaṇa*)	IX-28.
iii.	Renunciation (त्याग *Tyāga*)	XVIII-7.
36.	***Saṁnyāsī* (संन्यासी)**	
i.	Ever established in Renunciation (कर्मयोगी *Karma-yogī*)	V-3; VI-1.
ii.	Those who Renounce (त्यागी *Tyāgī*)	XVIII-12.

PRAYERFUL MEDITATION

Gītā Dhyānam - गीता ध्यानम्

ॐ पार्थाय प्रतिबोधितां भगवता नारायणेन स्वयम्
व्यासेन ग्रथितां पुराणमुनिना मध्ये महाभारतम् ।
अद्वैतामृतवर्षिणीं भगवतीं अष्टादशाध्यायिनीं
अम्ब त्वामनुसन्दधामि भगवद्गीते भवद्वेषिणीम् ॥ १ ॥

Oṁ pārthāya pratibodhitāṁ
bhagavatā nārāyaṇena svayam
vyāsena grathitāṁ purāṇa-muninā
madhye. mahā-bhāratam,
advait-āmṛta-varṣiṇīṁ bhagavatīṁ
aṣṭā-daśā-dhyāyinīṁ
amba tvām-anusanda-dhāmī
bhagavad-gīte bhava-dveṣiṇīṁ.

ॐ *Oṁ* = *Oṁ* (the mono-syllable indicative of Supreme *Brahman*); पार्थाय प्रतिबोधिताम् *pārthāya prati-bodhitām* = with which *Pārtha* (Arjuna) was enlightened; भगवता *bhagavatā* = by the Lord; नारायणेन *nārāyaṇena* = by *Nārāyaṇa*; स्वयम् *svayaṁ* = Himself; व्यासेन *vyāsena* = by *Vyāsa*; ग्रथिताम् *grathitām* = incorporated; पुराण मुनिना *purāṇa muninā* = by the ancient sage; मध्ये महाभारतम् *madhye mahābhāratam* = in the midst of *Mahābhārata*; अद्वैत अमृत वर्षिणीम् *Advaita amṛta varṣiṇīm* = the showerer of the nectarian philosophy of *Advaita*; भगवतीम् *bhagavatīm* = the Divine Mother; अष्टादश अध्यायिनीम् *aṣṭādaśa adhyāyinīm* = in the form of eighteen chapters; अम्ब *amba* =

O! Blessed Mother; त्वाम् *tvāṁ* = Thee; अनुसन्दधामि *anusandadhāmi* = I constantly meditate; भगवद्गीते *bhagavad-gīte = O Bhagavad-Gītā*; भवद्वेषिणीम् *bhava dveṣiṇīṁ* = which is an antidote to the experiences of change i.e., destroyer of *saṁsāra* (rebirth).

1. Oṁ, O! Bhagavad Gītā, *with which* Pārtha *(*Arjuna*) was enlightened by the Lord* Nārāyaṇa *Himself and which was incorporated in the* Mahābhārata *by the ancient* sage Vyāsa*—the Divine Mother, who is showering the nectarian philosophy of* Advaita *in the form of eighteen chapters, upon Thee, O! Blessed Mother, I constantly meditate—You are the sure antidote to the rocking experience of change i.e., the destroyer of* Saṁsāra *(rebirth).*

It is usual in the traditional of the *Aryans*, to pray to the Lord prior to the beginning of any auspicious undertaking, whether spiritual or secular. These nine stanzas, usually attributed to *Śrī Madhusūdana Sarasvatī*, are chanted by students devoted to the study of the *Gītā* in India before they start their daily lessons.

Usually, our mind is in a state of disintergration and exhaustion due to the daily tussles, competitions and tensions of life. Thus, when the mind reaches the study room, though it is efficient in the market place, it does not prove itself equally efficient to meet the subtle arguments to met with in philosophical discussions. The instruments of feeling and understanding need a general cleansing and adjustment. This is achieved generally by selecting the early period of the dawn for our studies and by physical preparations such as a bath, the atmosphere of the prayer room and the presence of the revered *guru* etc.

Even then, once in the *pūjā* room or at the study table, we still need to make some finer adjustments in our mental make-up to bring our entire faculties into play. We can find a beautiful example, of what I say, in modern laboratories. A scientist might have his laboratory assistant who would adjust the eye-piece and the object-piece of the microscope for him and yet the assistant would have adjusted the instrument only according to the assistant's own vission. There may be subtle differences in the powers of vision of the experimenting scientist and assistant, thus necessitating some still finer adjustments. These fine manipulations are to be made by the scientist himself in order that he may observe the slide for himself best. The general methods of *sādhanā* and the anxiety and urgency felt by the seekers to understand the *Gītā* may adjust the instruments of their feelings and thoughts, but a perfect integration between the mind and the intellect still remains to be achieved. This fine adjustment is gained by the seekers by singing these nine stanzas with thorough appreciation of their full significance and import.

Without reverence, respect and faith for the very textbook in hand, no serious study can ever take place; therefore, the very first stanza for meditation is dedicated to register our reverence and express our adoration to the Divine Mother *Gītā* Herself.

It is said that the *Bhagavad Gītā* is a scripture in which, as in the *Upaniṣad-s*, there is a glorious teacher who is teaching not a highly evolved student of the *Upaniṣadik* type, but an ordinary prince of the realm, an average man, an intellect riddled with a thousand desires and anxieties as in any of us—*Arjuna*. The *Pāṇḍava* prince, though generally famous and known as *Arjuna*, is also named *Pārtha* in *Mahābhārata*. Thus the very first line indicates that the teacher was the Master of masters and that no better qualified man could be found to give us a discourse upon the true way of living.

Again, as ordinary man is rather frightened of the very subject matter of philosophy since it is his experience that when a great teacher talks to a great students, an average person can only sit, listen and adore the talks but can never be able to understand the matter and be benefited by it. This difficulty will not be there in the *Gītā* as it is indicated that these discourses have been addressed to a below-average student and, therefore, we, hearing these discourses, would be highly benefited by these facile educative talks.

It is possible that the *Gītā* is an *Upaniṣadik* talk between a master mind and an everage man at the *Mahābhārata* time but, the theme being transcendental, it might have been misreported. This coversation which is supposed to have taken place in *Kurukṣetra* might have actually taken place elsewhere and at a different period of time. Since we have not ourselves directly overheard it, we have to depend entirely upon the good sense of the reporter.

It has been indicated in the second line that we have a dependable correspondent to report for us the *Gītā* which was sung, for the first time, before the very first arrow was shot in the *Mahābhārata* war. *Vyāsa,* the ancient seer, recorded and incorporated it in the centre of his classical work, the *Mahābhārata.* Every word here is important and the words bend down under the weight of their own heavy significances.

Vyāsa, the father of the *Vedā-s*, who, first collected, edited and published the *Veda* texts and who, thereafter, gave us the dialectics of *Vedānta* in his *Brahma Sūtra*, himself a great man of realisation, was indeed very well fitted for the job. This ancient seer had both the mastery of the theoretical science of religion—*Hindūism* and also practical experience of the Supreme.

Not only had he reported this conversation in the most enchanting lyrical poetry of the *Gītā* but had also found it worthy to be incorporated in the masterpiece of his matured age, the greatest classical piece of the world, the *Mahābhārata.* The *Gītā* occurs in the *Bhīṣma Parva* in the *Mahābhārata* and occupies almost the geometric center of that wonder-classic. In fact, any student of the *Mahābhārata* will willingly accept that the whole saga serves as a fitting background for the jewel of the *Gītā* to shine out.

Even if an Omniscient Being had discoursed to benefit an ordinary man, and even if a great mastermind had reported it and found it good enough to give to it an important place in his masterpiece, we, of the modern age, might not have felt at all imspired unless we knew that the subject matter was worthy of our attention. In the third line, it is described that the eighteen-chapters of the Divine Song discuss the immortal goal of oneness which is the theme of *Vedānta*—the *Upaniṣad*-s.

By the realisation of this goal, the sorrows and limitations suffered by an ordinary individual in his transactions with the world outside through the instruments of his body, mind and intellect, are dried up and the individual gets himself released to an ampler field of freedom, at once divine and joyous.

In the last line, the *Gītā* is addressed and approached as a mother and this is to be understood as very significant. The *Gītā* Mother, the divine womb, that gave birth to the universal religion, is the one to whom the children of any age can always confidently turn, expecting but total forgiveness and complete love, even after they have committed a million outrageous acts. Similarly, here the *Gītā*, the text book of life, is approached as our Mother because She never gives up anybody as completely lost, and every one who lovingly approaches Her courtyard calling out '*Mā...Mā...Mā*' can be sure that She will accept him in spite of all his past crimes and mischiefs.

Gītā adoration is not accomplished by a mere ritualistic worship of the text book; the Divine Song is a text book discussing *a way of living* to be lived and experienced. We generally live by our own convictions, and as our convictions, so are our thoughts; and as our thoughts, so are our actions.

The *Hindū* spiritual study accomplishes this necessary revolution in the intellectual levels and thereby carves out our thoughts into a more healthy pattern. These thoughts get projected out into the world as actions. Thereafter, our nature makes us master men in facing all our challenges in life. Constant rememberance of the way of life and the ideal goal of existence as indicated in the *Gītā* is, therefore, the surest and the best method of revering and respecting Mother *Gītā*.

नमोस्तु ते व्यास विशालबुद्धे
फुल्लारविन्दायतपत्रनेत्र ।
येन त्वया भारततैलपूर्णः
प्रज्वालितो ज्ञानमयः प्रदीपः ॥ २ ॥

Namo-'stu te vyāsa viśāla-buddhe
phullāravind-āyata-patra-netra,
yena tvayā bhārata-taila-pūrṇaḥ
prajvālito jñāna-mayaḥ pradīpaḥ.

नमः *namaḥ* = salutation; अस्तु *astu* = be; ते *te* = unto thee; व्यास *vyāsa* = O *Vyāsa*; विशाल बुद्धे *viśāla buddhe* = of mighty intellect; फुल्ल अरविन्द आयत पत्र नेत्र *phulla arvinda āyata patra netra* = with the eyes like the petals of a full-blown lotus-tree; येन *yena* = which; त्वया *tvayā* = by thee; भारत तैल पूर्णः *bhārata taila pūrṇaḥ* = full of the *Mahābhārata* oil; प्रज्वालितः *prajvālitaḥ* = lighted; ज्ञानमयः *jñānamayaḥ* = consisting of knowledge; प्रदीपः *pradīpaḥ* = lamp.

2. *Salutations unto thee,* O Vyāsa! *of mighty intellect, who has eyes like the petals of a full-blown lotus-tree, by whom was lighted the Lamp of Knowledge, filled with the* Mahābhārata *oil.*

After saluting the textbook as such, the students are encouraged to prostrate to its author, *Vyāsa*. We cannot easily bow down to anyone unless we are convinced that he has qualifications deserving our reverence. The great merits of *Vyāsa* are enumerated here in this meditation stanza.

Not only was his intellect mighty but he was completely tolerant and held in his infinite love-embrace the entire universe of living beings. *Vyāsa's* philosophical life is not sectarian; it is not a philosophy for the *Hindū-s* alone. It is universal in its application and addressed to man. Its anxiety is to bring to the people a sparkling life of joy and exuberance. Naturally, that philosopher, who can thus give us a universal scripture—the *Gītā,* the Bible of Man—should be not only brilliant in his culture but also supremely divine.

That this great wise seer had physical beauty of compelling charm is indicated in the second line. The arresting depth of serenity and joy, welling up in his eyes that have the magic of some mysterious love song about them, is suggested by the comparison of his eyes to the pools of beauty in each petal of a lotus in bloom.

However magnanimous his intellect may be or however compelling his beauty, no individual can command any respect in India, among the *Āryans,* unless he has contributed substantially to the gains in the happiness of the community. In this peculiar demand, the *Āryan* mind also can feel fully satisfied by the achievements of the poet-philosopher *Vyāsa.* It was he who, by his *Gītā,* lit up a Lamp of Knowledge flowing with the oil of the *Mahābhārata* stories.

All other *kinds of knowledge* that are known to us, contributed by different sciences, cannot in themselves be called knowledge since each one of them is a limited conditioned '*Knowledge.*' Knowledge of Physics, knowledge of Chemistry, knowledge of Astrology, knowledge of Mathematics—none of them is Knowledge in Itself but is knowledge of something or the other. In the *Gītā, the theme is Knowledge in Itself* in the light of which alone can all other kinds of knowledge be known.

The very metaphor used here has a very subtle indication inasmuch as it almost tells us how a study of the *Gītā* makes a scientist a better scientist and an artist a better artist. All other kinds of knowledge can be better acquired and creatively better digested in the light of the *Gītā.* Indeed, the Divine Song is the Lamp of Knowledge.

प्रपन्नपारिजाताय तोत्रवेत्रैकपाणये ।
ज्ञानमुद्राय कृष्णाय गीतामृतदुहे नमः ॥ ३ ॥

Prapanna-pārijātāya totra-vetraika-pāṇaye,
jñāna-mudrāya kṛṣṇāya gitāmṛta-duhe namaḥ.

प्रपन्न पारिजाताय *prapanna pārijātāya* = the *Parijāta,* or the *Kalpataru,* the tree of fulfilment i.e., the bestower of desires for those who take refuge in Him; तोत्र वेत्र एक पाणये *totra vetra eka pāṇaye* = who holds a cane, to drive cattle, in one hand; ज्ञान मुद्राय *Jñāna mudrāya* = the holder of knowledge symbol; कृष्णाय *Kṛṣṇāya* = to *Kṛṣṇa*; गीता अमृत दुहे *gitā amṛta duhe* = the milker of the *Gītā*-nectar; नमः *namaḥ* = salutations.

3. *Salutations to* Kṛṣṇa *: Who is a "tree of fulfilment" (i.e.,* Pārijāta *or* Kalpataru*—the bestower of all desries to all those who totally surrender to Him, who has milked the* Gītā*-nectar, the holder of* Jñāna-mudrā, *the wielder of the cane in one hand with which He drives home the herd of cattle under His protection.*

In the previous stanzas, *Śrīmad Bhagavad Gītā* and its author *Vyāsa* were meditated upon and their grace invoked. Herein, we have an invocation stanza in the name of Lord *Kṛṣṇa* who is the special *guru* in this scriptural textbook. In India, the highest philosophical textbooks have all been rendered more appealing by presenting them all in a conversational style.

All the *Upaniṣad-s* are discussions upon the Supreme between a man of realisation and one or a few seekers who had approached the teacher's feet. Copying the style of the eternal *Upaniṣad-s*, we have in the *Gītā*, Lord *Kṛṣṇa*, the Divine Charioteer giving His discourses upon the goal of life and the right values of living by which the consummate aim of Self-discovery can be gained by *Arjuna*, a typical seeker of his age. Unless we have respect and reverence for the teacher, it is impossible to practice and live, by ourselves, the themes of these discourses given by Him.

In the secular sciences, intimate relationship between a teacher and a taught is not very much needed since the studies are on objective themes and the student has only to learn to repeat what has been taught.

In spiritual science, however, there the need to achieve the perfection indicated by the teacher's theoretical discourses. When thus we want to become what we know, we will need the presence of an ideal teacher who has this very same perfection in himself.

We now salute *Kṛṣṇa*, the *guru* in the *Gītā* dialogue. Lord *Kṛṣṇa* is one who can fulfil all the desires of those who take refuge in Him. *Pārijāta* tree is a mythological conception in *Hindūism* and the belief is that it is a tree that can fulfil all the desires of those who go under its shade, what ever be their demands. Thus *Kṛṣṇa,* the Supreme in Its physical manifestation, carries in one hand the whip (stick) with which the cowherds drive the cattle to the pasture-land and back to their sheds. His other hand is described as holding the *Jñāna mudrā*, the 'Symbol of Knowledge.'

Mudrā is a physical symbol manipulated by the physical body expressing in itself some deep significance or meaning. *Jñāna mudrā* is described in our *Śāstrā-s* and is found in many painting and sculptures that have the *Hindū* mythology for their themes. It is generally indicated by the palm and the fingers. In this *Mudrā*, the middle, the ring and the little fingers are all held straight and upright, closely together and the index finger bends towards the thumb to touch with its tip the middle of the thumb. The thumb is generally held as upright as possible so that its lower portion, the entire arched index finger and the connecting portion of the palm together represent a complete circle.

Jñāna mudrā is described as representing the end and goal of human life and the means of attaining it. The three upright fingers held together represent the integrated physical, mental and intellectual personalities. Transcending them all (the physical, subtle and causal bodies) is the Self, symbolised here by the index finger which strives hard to discovers its identity with the self-in-all, the thumb. The 'thumb facing the fingures' is the highest state of evolution in the instruments of action and the thumb lends its efficiency to all other fingers. The Self in us (index finger), discovering its oneness with the *Brahman* (thumb), is the infinite experience (represented by the circle formed by the thumb and the index finger) which, in *Hindū* thought is declared as the experience divine.

This experience is the realisation of the One without a second, indicated in the *Jñāna mudrā* by the upper half of the thumb jutting out from the circle (the Infinite).

Kṛṣṇa is no doubt an objectified representation of the formless Infinite Truth and, therefore, we ever prostrate to *Śrī Kṛṣṇa*, the *Paramātman*. As such, in all these stanzas where *Kṛṣṇa* is invoked, we can actually read two interesting interpretations, one directly speaking of the manifested *Kṛṣṇa*, the other secretly indicating the Self which has manifested itself as *Kṛṣṇa*.

Our identification with the *matter* envelopments of the body, mind and intellect gives rise to the conception of a false-ego in us, suffering the endless sorrows of its finitude and limitations. It is this ego that is struggling hard to liberate itself from the shackles of its own limitations. Now, to the extent the ego strips itself of its *matter*-vestures, to that extent the essence in the ego, the Self, is realised.

The Self in us is the Perfect, the Infinite. Desires are our plans which our limited intellect conceives in order that it may escape from its own sense of imperfections and come to attain the imaginary joys of perfection. The Perfect can have no desires; the Perfect knows of nothing to desire for, nor can it be in want of anything. To the extent, therefore, the ego surrenders itself to *Kṛṣṇa* the Self, to that extent it is ending all its sense of desires. At last, when it has totally rediscovered that Lord *Kṛṣṇa* is its own Real Nature, it has surrendered completely and can no more have any desire that is not fulfilled.

The Life in us expresses itself in the world outside both in its choking monstrosities as well as in its throbbing beauties. Life it is, that drives the ego, the animal in us, into its varied fields of sense gratifications. The Life in us again is the very force that drives the aspiring part in us to the path of religion and philosophy and maintains us therein, making us march ahead till we reach the end of our evolution. Thus, *Kṛṣṇa* here is rightly indicated to be the Self by the symbolism of the cane with which He tends the cattle, and the *Jñāna mudrā* by which He instructs and guides seekers to discover their own esssential Personality Divine. To this great Self who had milked the nectar of the *Gītā* for all generatios to come, we offer our prostrations.

सर्वोपनिषदो गावो दोग्धा गोपालनन्दनः ।
पार्थो वत्सः सुधीर्भोक्ता दुग्धं गीतामृतं महत् ॥ ४ ॥

Sarvo-paniṣado gāvo dogdhā gopāla-nandanaḥ,
pārtho vatsaḥ sudhīrbhoktā dugdhaṁ gitāmṛtaṁ mahat.

सर्व उपनिषदः *sarva upaniṣadaḥ* = all the *Upaniṣad-s*; गावः *gāvaḥ* = the cows; दोग्धा *dogdhā* = the milkman; गोपाल नन्दनः *gopāla-nandanaḥ* = the cowherd's son i.e., *Kṛṣṇa*; पार्थः *pārthaḥ* = *Pārtha*; वत्सः *vatsaḥ* = the calf; सुधीः *sudhīḥ* = men of purified intellect; भोक्ता *bhoktā* = the enjoyers; दुग्धम् *dugdham* = the milk; गीता *Gitā* = *Gītā*; अमृतम् *amṛtam* = nectar; महत् *mahat* = the supreme.

4. *All the* Upaniṣad-s *are the cows, the son of the cowherd i.e.,* Kṛṣṇa, *is the milkman,* Pārtha *is the calf, men of purified intellect are the enjoyers, and the supreme nectar of the* Gītā *is the milk.*

In the last stanza it was only mentioned that *Kṛṣṇa* had milked out the nectar of *Gītā*. The metaphor suggested in the previous verse is beautifully elaborated by the fewest strokes into a complete word-picture here. Ordinarily milking needs at least a cow, a calf and a milkman.

'*All the Upaniṣad-s are the cows*':—The breed of the cow, we know, determines the quality of the milk. In procuring the milk of *Gītā*, it is indicated here—*Vyāsa* has not milked his own creative intellect but has gone to the very source of our scriptures of knowledge, the *Upaniṣad*-s.*

It is also interesting to note that the cow is that living organism through which the ordinary raw materials such as grass, water and other fodder get miraculously assimilated and converted into milk. The raw material for the seers of the *Upaniṣad-s* was but the sapless and colourless experiences of the ordinary everyday life, and yet, they, in their amplified vision, during moments fo contemplation, could cook, assimilate and secrete the 'wisdom-sparks' which represent the *Upaniṣadik mantrā-s*. The philosophy underlying them is *Vedānta* and to squeeze out of them a sure 'way of life' for the ready nutrition of the man in the market-place, is the service done by the author of the *Gītā*.

There is a great significance underlying the very joy in the metaphor, apart from the fact that it is quite in keeping with the essential agrarian background of Indian culture. Milk is a food that is nutritive and healthy not only to a newborn baby but also to the wrestler, to the sick man, to the convalescent, to the aged, to the dying; no other food is so universal in its blessing. Generally, that which is healthy and appropriate to one type is not equally efficient to serve all others. In comparing the *Gītā* with the milk, the verse is only declaring that the *Gītā* is an universal textbook, healthy for all the various races and types of men in their variegated walks of life, each one striving to maintain a variety of standards of living.

Of the innumerable names of *Kṛṣṇa*, the term chosen here, 'the son of the cowherd,' is quite appropriate inasmuch as

---

* Refer to Introduction in *Svāmījī's* Discourses on *Kenopaniṣad*.

a certain amount of efficiency and dexterity is necessary to milk-out the entire contents of an udder. As a cowherd boy, he was from his birth onwards observing, practising and living the profession, and was by instinct best fitted to do this job.

According to the science of animal husbandry, though now-a-days it is a fact very much ignored, the quality of the milk depends upon the emotional contents of the milch-cow. To no thinking man can the modern theory, which suggests the substitution of some music in place of the calf, be quite satisfactory. According to the *Hindū* scientists, the milk of the cow can be fully nutritive only when the mother cow, overflowing with love for her own calf, pours out her milk. Thus the calf is necessary to arouse the love of the mother cow, then alone can the overflowing udder supply the best type of milk. In the metaphor it is pointed out that *Arjuna* was the calf for the cow of the *Upaniṣad* to pour out its best milk which was then collected by the divine prophet, the Cowherd Boy of *Vṛndāvana*.

Though the cow, due to its love for the calf, pours out her best, the milk so gathered is not generally meant for the calf; it is enjoyed by those who can afford it. Similarly here the *Upaniṣadik* milk gathered and preserved in the *Gītā*, though facilitated by *Arjuna*, is not meant for *Arjuna* alone, but as the stanza says, it is meant 'for the enjoyment of all men of pure intellect.'

The universality of the *Gītā* is nowhere else so beautifully brought out and so openly declared as in this line. It is not said here that it is meant for the *brāhmaṇā-s* alone; nor does it make any concessional declaration such as that even the *śūdrā-s* can read it. In fact, the *Gītā* is not a text-book of the *Hindū-s*; it is a universal scripture and all men who are sincere and intelligent enough to perceive their own imperfections and courageously come to make a demand for perfection in themselves are the fit students on whom the *Gītā* pours out her best blessing.

वसुदेवसुतं देवं कंसचाणूरमर्दनम् ।
देवकीपरमानन्दं कृष्णं वन्दे जगद्गुरुम् ॥ ५ ॥

Vasudeva-sutaṁ devaṁ kaṁsa-cāṇūra-mardanam,
devakī-paramānandaṁ kṛṣṇam vande jagad-gurum.

वसुदेव सुतम् *vasudeva sutam* = the son of *Vasudeva*; देवम् *devam* = god; कंस चाणूर मर्दनम् *kaṁsa cāṇūra mardanam* = the destroyer of *Kaṁsa* and *Cāṇūra*; देवकी-परम-आनन्दम् *devakī parama ānandam* = the supreme bliss of *Devakī* (Mother of *Kṛṣṇa*); कृष्णम् *Kṛṣṇam* = to *Kṛṣṇa*; वन्दे *vande* = I salute; जगद् गुरुम् *jagad gurum* = the world teacher.

5. *I salute Lord* Kṛṣṇa, *the teacher of the Universe, the divine son of* Vasudeva, *the destroyer of* Kaṁsa *and* Cāṇūra, *the supreme joy of* Devakī.

Continuing our salutaions to the teacher of the *Gītā*, Lord *Kṛṣṇa*, we have this stanza which, as we said earlier, can be read as a direct glorification of the divinity manifested as *Kṛṣṇa*, or with its suggestiveness, it can raise an aspiring soul to adore the Eternal Life Spark—that is the one substratum for everything, everywhere.

Considering this stanza as a simple glorification of the Lord of *Vṛndāvana*, it has a direct meaning which reminds us of His parentage, of His adventurous and heroic service to the citizens of *Mathurā* in redeeming them from the tyranny of His uncle, *Kaṁsa* and of His status as a teacher of the world.

Reconsidering the same stanza, one certainly feels the impropriety of introducing a *Jagad-guru* as 'the son of his father, *Vasudeva*,' or as the apple of the eye of his own mother, *Devakī* or even as 'the murderer of his own uncle *Kaṁsa*!' None of these qualifications adds any glow to his being a teacher of the world, but, by recognizing *Kṛṣṇa* as nothing but the Self in us, the entire stanza starts breathing with a new thrill and pulsates with a new life, as it were.

Vasu-s[1], eight in number, are, in the *Vedik* literature, deities representing the seasons. The seasons march and in their parade runs out a year, therefore these eight deities in themselves rule the concept of time. The term *Deva* in *Saṁskṛta* indicates 'that which illumines,' *Vasudeva*, therefore means 'the illuminator of the concept of Time.' Time is conceived by the mind,[2] as the interval between two different experiences which it had lived through. Each experience is a perceptible mental disturbance (*manovṛtti*) and the illuminator of these *vṛttī-s* is the one that lights up the concept of Time. Evidently, therefore, it is the awareness in us that bathes our experiences in the light of its consciousness—that is, the illuminating factor in our mental life, the Self in us, the Pure Consciousness. The term *Deva* is again added, meaning the Illuminator, the Principle of Light.

The Self is the only power that can destroy the tyrant *Kaṁsa* and his henchmen like *Cāṇūra* who have usurped the Kingdom of *Mathurā* (Sweetness?) and imprisoned its real king *Ugrasena*. The names given to the personalities in the stanza, the very name of the kingdom : *Mathurā*—apart from the story of the cruel usurper and his tyranny—all remind us of the plight of man when the ego-centre usurps the inner kingdom of heaven. The Self in us identifying Itself with the *matter* envelopment creates the tyrant ego and it, with its criminal hosts of deputies—such as desires, anger, greed and passion—starts its ruthless persecution in our bossom. When the ego is ended along with its delusory attachment to its sheaths, the kingdom is redeemed. Lord *Kṛṣṇa* alone can throw *Kaṁsa* from his throne into the dust and usher in an era of joy and progress to the land of *Mathurā*.

1. *Vasu-s* are *Dhara, Dhruva, Soma, Āpaḥ, Anila, Anala, Pratūṣa and Prabhāṣa.*
2. In modern scientific terminology Time and Space are defined as :

"a) Separation of events intuits the cocnepts of time;

b) the extention of an object intuits the concept of space made of lengths;

c) and the gross structure of *matter* intuits concepts of Mass."

In the *Sāṅkhyan* philosophy, the terms *Prakṛti* and *Puruṣa* are used to indicate the world of *matter* and that of the Spirit. Matter is inert, and totally insentient. The layers of *matter* in us, the body, the mind and intellect, have no life of their own in them to react with the world outside and to eke out their joy from the world. All the joy that we know of are gained from these layers and we all know that we can do so only so long as life, the Consciousness, presides over them. Naturally, we, physical men, adore life more than anything else in the world because without life we are not capable of having any experience of joy.

The world of *matter*, *Prakṛti*, is represented here by the term *Devakī* who was the womb that gave birth to the manifestation of the Lord as *Kṛṣṇa*. If the Infinite is not conditioned by *matter*, It will not be able to express Its glories so vividly as we see It today in the pluralistic Universe. A violinist cannot express the music in his bosom without a violin. A dynamo can reveal the energy that it contains, only when harnessed. The flowing waters alone can manifest the electricity potential of the river. Indeed *Kṛṣṇa*, the Self should be the source of all joys and fulfilment to *Devakī*, the mother—the world of *matter* (*Prakṛti*).

In short, *Kṛṣṇa* is the Vital Life Principle in contact with which the insentient mineral compounds, bearing the shape and name of the body-mind-intellect, gain for themselves the scintillating look of intelligence and sentience. Indeed, the Self is the source of all the pleasures that *matter* seems to gather unto itself from its contacts with the world.

भीष्मद्रोणतटा जयद्रथजला गान्धारनीलोत्पला
शल्यग्राहवती कृपेण वहनी कर्णेन वेलाकुला ।
अश्वत्थामविकर्णघोरमकरा दुर्योधनावर्तिनी
सोत्तीर्णा खलु पाण्डवै रणनदी कैवर्तकः केशवः ॥ ६ ॥

Bhīṣma-droṇa-taṭā jayadratha-jalā gāndhāra-nīlotpalā
śalya-grāhavatī kṛpeṇa vahanī karṇena velākulā,
aśvatthāma-vikarṇa-ghora-makarā duryodhanā-vartinī
sottīrṇā khalu pāṇḍavai raṇanadī kaivartakaḥ keśavaḥ.

भीष्म द्रोण तटा *bhīṣma droṇa taṭā* = with *Bhīṣma* and *Droṇa* as its banks; जयद्रथ जला *Jayadratha jalā* = with *Jayadratha* as its water; गान्धार नील उत्पला *gāndhāra nīla utpalā* = with the king of *Gāndhāra* as the blue water-lily*; शल्य ग्राहवती *śalya grāhavatī* = with *Śalya* as the shark; कृपेण वहनी *Kṛpeṇa vahanī* = with *Kṛpa* as the current; कर्णेन वेल आकुला *karṇena vela ākulā* = with *Karṇa* as the breaker; अश्वत्थाम विकर्ण घोर मकरा *aśvatthāma vikarṇa ghora makarā* = with *Aśvatthāma* and *Vikarṇa* as the terrible crocodiles; दुर्योधन आवर्तिनी *duryodhana āvartinī* = with *Duryodhana* as the whirlpool in it; सः *saḥ* = that; उत्तीर्णा *uttīrṇā* = crossed over; खलु *khalu* = indeed; पाण्डवैः *pāṇḍavaiḥ* = by the *Pāṇḍavā-s*; रणनदी *rana nadī* = the river battle; कैवर्तकः *kaivartakaḥ* = the ferry-man; केशवः *keśavaḥ* = *Keśava* (*Kṛṣṇa*).

6. *The river of battle, with* Bhīṣma *and* Droṇa, *as its banks; with* Jayadratha, *as its waters; with the king of Gāndhāra, as the blue water-lily*; Śalya as the shark; Kṛpa as the current; Karṇa as the breaker; Aśvathāma and Vikarṇa as the terrible crocodiles; Duryodhana as the whirlpool in it—was indeed crossed over by the Pāṇḍavā-s with Keśava as the ferry-man.*

It is usual in *Saṁskṛta* to indulge in very elaborate metophor and here is a typical example wherein, the entire *Mahābhārata* war has been brought into the mental vision of the meditator through this elaborate picture of a river in flood. For an average man, at every moment of his life there is one challenge or the other to be faced. The greatest challenge of the *Pāṇḍavā-s* was the *Mahābhārata* war and *Arjuna*, who in

* A better rendering is *Nīlotpalā* which means "a dark blue rock."

the beginning felt it too much for his capacities to face, was helped by the *Gītā Ācārya*, Lord *Kṛṣṇa*, to meet this challenge gloriously and successfully. The ferocity of the threatening river of war is brought out very clearly by the suggestiveness of the picture which enumerates the mighty personalities and clearly brings out their individual heroism in the true classical style.

The two banks of the river of war are represented by *Bhīṣma*, the grandsire and *Droṇa*, the great teacher. The two banks are the limitations of a river for they alone decide its direction and flow. When bound by rocky banks rivers gush forth with terrific ferocity, while along the sandy banks they merely crawl and creep. Between *Droṇa* and *Bhīṣma*, the firm and steadfast banks, the waters of the river of war rose and fell with a velocity at once staggering and breath-taking. The implied significance is that it was they who decided the movements of the *Mahābhārata* war.

A river, even though flowing through rocky cliffs, cannot have any dynamic power unless it is full of waters. The contents of the river is its flowing water; *Jayadratha*, the commander-in-chief of the *Kaurava* forces is described here as the very waters. In a river two banks are constantly and continuously contacted by the waters that flow through it; also the nature and character of the waters flowing determine the nature and character of the river itself. As a true Commander-in-Chief and an efficient executive, *Jayadratha* was thus, so to say, in all places at all moments, executing each and every intention and plan of the Grandsire and the *Ācārya*; he worked as a perfect liaison officer between *Droṇa* and *Bhīṣma*.

The King of *Gandhāra*, who was the immediate kinsman of *Duryodhana*, served in the river of war as a 'dark and treacherous rock' (*Nīlotpalā*) upon which the waters splashed with a thunderous roar, exhibiting their otherwise imperceptible velocity and forces. However, there is another reading (*Nīlotpalā*) meaning 'a blue lotus.' The king of *Gandhāra* was, as it were, a noble decoration adding some beauty and fragrance to the *Kaurava* forces! *Śalya*, son of *Droṇa*, was the 'shark' who could swallow up the heroes even without their being aware of it because a shark can swallow without chewing. In the list of enumerations of the great heroes, the stanza says that *Kṛpa* was the very 'current' in the river that uprooted everything on its path and made it impossible for anyone even to hope to cross it. *Karṇa* was the 'mountainous waves' in this oceanic river. *Aśvathāma* and *Vikarṇa* were the 'terrible crocodiles' and *Duryodhana* was the tragic 'whirlpool' that sucked into its centre anything that happened to fall within the circumference of its play.

In short, the complete picture holds up to our vision a terrific challenge which is almost impossible for a mortal to meet, but the *Pāṇḍavā-s* did cross this formidable river, full of dangers, with *Keśava* as their divine ferry-man. The suggestion is that *Arjuna*, re-educated in the true philosophy of *Hindūism* as preached in the *Gītā*, was able to face the river of life, successfully, and ultimately to cross over it and reach the banks of success and glory.

A student of *Gītā* is thus made to appreciate the practical usefulness of *Hindūism* in facing one's own day-to-day problems. Compared to the problem so beautifully explained in this metaphor, we can say that even the worst of the challenges which we have to face now in our life is not even a fraction of what *Arjuna* had to face then. Such a reassuring suggestion encourages every student of *Gītā* to make a thorough study of the Song of Life in which the Lord delivered to *Arjuna* the entire philosophy of life.

पाराशर्यवचः सरोजममलं गीतार्थगन्धोत्कटं
नानाख्यानककेसरं हरिकथासंबोधनाबोधितम् ।
लोके सज्जनषट्पदैरहरहः पेपीयमानं मुदा
भूयाद्भारतपङ्कजं कलिमलप्रध्वंसिनः श्रेयसे ॥७॥

Pārāśarya-vacaḥ sarojam-amalaṁ
gītārtha-gandhot-kaṭaṁ
nānā-khyānaka-kesaraṁ-hari-kathā
saṁbodhanā-bodhitaṁ,
loke sajjana-ṣaṭ-padair-aharahaḥ
pepīya-mānaṁ mudā
bhūyād-bhārata-paṅkajaṁ kalimala-
pradhvaṁsinaḥ śreyase.

पाराशर्य वचः सरोजम् *pārāśarye vacaḥ sarojam* = born in the waters of the words of the son of *Parāśara* (*Vyāsa*); अमलम् *amalam* = spotless, stainless; गीता अर्थ गन्ध उत्कटम् *gītā artha gandha utkaṭaṁ* = sweet and pleasant fragrance of the significance of *Gītā*; नाना आख्यानक केसरम् *nānā ākhyānaka kesaram* = with many narratives as its inner soft petals (stamens); हरिकथा संबोधन आबोधितम् *harikathā saṁbodhana ābodhitaṁ* = fully blossomed by the stories of *Harī*; लोके *loke* = in the world; सज्जन षट्पदैः *sajjana ṣaṭpadaiḥ* = by the six footed (honey bees) of good men; अहः अहः *ahaḥ ahaḥ* = day by day; पेपीयमानम् *pepīyamānam* = drunk; मुदा *mudā* = joyously; बूयात् *bhūyāt* = may be; भारत पङ्कजम् *bhārata paṅkajaṁ* = the lotus of the *Mahābhārata*; कलिमल प्रध्वंसिनः *kalimala pradhvaṁsinaḥ* = (to us) who are eager to destroy and safely come out of the inner imperfections of the Iron Age (*Kali*); श्रेयसे *śreyase* = for the supreme good.

7. *May the spotless lotus of the Mahābhārata—born in the waters of the words of the son of Parāśara (i.e.,* Vyāsa*), having for its sweet and pleasant fragrance the significance of* Gītā, *with many narratives as its inner soft petals, fully blossomed by the stories of* Harī, *and joyously drunk day after day by the six footed (honey bees) the good men of the world—be productive of the supreme good to us who are eager to destroy and safely come out of the inner imperfections of the Iron Age.*

Here is yet another example of the elaborate figurative style in *Saṁskṛta* poetry which compresses in itself a vast storehouse of significances. The entire *Mahābhārata*, the greatest classic in the world, is being invoked here as a lotus which is considered in *Saṁskṛta* poetry as a symbol of beauty and auspiciousness. To the *Hindū* mind, the lotus is a symbol of peace and purity, the symbol of his 'goal of life,' and it is held symbolically by Lord *Viṣṇu* of the *Hindū* Trinity.

The lotus grows in the waters of ponds and lakes; the Lotus of *Mahābhārata* is born in the waters of *Śrī Vyāsa*'s pregnant and poetic words. *Vyāsa* was a great poet-philosopher and has become almost an institution representing all *Hindū-s* and no scriptural study or *Vedik* chanting is ever started without prostrations unto this greatest of saints and seers. If we must attribute *Hindūism* to any single individual, there is none else to whom we can most appropriately attribute its present existence and past glories except *Śrī Veda Vyāsa*.

Vyāsa is indicated here as the *Parāśara*'s son, perhaps to remind us of the traditional story of his birth and parentage. It is believed that he was born to the *brāhmaṇa Ṛsī*, *Parāśara*, by a fisher woman. The story need not be taken as a literal historical incident, but can be considered as significant. *Parāśara*, the *brāhmaṇa*, represents the *sāttvik* or the creative wisdom born out of a life of study and contemplation, while the fisher woman represents the daring adventurousness with which she has to sail forth day by day in her frail craft, riding over waves into the deep sea, from where to capture the unseen nutritive food and haul them to the shores where the dwellers can easily and cheaply get their nourishment at their own door steps. On the ocean of *Vedik* knowledge, *Vyāsa* had to sail in his frail life, fish out the best that it contained and bring to us the nutritive essence of *Hindūism* in the form of the great *Purāṇā-s*. In short, *Vyāsa* was not merely a man of realisation and perfection, but was also one who had the spirit of adventure to risk himself in serving the generation all through his life. He was a revivalist who contributed the maximum to the *Hindū* Renaissance of that critical era.

On the words of *Vyāsa*, grew the lotus of *Mahābhārata* whose very fragrance is the *Gītā*'s wisdom. A flower without fragrance is a China-paper reproduction—no doubt attractive and beautiful from a distance but without any capacity to influence the atmosphere of the room. The fragrance in a flower, it may be noted, is neither in its petals, nor in its sepals; it is not in the gross structure of the flower at all; and yet, it is everywhere. The fragrance is the quality in the atmosphere around the flower, rising no doubt from the flower, but not bottled in the flower. Similarly, here the fragrance of the Lotus of *Mahābhārata* is the fragrance of the *Gītā*...here again it is not the *Gītā* as such but true significance of the *Gītā* (*Gītārtha*).

The various stories in the classical work of *Mahābhārata* form the endless whirls of petals that constitute the beauty of a lotus. A flower opens by the soft touch of the wafting breeze; here the Lotus has been opened softly by the stories of *Harī*—the spirit of Devotion that permeates the entire text of the classic as its very life giving substance.

A flower may be beautiful and attractive in its fragrance and it may be opened up in its full maturity by the motherly breeze, but still it does not fulfil itself unless it is capable of attracting to itself the pollen-carriers—the courtiers in the floral world—that reach it, from all over, to sing their buzzing song of love. They must fertilise the flower. In the world it is "the good and the pure" that throng the lotus of *Mahābhārata* to enjoy its honey-contents, and it is quite appropriate that the devotees desiring to enjoy *Mahābhārata* are considered as the honey-bees. The five sense organs and the mind together cosntittute the six feet of the enjoyer of the *Mahābhārata.* Such devotees drink the honey contents of the *Mahābhārata* joyously, day after day, because, the more they drink, the more their thirst seems to increase.

May this Lotus Flower bless him who wants to destroy the moral weaknesses and ethical imperfections in his bosom which are the natural consequences of an age steeped in pure materialism and utter sensuality.

मूकं करोति वाचालं पङ्गुं लङ्घयते गिरिम् ।
यत्कृपा तमहं वन्दे परमानन्दमाधवम् ॥ ८ ॥

Mūkaṁ karoti vācālaṁ paṅguṁ laṅghayate girim,
yat-kṛpā tam-ahaṁ vande paramānanda-mādhavam.

मूकम् *mūkam* = the dumb, mute; करोति *karoti* = renders, makes; वाचालम् *vācālam* = eloquent; पङ्गुम् *paṅgum* = the cripple; लङ्घयते *laṅghayate* = crosses; गिरिम् *girim* = mountain; यत्कृपा *yatkṛpā* = whose grace; तम् *tam* = that; अहम् *aham* = I; वन्दे *vande* = salute; परमानन्द-माधवम् *paramānanda-mādhavam* = the Supreme Bliss, *Mādhava.*

8. *I salute that Supreme Bliss* Mādhava, *whose grace renders the mute eloquent and the cripple cross mountains.*

In its literal translation, it is only a prayer to Lord *Kṛṣṇa* with whose grace nothing is impossible for a devotee in this world. Even the dumb can come to discover speech and the lame may easily cross over mountains. But, subjectively reconsidered, the very same stanza has a still deeper meaning.

Kṛṣṇa is called *Mādhava* because he once destroyed a demon called *Madhu. Madhu,* in the *Vedik* symbolism, is the *Karma phala*—impressions of the past actions. Naturally, *Mādhava* means that which is experienced beyond the mind and intellect, and the Self is Supreme Bliss (*Paramānanda*) indeed, Lord, the consort of *Lakṣmī* (*mā*). Thus, the ego salutes the Eternal Blissful Self within and when the Self is realised—whose grace has flooded the heart of seeker—the mute life of that man becomes full of Music Divine. Compare the commercial agent *Narendra* and the eloquent *Vivekānanda*; the classroom talks of a Professor of Mathematics in Punjab and the resounding music of *Śrī Svāmī Rāma Tīrtha*; the simple lispings of a young child in Jerusalem and the brilliant Sermon of Jesus—examples can be multiplied into thousands wherein the same truth is amplified again and again that man, after the experience of the tranquil Self, becomes so full of the Music of Life that he must sing on, and the others must get enthralled.

An instrument of music, we all know, cannot sing by itself unless it is tenderly taken up, restrung and retuned before the musician can tickle out of it its music contents. The instruments of the mind and intellect are now, in any average man, almost mute, because it lies in our bosom neglected and dusty. To take it up and return it to the Eternal *Śruti* is the work of a seeker, and the man of perfection is one who has discovered the music in the erstwhile silent fiddle.

He is lame whose instruments of locomotion are not of equal strength or length. In such a case, the movement is impeded at every step and to such an individual even walking on plain grounds becomes a struggle. Subjectively viewed in our inner composition and structure, we are all lame at present inasmuch as the 'legs' of our inner personality, constituted of our mind and intellect, are never of the same dimension or of equal strength. The maladjustment between the mind and the intellect makes us "limping" personalities, who are thereby rendered incapable of facing any steep challenge or formidable obstacle in life. A man of perfection is he who has during his self-development and training, brought out a harmonious development of his emotional and intellectual equipments so that he can thereafter face any number of struggles and cheerfully and readily win over them all. This is but the grace of the Self that is realised.

It is only in *Saṁskṛta*, that we find so frequently one and the same verse talking at once in two languages, entertaining both the average man of faith and the greater man of philosophical thought.

यं ब्रह्मा वरुणेन्द्ररुद्रमरुतः स्तुन्वन्ति दिव्यैः स्तवैः
वेदैः साङ्गपदक्रमोपनिषदैर्गायन्ति यं सामगाः ।
ध्यानावस्थित तद्गतेन मनसा पश्यन्ति यं योगिनो
यस्यान्तं न विदुः सुरासुरगणा देवाय तस्मै नमः ॥ ९ ॥

Yaṁ brahmā varuṇendra-rudra-marutaḥ
stunvanti divyaiḥ stavaiḥ
vedaiḥ sāṅga-pada-kramo-paniṣadair
gāyanti yaṁ sāmagāḥ,
dhyānā-vasthita tad-gatena manasā
paśyanti yaṁ yogino
yasyāntaṁ na viduḥ surā-sura-gaṇā
devāya tasmai namaḥ.

यम् *yam* = whom; ब्रह्मा *brahmā* = *Brahmā*; वरुण: *varuṇaḥ* = *Varuṇa*; इन्द्र: *indraḥ* = *Indra*; रुद्र: *rudraḥ* = *Rudra*; मरुत: *marutaḥ* = the *Maruta-s*; स्तुन्वन्ति *stunvanti* = invoke, praise; दिव्यै: *divyaiḥ* = by divine; स्तवै: *stavaiḥ* = by hymns; वेदै: *vedaiḥ* = by *Vedā-s*; स: अङ्ग पदक्रम उपनिषदै: *sa aṅga pada-krama upaniṣadaiḥ* = with their *Aṅgā-s* in the *Pada* and *Krama* methods and by the *Upaniṣad-s* i.e., through their correct and appropriate chantings; गायन्ति *gāyanti* = invoke (lit. sing); यम् *yam* = whom; सामगा: *sāmagāḥ* = the singer of *Sāma* songs; ध्यान अवस्थित तद्गतेन मनसा *dhyāna avasthita tadgatena manasā* = with their mind absorbed in the goal of their contemplation through perfect meditation; पश्यन्ति *paśyanti* = see, realise; यम् *yam* = whom; योगिन: *yoginaḥ* = the *Yogī-s*; यस्य *yasya* = whose; अन्तम् *antam* = limits (lit. end); न *na* = not; विदु: *viduḥ* = know; सुर असुर-गणा: *sura asura-gaṇāḥ* = the hosts of *Devā-s* and *Asurā-s*; देवाय *devāya* = God; तस्मै *tasmai* = to that; नम: *namaḥ* = salutations.

9. *Salutations to that God-head whom the Creator* Brahmājī, *Lord* Varuṇa, *Lord* Indra, *Lord* Rudra *and the Lord of the* Maruta-s *invoke with their divine hymns; whom the singers of* Sāma *songs invoke*

through their correct and appropriate chantings, whom the Yogī-s *realise with their minds absorved in the goal of their contemplation through perfect meditation and whose limits are not known even to the denizens of the heavens or to the* Asurā-s *of the nether Kingdom.*

No cleverer words have ever tried to bring, in their embrace, a clearer invocation addressed to the Transcendental and this stanza can be a universal prayer, irrespective of the creed and the religion to which the devotee belongs. The invocation to the Supreme-most is undertaken here through a peculiar literary trick. The extent of the Infinite cannot be comprehended by anyone and therefore, it can be only indicated by suggestive terms. Even the Creator and the *Vedik* Deities representing the phenomenal powers must be praying to and invoking their own glorious powers only at the altars of the Infinite and so it is said that we invoke Him, whom the deities of the *Vedik* period invoke by their Divine hymns.

That must be the same Eternal Truth which the erudite scholars and master-minds of the world invoke through their learned chanting of the *Vedik mantrā-s.* Again, it must be the same that is experienced by the full-time seekers who have retired into their caves of meditation, wherein their minds get stilled in meditation and get dissolved with the theme of their contemplation—to that Lord which is the common theme in all the above instances, whose limits are not realised even by the dwellers of the heaven or the masters of the hell—to Him our Salutations.

These above-mentioned nine stanzas attributed traditionally to the pen of *Madhusūdana Sarasvatī* are generally chanted by the students of the *Gītā* before they start their daily studies.

MAHĀBHĀRATA IN BRIEF

The *Mahābhārata* and *Rāmāyaṇa* are the two great Epics of India. Of these, the *Mahābhārata* is even called the Fifth *Veda* because of the treasures of wisdom it contains. In fact, this colossal work of *Veda Vyāsa,* the compiler of the *Vedik* text-books, contains about one hundred thousand couplets and it is often said that what is not explained in the *Mahābhārata* is not worth knowing. It contains tales of high moral value, legends and myths that were prevalent at that time, philosophical discussions and historical scrap-bits, but all these are held together and worked out in elaborate detail with artistic frills upon the framework of the story of a fratricidal war which took place between two branches of a Royal family.

Before the Christian era, there flourished in North India a powerful *Bhārata* Kingdom, and at the time of the story, *Pāṇḍu,* the younger brother ruled the Kingdom, as *Dhṛtarāṣṭra,* the elder Prince was born blind. For, according to the *Āryan Sanātana Dharma,* such disability disqualified a Prince from becoming a king.

King *Pāṇḍu* had two wives, *Kuntī** and *Mādrī*. By the former he had three sons—*Yudhiṣṭhira, Bhīma* and *Arjuna* and by the other, the twins—*Nakula* and *Sahadeva*. The blind royal brother, *Dhṛtarāṣṭra,* had begotten hundred sons by his consort, *Gāndhārī,* a princess from the *Kandhāra* in Afghanistan. *Gāndhārī* was so devoted a wife that from the time she came to know that her husband was blind, she had voluntarily bandaged her own eyes and thus denied to herself permanently the joy of sight, which, by fate, was denied to her lord.

Pāṇḍu, the ruling brother accidently killed a *brāhmaṇa* and to atone for the sin thus incurred, retired to the forests for

* *Kuntī*, the adopted daughter of King *Kuntibhoja*, was the daughter of *Śūrasena* of *Yadu* clan and was also named *Pṛthā*..... Ed.

tapas, leaving the children to the care of his blind brother. Before *Pāṇḍu* came of age, *Bhīṣma* (uncle of *Pāṇḍu* and *Dhṛtarāṣṭra*) was acting as the regent of the kingdom and he was affectionately called "grandsire" by the offsprings of both the brothers. He supervised their education and development. *Droṇa Ācārya*, a *brāhmaṇa* by birth, but a master in the art of archery and war, was appointed the tutor of the boys.

Bhīṣma is one of the noblest characters in the *Mahābhārata*. He had renounced his right to the throne to enable his father to marry a maiden of his choice for whose love he was pining away and whose people had laid down as a condition precedent to marriage that the offspring by her should inherit the throne. In a spirit of sacrifice and filial duty, *Bhīṣma* further vowed not to marry lest his children should later reclaim the right renounced by their father. *Bhīṣma* was blessed by his father in ecstasy of joy thus... "You will not die without yourself wishing for it."

Droṇa Ācārya instructed them all (sons of *Pāṇḍu* and *Dhṛtarāṣṭra*) in the science of war. They all grew under the same roof as real brothers getting equal treatment from all. *Yudhiṣṭhira*, the eldest among the *Pāṇḍū-s*, was by common consent to be the next heir to the throne.

With the passage of time, all of them developed their independent personality and began expressing their own distinctive tendencies. *Yudhiṣṭhira* grew to be an embodiment of *Dharma*, wedded to truth and always straightforward and noble. *Bhīma* exhibited a recklessness and daring almost as stupendous as was his stregth in giving and taking blows! *Arjuna* was the type of his age, an ideal youth of chivalry and heroism. He had all the qualities that endear one to the masses in any civilised age. All the *Pāṇḍava* brothers were throughout noted for the nobility of their character, and the more they were crushed by the external adverse circumstances, the more they gave out a charming fragrance of serenity, enduring faith, love, tolerance and goodness.

In a sharp contrast to these noble Five, was the brood of the *Kaurava* Hundred; the eldest of them *Duryodhana* was malicious, treacherous, cruel, scheming and ever willing to stoop to any crookedness to gain his mean ends. To him the end justified even the immoral means. Even from his boyhood he was aware that *Yudhiṣṭhira* was a great obstacle in his way to the thrown; at the same time he realised that he was no match to *Bhīma* or *Arjuna*. Even in those early days, he tried once to poison *Bhīma* out of sheer malice and jealousy; but *Bhīma* survived it by dint of his gigantic stamina.

The time came when *Yudhiṣṭhira* was, in an elaborate public installation ceremony, declared as the heir-apparent to the *Bhārata*-throne. As the first prince, he even took charge of his Royal office, proclaiming necessary laws and generally administering justice—of course, in close consultation with and as advised by his grandsire, *Bhīṣma Pitāmaha* and teacher *Droṇa Ācārya*. He charmed everyone by his sparking qualities of the head and heart.

The smouldering embers of jealosy in the bossom of *Duryodhana* were leaping into flames as he watched the noble destiny of his cousin *Yudhiṣṭhira*. *Dhṛtarāṣṭra*, the blind elder, was no doubt quite impartial between his sons and his nephews. He equally loved all the children, but certainly the blind old king had one defect—he had a weakness for his eldest son, *Duryodhana*. Thus, when *Duryodhana* pleaded and argued, the old man relented and unwillingly yet helplessly he had many a time, to permit and sanction plans which aimed at the destruction of *Pāṇḍava* boys.

Once, *Duryodhana*, with the knowledge and permission of his aged father, contrived to invite the *Pāṇḍavā-s* and their mother to a buiding, specially constructed of lac, and the plan was to burn down the building at night, when the mother and her five sons would be in deep sleep.

The plan was worked out in detail and at night the building was brunt down; but the *Pāṇḍava* family was tipped off in time with the news by some faithful servant and so in the early hours of the night they escaped by a secret path to the jungles beyond. They roamed in the jungles as poor *brāhmaṇā-s*, dreading the avenging and merciless hand of *Duryodhana* pursuing them.

It was at this time that *Draupadī*'s *Svayamvara** was proclaimed. The *Pāṇḍavā-s* too, in their jungle hide-out heard of this great challenge. The daughter of *Drupada* was a famous beauty at the time in North India and King *Drupada* ruled over the *Pañcāla* (Agra-Gwalior) *Deśa*.

To the *Svayamvara, Duryodhana* and many other suitors came in the hope of winning this nobel beauty of the north as wife. King *Drupada* had arraged for a competition. The suitor winning *Draupadī's* hand was to shoot successfully at the eye of a fish fixed hanging in the air, through a wheel that revolved below it—and the shooting was to be done by looking at its reflection in a pool of water kept on the ground!

Each suitor came forward, tried his aim and failed. Then, from among the crowd, a *brāhmaṇa* came forward to try his luck. Everybody laughed in their royal sleeves at the ambitious *brāhmaṇa* youth! Nobody saw through the *brāhmaṇa*-dress, until the fish-eye was hit with ease and grace! Winner of *Draupadī*'s hand was none other than the master archer of the day, *Arjuna* himself.

Draupadī was accordingly given in marriage and the five brothers conducted the princess towards the hideout where *Kuntī* waited. As they approached the hut, rather late that day, the anxious mother heard the joyous brothers approaching the hut loudly calling "Come out *Mā*! See what we have brought today." The loving *Mā*, from within called back as always do, "whatever it be, share it equally among you all." Poor *Mā* thought it was some eatable, some hunt bagged. *Draupadī* thus became the wife of the brothers equally.

In the ceremony at *Drupada's* palace, there was *Kṛṣṇa* and *Balarāma*, both realted to *Drupada* and were in a way cousions

* A tradition in ancient India to invoke suitors—the Kings and Princes to claim the hand of a Princess in marriage after fulfilling stipulated conditions.....Ed.

to the *Pāṇḍavā-s*. They too followed them, for, *Kṛṣṇa* could recognise the *Pāṇḍavā-s* in spite of their *brāhmaṇa* make up.

Interrupting the story here, a few words about *Kṛṣṇa*:—

Kṛṣṇa was born in *Vṛṣṇi* clan to *Vasudeva* and *Devakī*, sister of *Kaṁsa* who was the cruel ruler of *Mathurā*. *Kaṁsa* tyrannised one and all, including his father *Ugrasena* whom he had imprisoned and usurped the throne. *Kaṁsa* was a despot of the worst type and crushed all opposition to his devilish ambition. He, however, had a soft corner for his sister *Devakī*, whose marriage, he celebrated in lavished style. After the marriage, his himself drove the chariot carrying *Devakī* and her husband to her new home. On the way a mysterious voice warned, "The eighth child by this couple shall kill thee." *Kaṁsa* flew into his most vicious temper at once and drew his sword to chop off the heads of *Devakī* and *Vasudeva* whom he had set out to escort so lovingly. *Devakī* begged for mercy and promised to surrender to him all the children that may be born to her. This appealed to him and thus were spared the lives of *Devakī* and *Vasudeva* who were, however, put into a strongly guarded jail.

One after the other, seven children were taken away from the parents, no sooner than they were born and done away with at the behest of the cruel *Kaṁsa*. *Devakī* was due to deliver the eighth child. This time the guards were doubled, chains were strengthened and the vigilant jail-officers were alerted. The day came, *Bhādrapāda Kṛṣṇa Aṣṭamī*. It was a dark night and the rain was pouring heavily. All the guards felt sleepy and lay down.

It was an easy delivery.

Vasudeva was aghast!.....!! Divine! Lord himself!..... speaking? What? ....!! "Take me to *Gokul* to *Nanda's* house; there a girl-child is born just now. Leave me there and bring that child back here." ....!! No. it must be all hallucination .... mere imagination! ......!!

But irresistibly *Vasudeva* lifted the child and went forward. How strange!....the chains dropped down!.... and the doors, of themselves, stood open!.... the flooded *Yamunā* river gave a clear way. He walked across. At *Nanda*'s house all lay fast asleep..... the children were exchanged and the prisoner returned.

The rain pelted on; the doors slowly clanged back and the chains became as they were. The girl-child started her innocent but incessant cry. The guard woke up. The news spread .....! *Kaṁsa* came and dragged the child by the feet, whirled her in the air and was about to dash her on a stone! She slipped from his hand and rose high up in the sky. As she went she said, "I would have killed you myself for your cruelty .... but I forgive you, for, you touched my feet even though to kill me. Remember, the boy who is kill you, is born; he is in *Gokul*. Be warned." So saying she disappeared into the Sky as lightning.

At *Gokul* all had a pleasant surprise. *Nanda* and *Yaśodā* were the most surprised but they forgot everything in their joy; after all, it was a boy and not a girl as they thought.

Kaṁsa would not stop at anything. He hatched many a diabolic plot to kill all the children of *Kṛṣṇa*'s age. Many were killed. But the Blue-boy seemed to thrive on such plots. When some of *Kaṁsa*'s cruel and crafty emissaries reached Him, on the pretext of play, *Kṛṣṇa* each time turned their plots back upon themselves, as though in child's play.

Time passed on. This child showed many divine miracles to *Yaśodā* and others. But all of them, in the quick delusions, thought it all to be some strange hallucination.... and again considered Him to be only their lucky Blue-Boy.

The boy grew up. He was sent out with the cowherd boys to tend the cattle. *Kṛṣṇa*, from childhood, was full of an irrepressible energy and activity. He was all fun, frolic and adventure. So restless and mischievous in childhood... He would steal or loot the "haves" of all their milk, curd and butter and share these with his *Gopā* friends, the "have-nots." Complaints used to pour in at *Yaśodā's* door. *Yaśodā* compensated the complainants but she would invariably forget to punish the Divine Child.

Once the *gopī-s* complained collectively to *Yaśodā* and suggested tying him down. *Yaśodā* allowed them to have their way, but lo! no rope would suffice to encircle Him, the *Viśvarūpin*! Despaired, the *gopī-s* sought *Yaśodā's* help. *Yaśodā* acceeded and took a very small rope for the purpose, but that was enough to tie the Lord who succumbed to *Yaśodā's* love rather than to the *gopī's ahaṅkāra*. On another occasion, it was complained that *Kṛṣṇa* had eaten mud. To *Yaśodā's* order he opened His mouth where she saw the entire universe and turned her face away from this, yet another so called hallucination.

Kṛṣṇa continued to grow to chagrin of *Kaṁsa*. *Nanda*, the chieftain and his friend moved to the forests of V*ṛndāvana*. There along the banks of the *Yamunā*, the Divine Blue Boy frisked about and indulged from one pleasant mischief into another. *Kṛṣṇa* in *Vṛndāvanam* was an embodiment of *joie-de-vivre*. His flute, shepherd's reed to be precise, was the symbol of his care-free, light-hearted life of chaste joys and unearthly bliss. *Kṛṣṇa* is perhaps, the only prophet (*Avatāra*) that was never known to have wept—ever laughing, ever active, ever ethusiastic, thirsty to live, hungry to exprience. He was in love with life—-be it on the *Yamunā* banks, in political discussions, in the home, in the forest or on the war front. He was Life itself—the warm, radiant Life! He led the hectic crowd of the gay *gopā*-boys and the giggling bunch of *gopī*-girls aways followed Him.

Kṛṣṇa was twelve now. All attempts of *Kaṁsa* to remove the dread that weighed so heavy on him failed. So he planned a huge festival at *Mathurā* to which many nobles and chieftains were invited—*Kṛṣṇa* and *Balarāma* were also among the distinguished guests. Many games and feats were on the agenda—naturally the entire cowherd folk also thronged there to see the *Tamāśā* (fun-fair).

Kṛṣṇa and *Balarāma* entered the festival and as they were taking their appropriate place among the assembled nobles, a wrestler came forward to challenge *Kṛṣṇa* for a mock wrestling match. This was another scheme to kill *Kṛṣṇa*, but the Lord of all Hearts understood it, accepted the challenge, and in the ensuing bout, killed the challenging wrestler. Immediately therafter, *Kṛṣṇa* ran up to the Royal balcony—wherefrom his uncle, speechless and staggered was looking down at the failure of his plans—and in a split moment *Kaṁsa* was hurled down from the heights to the grounds, where he lay dead. The kingdom was given away to *Kaṁsa's* father, *Ugrasena*, who was languishing in a prison where his tyrant son had imprisoned him.

This marks a turning point in His programme of activities. All the chidish pranks, the mischievous rustic games, the love-plays, dancing and music suddenly came to an end. *Kṛṣṇa* did not return to *Vṛndāvana*. From *Mathurā* He went to *Dvārakā*, built the city and consolidated a kingdom there. From then onwards, he intervened in many a dispute; many a king he made; in many a kingdom he decided either in favour of the one or the other—but he remained ever a king-maker, never aspiring to annex others' territories. He advised on diplomacy, statecraft, war, etc., but never Himself sat on any throne, won or saved through influence and might. In fact, *Kṛṣṇa* did not rule even *Dvārakā*. He was all the time engaged in putting down the wrong and propping up the right.

Again ever-energetic and enthusiastic, he courted all those in trouble with His Infinite cheer, solved all their problems and lived tirelessly serving others. He constantly remained in everything and yet far away from all! He was the Centre of attraction—he was the most important pesonality in all the major political events of His time! He advised but never imposed His will upon others. He seemed to watch from afar though living under the same roof. He actually lived all His life what he preached in the *Gītā* later, without attachment, loving, serving and working but caring not for the fruits, he ever mingled with everything, yet was always far away from all, always. A perfect *Yogī*, he lived a life full of activity serving all at all times—but keeping Himself more as a spectator of all happiness. He lived here amidst all, more as a sojourner upon the earth than as a native of it!

Now continuing the main story ......

Kṛṣṇa thus reached the hut of *Kuntī* to bless the newly married *Draupadī*. With the new marriage alliance and with *Kṛṣṇa*'s friendship, the *Pāṇḍava* brothers gathered courage and reappeared. *Dhṛtarāṣṭra* was informed. At the compulsion of *Bhīṣma*, the blind king agreed to give them half of the kingdom, while the other half would be ruled by his own sons.

Yudhiṣṭhira had exhibited his fine sense of vision and foresight when he built his splendid new Capital at *Indraprastha* near the present metropolis of Delhi. The remnants of the ancient fort (*Purāṇā Quilā*) built by *Yudhiṣṭhira* still stand as monuments of Indian architectural perfections, in spite of the vicissitudes of time and elements. It is a 'must see' for the modern tourist.

This comparatively small kingdom ruled by such a far-sighted economist and administrator as *Yudhiṣṭhira*, soon became a prosperous unit, self-sufficient in all their needs. With plentitude of cattle and good harvests people prospered. *Kṛṣṇa* bacame a very close friend of the royal family and advised *Yudhiṣṭhira* in every department of his administration. *Arjuna* soon grew to be the dearest friend of *Kṛṣṇa*. They were both seen cosntantly together in close companionship.

Duryodhana and his brothers were also among the distinguished guests at the coronation ceremony of *Yudhiṣṭhira* as King of *Indraprastha*. *Yudhiṣṭhira's* glory kindled again the flames of jealousy in *Duryodhana*'s breast. He decided to bring about dishonour to and down-fall of his cousion's popularity and fair name, by any means whatsoever, fair or foul.

For his diabolical plans, *Duryodhana* found in his uncle—one of his mother's cousins—*Śakunī*, a notorious sharper in dice-play, a fit and reliable friend. *Śakunī* also knew no scruples; nor respected any; to him fair play was anathema.

For all his goodness, *Yudhiṣṭhira* had one great weakness—playing dice and once he entered the game, his chivalrous nature prompted him to be reckless in his stakes. *Duryodhana* knew this and he decided to invite his cousin to play a game of dice. *Dhṛtarāṣṭra* was soon persuaded to give his consent and royal brothers from *Indraprastha* were invited. The *Pāṇḍavā-s* arrived—the game started. Of course *Śakunī* was to play the specially loaded dice for *Duryodhana.*

Game after game, the visiting team, naturally, lost. Each loss whetted *Yudhiṣṭhira's* zest for the game and he bacame more and more reckless in his stakes. He staked his kingdom, brothers, wife—all, but the loaded dice, played by the heartless sharper, always won!

Duryodhana's joy knew no bounds. He ordred one of his younger brothers, *Duḥśāsana* to bring *Draupadī* to the court and to insult her publicly; she was now his as the *Pāṇḍavā-s* had lost her to him in the game. The shamelss brute, intoxicated with his ill-gotten victory, did not hesitate to order that *Draupadī* be stripped naked in public. *Duḥśāsana* tugged at *Draupadī*'s *sārī** and kept on tugging. But the *sārī* miraculously proved endless. A mountain of cloth was collected. *Duḥśāsana* perspired. *Draupadī*'s prayers were answered and by the grace of the Lord she remained draped as before.

All the elders in the court were horrified at this unexpected turn of events. Everybody felt that it was a high-handed excess; but when one is drunk with power, no reason can influence the animal in such a victor. *Dhṛtarāṣṭra*, the blind royal father, trembled with fear; he knew deep within him that woman outraged can effectively curse and bring immediate disaster to the royal family. The grand old blind king called *Draupadī* to his side and requested her to ask of him three boons, as atonement for the outrage committed by his sons.

With her first boon, she demanded freedom for *Yudhiṣṭhira*; with the second, freedom for the rest of the *Pāṇḍava* brothers together with their weapons. These were granted. When *Dhṛtarāṣṭra* asked, "What about the third boon?' she paused

* A traditional Indian dress .... having 5.5 to 8 metres of length .... wrapped around waist, worn by women in India. ---Ed.

and replied, "The *Pāṇḍavā-s*, once freed, can look after themselves—they need no help from anyone."

Finding his plans unsuccessful, *Duryodhana* again persuaded his father to permit him to invite *Yudhiṣṭhira* once more for a game of dice. *Dhṛtarāṣṭra* yielded; the old father was helpless in yielding to his eldest son—that was his weakness and the cause of his sorrows, and ultimate doom.

Yudhiṣṭhira was invited to play again. He accepted as it was a point of honour to *Dharmaputra*. This time the stake was that he who loses will leave his kingdom and go into the forests to live there a recluse-life for twelve years, at the end of which the losing party will live incognito for one year in some city or town. If they were recognised during the thirteenth year, they would again have to go for a twelve-year sojourn in the forests. This was accepted; the game progressed; *Yudhiṣṭhira* lost!

The *Pāṇḍava* brothers, righteous as they were, got ready to go to the forest. They took leave of the elders and when they came to *Dhrtarāṣṭra*, he said, "Children! when you come back after the thirteenth year successfully living all the terms, you shall walk into your kingdom as you came out of it today, to play the dice. "Promise was that there would be no hitch to their regaining their kingdom and for the thirteen years during which the *Pāṇḍavā-s* were to remain in exile *Duryodhana* was to administer *Indraprastha* as a trustee only.

The *Pāṇḍava* brothers spent their twelve years of life in the forests, practising austerities, spending their time among the ascetics and generally living a Life Divine. *Kṛṣṇa* and *Arjuna* had, during these years, spent together many a day and night discussing matters religious and spiritual. They discussed life, world, God and Soul. Very interesting philosophical passages occur in the *Mahābhārata* dealing with this period of the *Pāṇḍavā-s*' life.

The thirteenth year arrived and it was spent in the palace of the King of *Virāta*, where the five brothers and *Draupadī* worked as domestics. At long last, the stipulated time was over. *Duryodhana* was making frantic efforts to discover the *Pāṇḍavā-s* during this last year of their exile—so that he could condemn them again for another twleve years—but all his plans proved futile.

The *Pāṇḍavā-s* returned claiming their kingdom back. The royal father's words at the time of their departure was their only sanction and guarantee; but *Duryodhana* had enjoyed the empire without a rival for so long that his lusty and greedy nature would not yield even a jot! He had made powerful alliances with all other neighbouring kings; the exchequer was his; the army was his to command. *Droṇa* and *Bhīṣma* were insisting that *Yudhiṣṭhira* must be given back his kingdom; *Kṛṣṇa* pleaded for reconciliation but *Duryodhana* would not yield. According to him, he had won the kingdom by the rules of *Dharma* and *Yudhiṣṭhira* who lost it in dice, had no right to demand back. "No, not even shall I give them five houses, nay, not even one house—Why, not even enough land to carry on the tip of a needle!"

Thus, war became inevitable. Feverish preparations soon started. The *Pāṇḍavā-s* also sent out their appeal to their friends and well-wishers. Many answered their call for help in a just war. *Kṛṣṇa* was approached by both *Arjuna* and *Duryodhana*; *Kṛṣṇa* said, "Since you both demand my help. I divide myself like this— my army and all my weapons for one and myself unarmed for the other." He asked *Duryodhana* what choice he would make. *Duryodhana*, of course, chose to have the forces; *Arjuna* was happy to have *Kṛṣṇa* as his charioteer.

Before the war, *Dhṛtarāṣṭra* sent a hesitant half-hearted *Sañjaya* to *Arjuna* with a secret message full of psychological implications and diabolical auto-suggestions which were calculated to undermine his morale. And actually it did....the very same words came tumbling out of his mouth in the second chapter of the *Gītā* as his arguments against fighting this war! When well-aimed and intelligently used, perhaps, psychological weapons are more powerful and deadly than even the modern nuclear-weapons.

Just at the outset of the war, when the preparations were made frantically by both the parties, *Yudhiṣṭhira* had an emotional break-down and felt stricken by his conscience; but *Kṛṣṇa* ran to him and explained how hard he had tried to avoid the war; but it was irresistible and that destiny must be fulfilled. *Dharmaputra* was assured that none would ever accuse him of being the aggressor because it was a war of righteousness. Hearing this, *Yudhiṣṭhira* took heart and thereafter never during the war showed any sign of losing his morale.

Bhīṣma, the grandsire, *Droṇa*, the *brāhmaṇa* teacher of millitary art of all the royal boys, *Karṇa*, the half-brother of *Arjuna*, were all in the *Kaurava* forces. *Bhīṣma* and *Droṇa*, wise and far sighted, as they were, must have felt what would be the final outcome of this fraticidal war. They were helpless as they were in the service of *Dhṛtarāṣṭra* for so long. "To be true to the salt one has eaten" was a great rule of conduct which the loyal *Hindū* always respected. *Karṇa* had a chivalrous rivalry with *Arjuna*, who was an equally great hero; it was the rivalry of two equally great arches! One world was too small a place for such two great men of such might, ambition and prowess!

On the fateful day, both the armies assembled. *Bhīṣma* commanded the *Kaurava* forces and *Dhṛṣṭadyumna*, son of *Drupada* king of *Pañcāla*. *Pāṇḍavā-s* own brother-in-law was the Commander-in-Chief of their forces. No doubt, *Duryodhana*'s army was overwhelming in its number, equipment and supplies; the *Pāṇḍavā-s* forces were less in number, meagre in war-materials and fewer in the number of their available real heores and notable men-of-war, yet....the *Pāṇḍavā-s* could fight with inspiration, while the *Kauravā-s* had to bear a heavy conscience and plan their moves with a guilty conscience.

As the armies stood in battle array—the *Kauravā-s* in the Bird-design and the *Pāṇḍavā-s* in Wheel-design—*Arjuna*, thrilled to the tip of his fingers with his impatience to start the game of war, asked *Kṛṣṇa* to drive his chariot around and stop it for a while in between the two armies so that he might inspect their strength and observe who all were the champions in his enemy lines.

He reviewed. He saw, He was bewildered. The voice of *Sañjaya* conveying the message of *Dhṛtarāṣṭra*, was faithfully clamouring in his brain! Uncles, brothers, relations, friends, teachers, and grand-sire *Bhīṣma* himself—all stood arrayed in the enemy lines. To kill them all was the duty—if *Arjuna* wanted the kingdom and the joys of ruling over it, glory and power, joys of wealth and riches all smeared with the blood of the dear and near, the revered and the respected, the adored and the loved!....!!

The challenge was too much for *Arjuna.* He broke down. He was in tears. His bow, *Gāṇḍīva*, slipped off from his dejected hands! Trembling in his limbs, pale and haggard in his looks, he stared at *Kṛṣṇa*—a psychological wreck, a man of ruined morale! He started protesting—in broken words—blabbering. He talked of the ignominies of war. He repeated all the arguments of all pacifists. He quoted *Dharma Śāstrā-s* and at last he declared, "It is better to eat by begging alms than rule over this kingdom after killing all these men in battle."

Kṛṣṇa saw the state of delusion in which *Arjuna* was. As a true and able psychologist, *Kṛṣṇa* read the confusion in *Arjuna*'s heart, diagnosed its causes and decided that immediately he must be whipped to activity by sharp words that will really go home. A psychological surgery was needed and He used the sharpest of knives: "Oh! *Arjuna*, this cowardly nervousness in the face of a crisis is not fit for an Aryan and is an impediment to your welfare hereafter," etc.

This shock-therapy, through sudden insult, had an evident effect. *Arjuna* started again noisy blabberings. The Lord allowed him to exhaust himself and then started His more thorough treatment of the shattered mental constitution of *Arjuna* through His Divine Song, *Śrīmad Bhagavad Gītā*. No better setting could have been given to the Philosophy of Life—Which is true *Hindūism*—than this battlefield.

Religion is easier and simpler to live and practise in secluded forests, it can be considered even a luxury if it were to be lived only in the sanctum of a church or a temple; but a philosophy that has no bearing on life has no pith. Here in the *Gītā*, *Hindūism* is in action—the dynamism of the wisdom of the seers brought to bear upon a crisis in one single individual's life! How the entire history of the country was made by the successful rehabilitation of one erring, deluded hero, was amplified in the *Mahābhārata*. That which could then revive a normal man, *Arjuna*, from his derangements into an integrated whole being, can be made use of even now in reviving everyone who is in the state of *Arjuna*, if he but approaches the *Gītā* with the faith and ugency of *Arjuna*.

What *Kṛṣṇa* taught *Arjuna*—perhaps with a look or a few words—has been given to us by *Vyāsa*, in the *Gītā* of seven hundred stanzas, put in the mouth of *Sañjaya*.

At the outset of the war, *Vyāsa* offered the born-blind *Dhṛtarāṣṭra* a divine power of vision—so that he might satisfy personally his desire to see the war with his own eyes, but the old royal-father, who instinctively dreaded the outcome of the unjust war, refused to accept the kind offer, but wanted to get reports of what was happening on the war-front. Hence, *Vyāsa* gave *Sañjaya* both the powers of seeing and hearing all that was happening in *Kurukṣetra*, even while sitting in the palace at *Hastināpura*.

Sañjaya's sympathies were evidently on the side of the *Pāṇḍavā-s*. He was evidently feeling very guilty for having had to play as an unwilling cat's-paw, in the old king's mean plot for undermining *Arjuna*'s nerves and fire. No greater soul of nobler sympathies could we ever get for reporting the *Gītā* to posterity than *Sañjaya*—"our own Special Correspondent."

How far the *Gītā* had been effective in the case of *Arjuna* was evidently clear from his own admission, "My delusions have dropped, I now remember my true nature" (in Chapter XVIII-73). The heroic actions that followed clearly showed that *Arjuna* had been cured of all his emotional derangements from which he had been suffering—we might say all his life-time. From childhood onwards, he had been smarting under the injustices and wrongs he had had to put up with and perhaps, he was bitterly jealous of *Duryodhana*'s palpable success even though his means were low and unfair. These repressed emotions, released a volume of energy, which *Arjuna* could not direct into proper channels at this critical hour and hence his confusions, grief and even cowardice.

Once *Kṛṣṇa* set *Arjuna*'s psychological equipments right, through the wisdom of the *Gītā*, he, the indomitable hero, sprang to his feet, bow in hand and thereafter he was death to all; he was annihilation to the outnumbering *Kaurava* forces. After eighteen days of unceasing warfare, *Duryodhana* was laid low by *Bhīma's* club, *Droṇa* was killed by *Dhṛṣṭadyumna*, who in turn was stampeded and killed by *Droṇa's* son. *Draupadī* lost all her five children: both sides lay waste in Death's own courtyard! The flames died down to embers; the flight of arrows stopped in panting weariness.

Kings lay dead among the dying animals, between broken chariots, among broken limbs and headless trunks! Vultures hovered around impatiently hungry, perhaps never before had they a feast of such pure royal flesh and blood. The heart-tearing wailing of the survivors'—mothers, wives, children, aged fathers and grand-fathers—rent the skies. They miserably waded through human blood and torn flesh and bones searching for their husbands, sons, fathers and brothers—all cursing the ambitious war-mongers who brought about such total havoc to society...!

Gāndhārī, mother of the *Kaurava* brothers, came forward to embrace her dead children. She heard *Kṛṣṇa*'s approaching feet. With the burning fire of a mother's bleeding heart, she cursed : "*Kṛṣṇa*, you stood by and saw the entire family being killed. It was all due to Thy indifference. You too shall, similarly, become the slayer of your own kinsmen. As the women now weep here in *Kurukṣetra*, your own women-folk shall weep in desolation—and you too shall perish by foul means, in wilderness, in the thiry-sixth year from now!"

Kṛṣṇa replied: "May all these be blessings of thine, *O! Gāndhārī*, for thus helping me to find a way out. The *Vṛṣṇī-s* have become so powerful that they must now end by fighting among themselves. I too must quit, "my temporary mission is now over!"

Thereafter *Kṛṣṇa* gave her a discourse, hearing which the bereaved mother's inner eye opened to see the whole incident in its true perspective. She was consoled and she realised that Royal boys, born of Royal parents, could have no better end than in the war-field fighting for power and wealth.

Yudhiṣṭhira was crowned as King. *Dhṛtarāṣṭra* and *Gāndhārī* retired to the forests to spend the rest of their life in retirement and prayers. For thirty-six years, the eldest of the *Pāṇḍavā-s* ruled the kingdom true to his name, *Dharmaputra*. Never was North India so happy and so prosperous, so justly ruled and so faithfully served in all aspects of her cultural aspirations.

The time had come for *Gāndhārī*'s curse to be fulfilled. Civil war broke out in *Dvārakā*. All able-bodied men died, Lord *Kṛṣṇa* sent a message to the *Pāṇḍavā-s* to come and take charge of the womenfolk. He himself knew that His time had come to fold up his *Māyā*-made manifestation. He retired and lay down under a tree with mind gathered and attention fixed upon His *Sahaja* Nature—as the Infinite, Eternal Self of all.

A hunter saw the Lord's red-heels, and mistaking them for a deer lying curled up in rest, shot his arrow—when he came near he realised the mistake he had made..... he wailed, and penitently asked for forgiveness. The Lord consoled him with a smile of blessedness. Even when He in His *Līlā* assumes a form to re-establish *Dharma* from time to time, He strictly follows the rules of the game. There must be a cause for ending His embodiment. He ascended back to His Infinite Nature.

Thus, Lord *Kṛṣṇa* of *Vṛndāvana*, the beloved of the *Gopī-s*, the Hero of *Mathurā* and Annihilator of *Kaṁsa*, the Killer of *Jarāsaṁdha*, the Architect of *Dvārakā*, the friend of

Arjuna, the central fingure in the *Mahābhārata* war—after finishing His game of hastening the doom of the bad and the redemption of the good; His game of declaring to the world that He can love as Love alone can, and yet can ever remain completely and divinely detached; His game of making kingdoms and giving them away to the rightful to rule over and enjoy; His game of being in everything and yet identifying with nothing....He dissolved His manifestation and made an exit from this stage of life to enter the Life Eternal Beyond!

When *Arjuna* reached *Dvārakā*, he found there a scene of utter devastation and misery. He gathered all the desolate women and started for his capital. On the way, some dacoits pounced upon the party and carried away many women. *Arjuna* found that he had not even the strength to wield his mighty bow *Gāṇḍīva*! He realised that with *Kṛṣṇa*'s departure his strength and might had also vanished.

The five brothers decided to retire. They set *Arjuna*'s grandson, *Parīkṣita*, on the throne and leaving the kingdom under his care, the brothers along with *Draupadī* started towards the *Himālayās*. As they went, one by one the brothers fell on the way to breathe their last. *Yudhiṣṭhira* plodded along with *Draupadī* and a stray dog both of whom accompanied him faithfully, all along. At last *Draupadī* also fell to join her forefathers. *Yudhiṣṭhira* was alone now ascending the peaks beyond *Badrīnātha*, when celestial Angels brought a Divine Chariot for him to go bodily to heaven.

But the dog.....No!....Dogs were not allowed to get into celestial chariots.....much less could they go to heaven bodily!.... The embodiment of rightousness *Yudhiṣṭhira* unhesitatingly said, "All right, then, I too do not want the enjoyment of heaven if I have to discard it for a faithful friend—be it a dumb animal, a dog."

At this, the dog assumed its real from; it was Lord Death—*Dharma Rāja* Himself—wanting to test *Dharma-Niṣṭhā* of *Yudhiṣṭhira*. He went to heaven, where he met all his brothers and many of his relations.

GENERAL INTRODUCTION

Śrīmad Bhagavad Gītā, the Divine Song of the Lord, occurs in the *Bhīṣma Parva* of the *Mahābhārata*, and comprises eighteen chapters, from the 25th to the 42nd. This great handbook of practical living marked a positive revolution in *Hindūism* and inaugurated a *Hindū* renaissance for the ages that followed the *Paurāṇik* Era.

Veda Vyāsa, the author of *Mahābhārata*, was the most daring religious revolutionary that ever appeared on the horizon of the *Hindū* cultural history. By his time the glorious *Vedik* law had fallen into much disuse, and perhaps into a lot of misuse, the orthodox divided each *Veda* into three sections: the *Karma Kāṇḍa* (the ritualistic section), the *Upāsanā Kāṇḍa* (the section dealing with methods of worship and concentration) and the *Jñāna Kāṇḍa* (the section dealing with pure philosophy). These had come to be mere formal names, carrying with them only the charm and novelty of museum exhibits rather than the joy and utility of any practical lessons to live a better life.

In the Song of the Lord, the *Gītā*, the Poet-Seer *Vyāsa* has brought the *Vedik* truths from the sequestered Himalayan caves into the active fields of political life and into the confusing tensions of an imminent fratricidal war. Under the stress of some psychological mal-adjustments, *Arjuna* got shattered in his mental equipoise and lost his capacity to act with true discrimination. Lord *Kṛṣṇa* takes in hand that neurotic mind of *Arjuna* for a *Hindū* treatment with *Vedik* truths.

Religion is philosophy in action. From time to time an ancient philosophy needs intelligent re-interpretation in the context of new times, and men of widsdom, prophets, and seers guide the common man on how to apply affectively the ancient laws in his present life.

Almost for the first time, therefore, *Vyāsa* depicted the story of the divine incarnation, *Kṛṣṇa*, who is called as the *Vāsudeva*, the *Parmātman*. And Lord *Kṛṣṇa* was made to declare the new message of the *Gītā* which is, we shall find, nothing but a reinterpretation of the ancient wisdom of the *Upaniṣad-s* with proper emphasis upon certain vital concepts which were distorted out of all recognition.

Great research scholars have now brought to light the fact that long before the *Mahābhārata* was written, there was in existence a deity, worshipped by the *Vṛṣṇi* clan, called *Vāsudeva*. Thus identifying *Kṛṣṇa* as *Vāsudeva* meant more than that he was the son of *Vāsudeva*. It is a direct attempt at deification of *Kṛṣṇa* into the status and dignity of an incarnation. With this *Hindūism* enters its theistic era of recognising a God-man as the Lord, the Supreme *Puruṣottam*, descending in the form of a mortal for the reorientation of our forgotten *Dharma* and to put our decadent culture back again on its high pedestal.

Thus, as we said earlier, if the *Upaniṣad-s* are the text-books of philosophical principles discussing man, world and God, the *Gītā* is a handbook of instructions as to how every human being can live the subtle philosophical principles of *Vedānta* in the actual work-a-day world and thus be a true citizen of the incomparable *Ārya Varta—Hindūstān*.

Arjuna is no new character in the *Mahābhārata*. Pages after pages of descriptions have painted thick the valour and glory, the beauty and strength, the nobility and chivalry of the greatest of the archers of his time, *Arjuna*. And yet, we find in the *Gītā* that we have one whole chapter dedicated in bringing out the character of *Arjuna*, to whom this immortal Song of Truth was sung by the divine teacher, *Kṛṣṇa*.

On this score, there are a few critics of the *Gītā* who claim that the first chapter is but a connecting link between the

Gītā proper and the *Mahābhārata*. To reject thus the opening chapter would be to blockade our true understanding of the deeper significances of the message of the *Gītā*. No doubt, *Arjuna*, the man—his physical status, beauty, strength and capacity—has been fully brought out earlier in the great classic but the *Gītā* is not addressed to the physical entity in *Arjuna* but to the mental and intellectual constitution of that heroic prince. Under the stress of some psychological maladjustments, *Arjuna* got shattered in his mental equipoise and lost his capacity to act with true discrimination. Lord *Kṛṣṇa* takes in hand that neurotic mind of *Arjuna* for a *Hindū* treatment with *Vedik*-truths. Such a practical application of *Hindūism* was almost unknown at the time of the *Mahābhārata*. By the Song of the Lord, the *Gītā*, *Vyāsa* has brought out the *Vedik* truths from the sequestered Himalayan caves into the active fields of political life and into the confusing tensions of an eminent fratricidal war.

There are many commentators, who, in their own style, proclaim that the Message of the *Gītā* is the 'Message of Action.' Hasty students, in their half-digested understanding of the *Gītā*, repeat this slogan but when, they try to translate it into their own actions, they find themselves unable to live the *Gītā* in life. Thus, we have today more people who *talk* on the *Gītā* than those who *learn* the *Gītā*; more who *read* the *Gītā* than *understand* the Divine Song; and indeed, very few who try to live the *Gītā*.

Especially, among the educated classes, many sincere students of the *Bhagavad Gītā*, after their best efforts to appreciate its decalrations, have come to the conclusion viz., "*Gītā* is one of the greatest books in the world explaining a wondorous philosophy to read and appreciate rather than to live and benefit by." Though we may meet a few who would, in their sentimental devotion to the *Gītā*, verbally declare that the *Gītā* can be lived, we will find that a few questions to them would reveal that, in their inner most hearts, they have their own doubts as to how 'desireless activity' without egoism would purify man's inner nature and help him to evolve more and more to the status of a God-man

If we try to digest properly the implications of the *Gītā*'s advice in the light of *Vedik* lore, it becomes amply clear how actions performed without ego-centric desires purge the mind of its deep-seated impressions and make it increasingly subtle in its purification and preparation for greater flights into the Infinite Beyond. To explain this, we will just try to review a little the conception of the mind and its functions in our day-to-day life.

Mind is man. *As the mind, so is the individual.* If the mind is distrurbed, the individual is disturbed. If the mind is good, the individual is good. This mind, for purposes of our study and understanding, may be considered as constituted of two distinct sides---one facing the world of stimuli that reach it from the objects of the world, and the other facing the "within" which reacts to the stimuli received. The outer mind facing the object is called the objective mind---in *Saṁskṛta* we call it the *Manas*— and the inner mind is called the subjective mind---in *Saṁskṛta*, the *Buddhi*.

That individual is whole and healthy in whom the objective and subjective aspects of the mind work in unison with each other, and in moments of doubt, the *objective mind* readily comes under the disciplining inflluence of the *subjective mind*. But unfortunately, except for a rare few, the majority of us have minds that are split. This split between the *subjective* and the *objective* aspects of our mind is mainly created by the layer of egoistic desires in the individual. The greater the distance between these two phases of the mind, the greater is the inner confusion in the individual, and the greater the egoism and low desires which such an individual comes to exhibit in life.

Through the five "gateways of knowledge," the organs of perception, all of us experience the world of objects around us at all moments of our waking state. The innumerable stimuli that react with our sense organs (receptors), create impulses which reach the *objective* mind and these impulses filter deep down to the *subjective* stratum through the intervening layers of individual ego-centric desires. These impulses, thus reaching the *subjective* mind of a person, react with the existing impressions of his own past actions that are carefully stored away in the *subjective* layer and express themselves in the world outside through the five organs of action (effectors).

The Diagram "A" gives figuratively the design of each activity that man performs in the world outside when he consciously comes to react with a given set of stimuli.

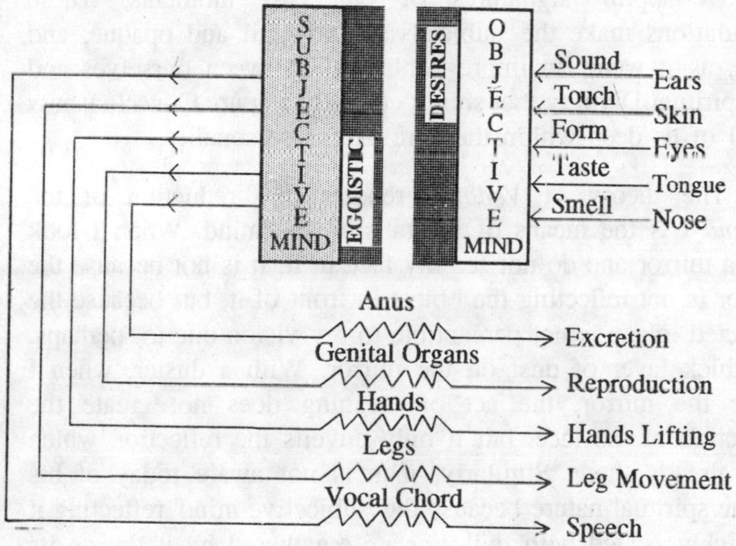

DIAGRAM " A "

At each moment, man meets with different patterns of these stimuli, and thus constantly gathers new impressions in the 'subjective mind.' Every set of impulses reaching it not only adds to the existing layers of impressions already in it, but also gets coloured by the quality of these *Vāsanā-s* hoarded within. When these are translated into action, the actions carry a flavour of the existing *Vāsanā-s* in the 'subjective mind.'

All of us live constantly meeting a variety of experiences; and at each incident, we perceive, react with the perceived and come to act in the outer field. In this process, we unwittingly come to hoard in ourselves more and more dirt of new impressions. The 'subjective mind' gets increasingly granulated by overlapping signatures of our past moments. These granulations make the 'subjective mind' dull and opaque, and form, as it were, an impregnable wall between ourselves and the spiritual Divinity that shines eternally as pure Consciousness in all of us deep within the core of our personality.

The theory of *Vedānta* repeats that reduction of the *Vāsanā-s* is the means of volatalising the mind. When I look into a mirror and do not see my face in it, it is not because the mirror is not reflecting the object in front of it, but because the reflected image is not perceptible to my vision due to, perhaps, the thick layer of dust on the mirror. With a duster, when I clean the mirror, the act of cleaning does not create the reflection of the face, but it only unveils the reflection which was already there. Similarly, man is not aware today of his divine spiritual nature because the 'subjective mind' reflecting it is thickly coated with dull *Vāsanā-s* gathered by it during its ego-centric, passionate existence in the world.

To bring the subjective and the objective aspects of the mind together into a happy marriage where the 'objective mind' is well-disciplined to act faithfully as per the guidance of the 'subjective,' is the *Yoga* pointed in the *Gītā*. This is accomplished only by the removal of the dividing factor—the ego-centric desires. The typical word used in the *Gītā* to indicate this practical implication of *Yoga* is self-explanatory—*Buddhi Yoga.*

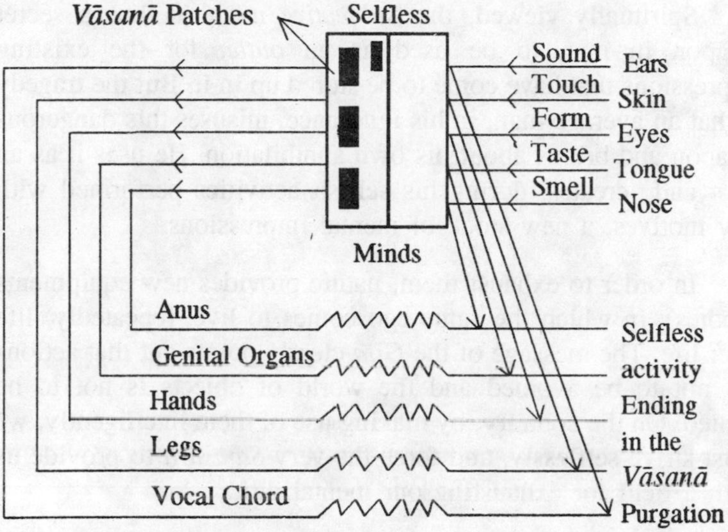

DIAGRAM "B"

As represented in Diagram "B," when this happy marriage between the subjective and the objective aspects of the mind has taken place, thereafter that equanimous *Yogin* becomes skilled in action,* and he, with his 'objective-mind,' reacts intelligently and faithfully to the external stimuli; his actions become, as it were, a purgation of the already existing *Vasanā-s* in his 'subjective mind.' Thus, through intelligent action, an individual can exhaust his existing impressions and ultimately redeem his 'subjective-mind' from the granulations and make it more clear and crystalline.

This idea has been emphasised by great commentators like *Śaṅkara*, who tirelessly repeat that selfless activity, performed in a spirit of egoless adoration and reverence to the divine ideal, would ultimately result in inner purification. This,

* *Yogaḥ karmasu kauśalam*—"Dexterity in action is *Yoga*"—II-50.

according to *Śaṅkara*, is the most unavoidable pre-requisite before the subjective mind can turn inward seeking to re-discover the sanctuary of the Self, the Spiritual Reality.

Spiritually viewed, the '*subjective mind*' is thus a secret weapon in man to be used as an *outlet* for the existing impressions that have come to be stored up in it. But the tragedy is that an average man, in his ignorance, misuses this dangerous weapon and brings about his own annihilation. He uses it as an *inlet* and creates, during his selfish activities performed with low motives, a new stock of mental impressions.

In order to exhaust them, nature provides new equipments (bodies), in which the same ego comes to live, repeatedly, life after life. The message of the *Gītā* clearly points out that actions are not to be avoided and the world of objects is not to be denied. On the contrary, by making use of them intelligently, we must strive selflessly, and force the very *Saṁsāra* to provide us with a field for exhausting our mental dirt.

Just as a misconceived *Hindūism* of today has come to bray forth many unhealthy idealisms as its cardinal virtues, so too, evidently, at the time of the *Mahābhārata*, the average intelligent educated man in India must have had many mis-conceptions about the *Vedik* ideologies. A philosophy, however noble and healthy, cannot maintain itself for long unless those, who are the custodians of it, are vigilantly kept under the whip of a kingly patronage. No Government in the world can dare claim to have fulfilled their responsibilities if they leave the religion of the country in the hands of an ill-disciplined uneducated class, who, by the mere accident of birth, claim to be the priests of that religion. It is the sacred duty of any Government to see that the philosophy of their ancient culture gets healthy interpretations from the priests. To fight shy of religion may be covenient for a modern Government in certain extraordinary political conditions, but in the long run they shall be impeached by history as the culprits who were the cause of the cultural havoc of the nation.

At the time of the *Mahābhārata*, religion had become a special portfolio for the learned *paṇḍita-s* to chant and to minister its ritualisms and all others, with faith in their hearts, were to listen to the chantings, although they understood from them precious little. In the *Gītā*, we have a translation of the *Vedik* Truth in the language of the *Mahābhārata* times—the age of chivalry and heroism.

An unhealthy mind divided in itself, as we explained earlier, becomes an easy prey to a host of psychological diseases. Weakened in its constitution, it easily becomes a victim to all contagions. *Arjuna* was an average educated man, and from the details of the *Mahābhārata*, we know the environments in which he grew up. But for the entire *Mahābhārata*, we would not appreciate so fully *Arjuna*'s mental condition, without which *Kṛṣṇa's* message would have fallen flat upon the readers. Therefore, the *Gītā* is an intrinsic part of the entire *Mahābhārata* and the classic would have been a hotch-potch story, without pith and dignity, if *Śrīmad Bhagavad Gītā* was not in it—and the *Gītā* would have been a mere philosopher's riddle-poem without the *Mahābhārata* background. The story and the poem together are an organic whole; each devoid of the other would be ineffectual and empty.

Modern psychology exhausts volumes in describing to us the dreary results of suppression and repression of emotions. There are many moments in our lives when we *knowingly* suppress many of our emotions; but more often in our day-to-day life, we, *unconsciously*, repress many of our sentiments. Repressed emotions accumulate a tremendous amount of dynamic energy which must necessarily seek a field for expression, and unless they are properly guided they would boomerang back to destroy the very individual. Though there are no direct explanations of any repressions of emotion in *Arjuna*, a careful student of the story can easily diagnose that the great hero on the battle-field came under the influence of his repressed conditions and behaved as a victim of perfect neurosis.

The causes for his emotional repressions are not far to seek. A great hero, confident of his own strength, was made to live amidst the unjust tyranny of his Machiavellian cousins. At the same time the great archer could not give vent to his nature because of the righteous policy of "peace at all costs" of his eldest brother, *Yudhiṣṭhira*. These repressed emotions found a healthy field for expression in the severe *Tapas* which he performed during his life in the jungles.

During the last year of their lives *incognito*, the *Pāṇḍava* family had to serve as menials in the palace ofthe *Rājā* of *Virāṭa*. The carping injustice and the cruel indignities of the situation caused, no doubt, a lot of repression in *Arjuna*'s mind. But even these found a healthy field of expression in the battle that he had to wage against *Duryodhana*'s forces that came to challenge the *Virāṭa*-might.

After their long and strenuous trials, when the *Pāṇḍavā-s* at last reached their native kingdom, their tyrant cousin, with no rhyme or reason, denied them not only their right to half the kingdom, but also all terms of conciliation. The conciliatory policy of *Yudhiṣṭhira* went to the extent of even requesting at least five houses for the five brothers to live in, but the lusty and greedy *Duryodhana* declared that "he would not give them even as much land as could be raised upon the head of a pin." Thus, war became inevitable.

The shrewd, blind *Dhṛtarāṣṭra*, father of the *Kauravā-s*, probably understood the psychological condition of the great warrior, *Arjuna*, and on the day previous to the great war, he sent *Sañjaya*, his emissary, to *Arjuna* with a secret message. This message, full of mischievous import, sowed the seeds of dangerous ideas in the mind of *Arjuna*, directing his energies caused by the repressions of his emotions into wrong channels, so that he became a hapless neurotic in the face of the great challenge. We shall read in the First Chapter the very same arguments and ideas repeated by *Arjuna* faithfully from the message, he had received the previous day from his uncle.

On that fateful day, when both the armies were getting into formation, *Arjuna* asks his charioteer, Lord *Kṛṣṇa*, to drive the chariot to a point between the two forces, so that he may review the enemy lines. Larger in number, better equipped, more liberal in supplies and commanded by well-known personalities, the *Kaurava* formation, expanding itself like an "eagle," stood poised to swoop down upon the smaller army of the *Pāṇḍavā-s*. This was a sight severely challenging the mental stamina of the *Pāṇḍava* hero. His 'objective-mind,' under the impact of the stimuli, could not find any reaction from its 'subjective-mind' (*Buddhi*), because the shattering of these two aspects was complete due to the intervening layers of his ego-centric assumptions and desire-prompted anxieties. The dynamic forces released in his mind, due to the repressions, were not properly channelised, but were mis-directed by the suggestions of *Dhrtarāṣṭra's* words, and therefore, the greatest hero of the times, *Arjuna*, suddenly became a despondent, bewildered, neurotic patient.

The '*Kṛṣṇa*-treatment' of this patient of psychological derangement was certainly a specific cure, inasmuch as, in the last chapter we definitely hear *Arjuna* declaring that all his "delusions have ended." The rest of the story of how, having come into his own, he became a rejuvenated warrior of tremendous strength and valour, is quite well-known to all students of this great classic.

In varying degrees, every man is a victim of this '*Arjuna*-disease,' and the '*Kṛṣṇa*-cure,' being specific, is available to all of us at all times in the philosophy of the *Gītā*.

In the Second Chapter, which is almost a summary of the entire *Gītā*, *Kṛṣṇa* indicates the two main lines of treatment. One is a "treatment of idealism" wherein *Arjuna* is directed to a greater reality than his mind, ego and intellect and thereby the divorce between the 'subjective' and the 'objective' aspects of his mind is eliminated to some extent. In the second half of the same chapter, we shall read and come to understand how selfless activity will purge the existing *Vāsanā-s* in the individual. *Arjuna* being a *Kṣatriya*, his mind was coloured by the impression of *Rajo-guṇa* (activity), and so he needed a battle-field to exhause those impressions.

Thus, we find *Kṛṣṇa* repeatedly goading his friend with the words, "Get up and fight." This need not necessarily mean that the *Gītā* is a war-mongering scripture of the ruling-class. It is a call to each one of us to get up and fight the battle of our own life, according to our own *Vāsanā-s* (*Sva-dharma*), so that we may exhaust them and thus gain inner purity. As we take it up, stanza by stanza, for a close study of the entire Song, we shall try to see how *Kṛṣṇa* indicates the same truth from the different angles of vision and explained the same in different words.

Chapter I

ARJUNA'S GRIEF

Introduction

No other race in the world had ever harnessed so successfully the scintillating possibilities of the drama in literature for the purposes of philosophical exposition as the ancient *Hindū*-s. The *Upaniṣad-s* were recorded in the form of conversations between the teacher and the taught, in the quiet atmosphere of the silent and peaceful Himalayan valleys. In the *Gītā*, however, the highest and the best in *Hindū* philosophy has been reiterated, in a more elaborate and detailed dramatic layout amidst the din and roar of a total-war. *Kṛṣṇa* gives his message of manly action to *Arjuna* amidst the breathing, palpitating environment of the clash and carnage of a battle-field.

There are some commentators who struggle to find an allegorical significance in not only the characters in the *Gītā* but in almost every line of the great Immortal Song. This extra pre-occupation to discover some secret meaning in many of the lines has crushed the *Gītā* out of its natural and sweet shape. No doubt, *Vyāsa*, the author of he *Mahābhārata*, was a child of the *Vedā-s*, and soaked as he was in the literary style of the *Vedik* mysticism, he had employed symbolism to a certain extent in his *Paurāṇik* works. The entire *Mahābhārata*, in the development of its theme, represents a huge literary canvas upon which he had successfully brought out *Vedānta*, in speaking objective representations.

The *Kauravā-s*, hundred in number, represent the innumerable un-godly forces of negative tendencies within man's bosom, and the *Pāṇḍavā-s,* no doubt, represent the divine impulses in him. A constant *Mahābhārata* war is being waged within every one of us at all our crucial moments of action; and in all cases the negative forces in each one of us are larger in number and usually mightier in their effectiveness, while the inner divine army is ever lesser in number and apparently, comparatively weaker in efficiency. Therefore, every single individual, at the moment of his inward checking up, must necessarily feel the desperations of *Arjuna.*

The story of the *Mahābhārata* sounds an optimistic note of hope to man that, even though the diviner impulses are seemingly less in number, if the same are organised fully and brought under the guidance of the Supreme Lord, *Kṛṣṇa,* the Self, then, under His guidance, they can easily be ushered into a true and permanent victory over the out-numbering forces of lust and greed.

Any careful student of the *Gītā* cannot but be reminded of the famous analogy of the chariot in the *Kaṭhopaniṣad.* The *Mahābhārata,* was written in an age, when the *Vyāsa*-generation was fully conversant with atleast the famous passages in the *Vedā*-s and particularly of the *Upaniṣad-s.* Any young man of that age reading the *Gītā* could not but be reminded of the corresponding picture that had been so beautifully painted by the words of Lord of Death to *Naciketā.**

In the famous analogy of the Chariot, the physio-spiritual theory of the *Vedāntik Sādhanā* had been most effectively described. The body is the Chariot, which is pulled forward by five steeds, the sense-organs each trotting along its path laid out by the sense-objects. The discriminative intellect is the ideal charioteer who holds the lusty steeds in perfect control and, therefore, drives the chariot and the Lord of the chariot—the ego—to its destination, the haven of peace. When a student of the *Kaṭhopaniṣad* enters the description of the *Gītā* setting,

---

* Refer Introduction to Discourses on *Kaṭhopaniṣad* by *Svāmījī's.*

the very picture of Lord *Pārthāsārathy*, in the chariot advising *Arjuna*, speaks to him a greater significance than it would to a raw reader.

The *Kauravā-s*, representing the negative tendencies and the sinful motives in a mortal's bosom, are born as children to the old king, *Dhṛtarāṣṭra*, a born-blind prince, wedded to *Gāndhārī*, who had *voluntarily* blinded herself by putting bandages over her eyes! Commentators are tempted to see in this a very appropriate significance. Mind is born-blind to truth, and when it is wedded to an intellect which also has assumed blindness, the negative instincts yoked with low motives can only beget a hundred criminalities and sins!

When, upon the spiritual field of self-development within (*Dharma-kṣetra*), the lower instincts and the higher ideals array themselves, ready to fight, a true seeker (the captain of the latter), under the guidance of his divine discriminative intellect, takes himself to a point on no-man's land between the two forces for the purpose of reviewing the enemy lines, without identifying himself with either the good or the evil in him. And, at that moment of his introspective meditations, the egoistic entity comes to feel a morbid desperation and feels generally incapacitated to undertake the great spiritual adventure of fighting his inner war with any hope of victory.

This peculiar mental condition of a seeker is beautifully represented in the vivid picture of *Arjuna*'s dejection in the opening chapter.

In *Saṁskṛta* works, it is a recognised tradition that the opening stanza should generally indicate the whole theme of the text. The bulk of the book then discusses at length the different views and gives all possible arguments, until in its concluding portion the last stanza generally summarises the final conclusions of the *Śastra* on the theme indicated in the opening section of the book. In this way, when we consider the *Gītā*, we find that the Divine Song starts with the word "*Dharma*" (I-1) and concludes with the term *Mama* i.e., "Mine" (XVIII-78); and therefore, the contents of the *Gītā*, we may conclude, are nothing but "My *Dharma*" (*Mama Dharma*).

The term *Dharma* is one of the most intractable terms in *Hindū* philosophy. Derived from the root *dhar* (*Dhṛ*) to uphold, sustain, support, the term *Dharma* denotes "that which holds together the different aspects and qualities of an object into a whole."* Ordinarily, the term *Dharma* has been translated as religious code, as righteousness, as a system of morality, as duty, as charity, etc. But the original *Saṁskṛta* term has a special connotation of its own which is not captured by any one of these renderings. The best rendering of this term *Dharma* that I have met with so far is "the Law of Being" meaning, "that which makes a thing or being what it is." For example, it is the *Dharma* of the fire to burn, of the sun to shine, etc.

Dharma means, therefore, not merely righteousness or goodness but it indicates the essential nature of anything, without which it cannot retain its independent existence. For example, a cold dark sun is impossible, as heat and light are the *Dharmā-s* of the sun. Similarly if we are to live as truly dynamic men in the world, we can only do so by being faithful to our true nature, and the *Gītā* explains "to me my *Dharma*."

In using thus the first person possessive noun, this scripture perhaps indicates that the Song Divine sung through the eighteen chapters is to be subjectively transcribed, lived, and personally experienced by each student in his own life.

---

* *Dhāranāt dharma ityāhu, dharmeṇa vidhṛtaḥ prajaḥ*

ॐ

श्री परमात्मने नमः

अथ प्रथमोऽध्यायः

धृतराष्ट्र उवाच-

धर्मक्षेत्रे कुरुक्षेत्रे समवेता युयुत्सवः ।
मामकाः पाण्डवाश्चैव किमकुर्वत सञ्जय ॥ १ ॥

Dhṛtarāṣṭra Uvāca—

Dharma-kṣetre kuru-kṣetre samavetā yuyut-savaḥ,
māmakāḥ pāṇḍavāś-caiva kimakurvata sañjaya.

धर्मक्षेत्रे *dharmakṣetre* = on the holy plane (field); कुरुक्षेत्रे *kurukṣetre* = at *Kurukṣetra;* समवेताः *samavetāḥ* = assembled together; युयुत्सवः *yuyutsavaḥ* = desirous to fight; मामकाः *māmakāḥ* = my people; पाण्डवाः *pāṇḍavāḥ* = the sons of *Pāṇḍu*; च *ca* = and; एव *eva* = also; किम् *kim* = what; अकुर्वत *akurvata* = did do; सञ्जय *sañjaya* = O *Sañjaya.*

Dhṛtarāṣṭra said:

1. *What did the sons of* Pāṇḍu *and also my people do when, desirous to fight, they assembled together on the holy plane (field) of* Kurukṣetra, O Sañjaya?

In the entire *Gītā* this is the only verse which the blind old king *Dhṛtarāṣṭra* gives out. All the rest of the seven hundred stanzas are *Sañjaya's* report on what happened on the *Kurukṣetra* battle-field, just before the war.

The blind old king is certainly conscious of the palpable injustices that he had done to his nephews, the *Pāṇḍvā*-s. *Dhṛtarāṣṭra* knew the relative strength of the two armies, and therefore, was fully confident of the larger strength of his son's army. And yet, the viciousness of his past and the consciousness of the crimes perpetrated seem to be weighing heavily upon the heart of the blind king, and so he has his own doubts on the outcome of this war. He asks *Sañjaya* to explain to him what is happening on the battle-field of *Kurukṣetra*. *Vyāsa* had given *Sañjaya* the powers to see and listen to the happenings in far-off *Kurukṣetra* even while he was sitting beside *Dhṛtarāṣṭra* in the palace at *Hastināpura*.

Vyāsa was a complete artist. Unhurriedly he works on; nowhere is he hasty. In almost every stanza, he not only exhibits his literary mastery over the use of words, but also employs them with such precision that his simple-looking words, in their right context, talk volumes to all careful students. In the second line, where *Dhṛtarāṣṭra* enquires as to what had happened on the battle-field by putting "my-people" before "*Pāṇḍvā-s,*" he gave out a clear note of his greater love for his own children than for his nephews.

सञ्जय उवाच—

दृष्ट्वा तु पाण्डवानीकं व्यूढं दुर्योधनस्तदा ।
आचार्यमुपसङ्गम्य राजा वचनमब्रवीत् ॥ २ ॥

Sañjaya Uvāca—

Dṛṣṭvā tu pāṇḍavā-nīkaṁ vyūḍhaṁ duryodhanas-tadā,
ācāryam-upasaṅgamya rājā vacana-mabravīt.

दृष्ट्वा *dṛṣṭvā* = having seen; तु *tu* = indeed; पाण्डवानीकम् *pāṇḍavānīkam* = the army of the *Pāṇḍavā-s*; व्यूढम् *vyūḍham*= in battle array; दुर्योधन: *duryodhanaḥ* = *Duryodhana*; तदा *tadā* = then; आचार्यम् *ācāryam* = the teacher; उपसङ्गम्य *upasaṅgamya* =

having approached; राजा *rājā* = the king; वचनम् *vacanam* = speech; अब्रवीत् *abravīt* = said.

Sañjaya said :

2. *Having seen the army of the* Pāṇḍavā-s *drawn up in battle array, King* Duryodhana *then approached his teacher (*Droṇa*) and spoke these words.*

From this stanza onwards, we have the report of *Sañjaya* upon what he saw and heard on the war-front at *Kurukṣetra*. When *Duryodhana* saw the *Pāṇḍava*-forces arrayed for battle, though they were less in number than his own forces, yet the tyrant felt his self-confidence draining away. As a child would run to its parents in fright, so too *Duryodhana*, unsettled in his mind, runs to his teacher, *Droṇācārya*. When our motives are impure and our cause unjust, however well-equipped we may be, our minds should necessarily feel restless and agitated. This is the mental condition of all tyrants and lusty dictators.

By using the simplest of words, *Vyāsa* has a knack of bringing out a wealth of detail regarding the mental traits of his characters. The stanza says that *Duryodhana* approched his teacher, and "the King said." The implication is that although *Duryodhaṇa* as a disciple ran to seek the protection of his teacher, he started taking with kingly vanity and not with the modesty and reverence that a disciple should show towards his teacher.

पश्यैतां पाण्डुपुत्राणामाचार्य महतीं चमूम् ।
व्यूढां द्रुपदपुत्रेण तव शिष्येण धीमता ॥ ३ ॥

Paśyaitāṁ pāṇḍu-putrāṇām-ācārya mahatīṁ camūm,
vyūḍhāṁ drupada-putreṇa tava śiṣyeṇa dhīmatā.

पश्य *paśya* = behold; एताम् *etām* = this; पाण्डु-पुत्राणाम् *pāṇḍu-putrāṇām* = of the sons of *Pāṇḍu*; आचार्य *ācārya* = O teacher; महतीम् *mahatīm* = great; चमूम् *camūm* = army; व्यूढाम्

vyūḍhām = arrayed; द्रुपद-पुत्रेण *drupada-putreṇa* = by the son of *Drupada*; तव शिष्येण *tava śiṣyeṇa* = by your disciple; धीमता *dhīmatā* = wise.

3. *Behold, O Teacher! this mighty army of the sons of* Pāṇḍu, *arrayed by the son of* Drupada, *thy wise disciple.*

It is indeed stupid of *Duryodhana* to point out to *Droṇa* the army formation of the *Pāṇḍavā-s*. Later on also we shall find *Duryodhana* talking too much and that is a perfect symptom indicating the inward fears of the great king over the final outcome of the unjust war. There is an instinctive taunt in *Duryodhana*'s words to his aged teacher, from which the cruel tyrant could not keep away. At moments of high tension, an individual's words give clear indications of his essential mental nature. He hints at the foolishness of his teacher who had taught the science of war to undeserving student like the son of *Drupada*, who was now standing ready to make use of his knowledge of war to fight against his own teacher.

अत्र शूरा महेष्वासा भीमार्जुनसमा युधि ।
युयुधानो विराटश्च द्रुपदश्च महारथः ॥ ४ ॥

Atra śūrā maheṣvāsā bhīmārjuna-samā yudhi,
yuyudhāno virāṭaś-ca drupadaś-ca mahārathaḥ.

अत्र *atra* = here; शूरा *śūrā* = heroes; महेष्वासा *maheṣvāsā* = mighty archers; भीम अर्जुन समा *bhīma arjuna samā* = equal to *Bhīma* and *Arjuna*; युधि *yudhi* = in battle; युयुधानः *yuyudhānaḥ* = *Yuyudhāna*; विराटः *virāṭaḥ* = *virāṭa*; द्रुपदः *drupadaḥ* = *Drupada*; च *ca* = and; महारथः *mahārathaḥ* = the great chariot-warrior.

4. *Here are heroes, mighty archers, equal in battle to* Bhīma *and* Arjuna; Yuyudhāna, Virāṭa *and* Drupada, *the great chariot-warrior. ...*

धृष्टकेतुश्चेकितानः काशिराजश्च वीर्यवान् ।
पुरुजित्कुन्तिभोजश्च शैब्यश्च नरपुङ्गवः ॥ ५ ॥

dhṛṣṭaketuś-cekitānaḥ kāśirājaś-ca vīryavān,
purujit-kuntibhojaś-ca śaibyaś-ca nara-puṅgavaḥ.

धृष्टकेतुः *dhṛṣṭaketuḥ* = *Dṛṣṭaketu*; चेकितानः *cekitānaḥ* = *Cekitāna*; काशि-राजः *kāśi-rājaḥ* = king of *Kāśi*; च *ca* = and; वीर्यवान् *vīryavān* = valiant; पुरुजित् *purujit* = *Purujit*; कुन्तिभोजः *kuntibhojaḥ* = *Kuntibhoja*; च *ca* = and; शैब्यः *śaibyaḥ* = son of *Śaibya*; च *ca* = and; नर पुङ्गवः *nara puṅgavaḥ* = the best of men.

5. Dhṛṣṭaketu, Cekitāna, *and the valiant king of* Kāśi, Purujit, Kuntibhoja *and* Śaibya, *the best of men. ...*

युधामन्युश्च विक्रान्त उत्तमौजाश्च वीर्यवान् ।
सौभद्रो द्रौपदेयाश्च सर्व एव महारथाः ॥ ६ ॥

Yudhāmanyuś-ca vikrānta uttamaujāś-ca vīryavān,
saubhadro draupadeyāś-ca sarva eva mahārathāḥ.

युधामन्युः *yudhāmanyuḥ* = *Yudhāmanyu*; च *ca* = and; विक्रान्तः *vikrāntaḥ* = the strong; उत्तमौजाः *uttamaujāḥ* = *Uttamaujā*; च *ca* = and; वीर्यवान् *vīryavān* = the brave; सौभद्रः *Saubhadraḥ* = the son of *Subhadrā*; द्रौपदेयाः *draupadeyāḥ* = the sons of *Draupadī*; च *ca* = and; सर्व *sarva* = all; एव *eva* = indeed; महारथाः *mahārathāḥ* = the great chariot-warriors (men commanding each 11000 archers-mighty worriors).

6. *The strong* Yudhāmanyu *and the brave* Uttamaujā, *the son of* Subhadrā (Abhimanyu) *and the sons of* Draupadī, *all of them—indeed great chariot-warriors (divisional commanders).*

In these three stanzas, we have a list of names of all those who were noted personalities in the *Pāṇḍava* army. *Duryodhana*, reviewing his enemies standing in formation, recognises very many noted men of war functioning as *mahārathā-s* in the *Pāṇḍava* forces. A *mahārathī* was in charge of a group of 11,000 archers, which formed a division in the ancient *Hindū* army.

Arjuna and *Bhīma* were accepted men of war, noted for archery and strength. These enumerated heroes were, says *Duryodhana*, each as great as *Arjuna* and *Bhīma*, the implication being that though the *Pāṇḍava* forces were less in number, their total effectiveness was much greater than that of the larger and better equipped army of the *Kauravā-s*.

Yuyudhāna was *Kṛṣṇa's* charioteer who was also called later on in the *Gītā* by his other name—*Sātyaki*. *Virāṭa* was the king of the *Matsya*, living on the sacred land between the *Yamunā* and the *Sarasvatī* and in whose palace the *Pāṇḍava* brothers, with their wife *Draupadī*, took shelter during their one year's life incognito. *Drupada* was the king of the *Pañcāla Deśa* (between Delhi and Gwalior), father-in-law of the *Pāṇḍvā-s*.

Dhṛṣṭaketu was the king of *Cedis* and the brother-in-law of *Nakula*. *Cekitāna* was the warrior in the *Pāṇḍava* forces. The king of *Kāśi* was a tribal chieftain whose capital was on the banks of the *Ganges* near modern *Banārasa*. *Purujit* and *Kuntibhoja* were both brothers, and the latter had adopted *Kuntī*, who later married King *Pāṇḍu* and became the famous mother of the *Pāṇḍavā-s*. *Śaibya* was the king of the *Śibī* tribe.

Yudhāmanyu and *Uttamaujā* were both prominent local chieftains who and thrown in their lot with the *Pāṇḍava* forces. *Saubhadra*, the son of *Subhadrā*, the sister of *Śrī Kṛṣṇa* given in marriage to *Arjuna* and the son born of her for *Arjuna* was *Abhimanyu*, who exhibited in the great war, super-human heroism and ultimately died fighting against terrible odds. *Draupadeyā-s* were the sons of *Draupadī*, the five *Pāṇḍavā-s* had each a son born to them of *Draupadī*.

All these 17 warriors were Divisional Commander each in charge of a battalion constituted of 11,000 archers.

अस्माकं तु विशिष्टा ये तान्निबोध द्विजोत्तम ।
नायका मम सैन्यस्य संज्ञार्थं तान्ब्रवीमि ते ॥ ७ ॥

Asmākaṁ tu viśiṣṭā ye tānni-bodha dvijottama,
nāyakā mama sainyasya saṁjñārthaṁ tānbravīmi te.

अस्माकम् *asmākam* = ours; तु *tu* = also; विशिष्टा: *viśiṣṭāḥ* = the best, distinguished chiefs; ये *ye* = who; तान् *tān* = those; निबोध *nibodha* = know (thou); द्विजोत्तम *dvijottama* = (O) best among the twice-born; नायका *nāyakā* = the leaders; मम *mama* = my; सैन्यस्य *sainyasya* = of the army; संज्ञार्थम् *saṁjñārtham* = for information; तान् *tān* = them; ब्रवीमि *bravīmi* = (I) speak; ते *te* = to thee.

7. *Know also, O best among the twice-born, the names of those who are the most distinguished amongst ourselves, the leaders of my army; these I name to thee for thy information. ...*

Addressing his Master as "the best among the twice-born," *Duryodhana* now repeats the names of the distinguished heroes in his own army. A weak man, to escape from his own mental fears, will whistle to himself in the dark. The guilty conscience of the tyrant king had undermined all his mental strength. The more he realised the combined strength of the great personalities arrayed in the opposite enemy camp, the more abjectly nervous he felt, in spite of the fact that his own army was also manned by highly competent heroes. In order to revive himself, he wanted to hear words of encouragement from his teachers and elders. But when *Duryodhana* met *Droṇa*, the *Ācārya* chose to remain silent and the helpless king had to find for himself new means of encourgement to revive his own drooping enthusiasm. Therefore, he started enumerating the great leaders in his own army.

When a person has thus completely lost his morale due to the heavy burden of his own crimes weighing on his conscience, it is but natural that he loses all sense of proportion in his words. At such moments of high tension an individual clearly exhibits his true mental culture. He addresses his own teacher as "the best among the twice-born."

A *brāhmaṇa* is considered as "twice-born" because of his inner spiritual development. When born from his mother's womb man comes into the world only as the animal called man. Thereafter, through study and contemplation he gains more and more discipline, and a cultured *Hindū* is called a *brāhmaṇa* (*Brahmin*).

In an earlier stanza,* *Duryodhana* had indicated that the officers meaning the *Pāṇḍava* forces, were almost all of them students of *Droṇācārya*. These statements together imply that his teacher's *brāhmaṇa*-heart should necessarily beat softly in love for his own great disciples. A hint was thus thrown in the earlier stanza to suggest *Duryodhana*'s lack of confidence in his own teacher. Here, in the couplet under discussion, this doubt is confirmed. After all, *Droṇa* is a *brāhmaṇa* by birth and as such he must have a greater share of softness of heart. Moreover, the enemy lines are fully manned by his own dear students. As a shrewd dictator, *Duryodhana* entertained shameless doubts about the loyalty of his own teacher.

This is but an instinctive fear which is natural with all men of foul motives and crooked dealings. When we are not ourselves pure, we will project our own weaknesses and impurities on others who are working around us as our subordinates. The stanzas throw more and more light and shade upon the ugly features of the distorted mental picture of the *Kaurava* chief.

भवान्भीष्मश्च कर्णश्च कृपश्च समितिञ्जयः ।
अश्वत्थामा विकर्णश्च सौमदत्तिस्तथैव च ॥ ८ ॥

Bhavān-bhīṣmaś-ca karṇaś-ca kṛpaś-ca samitiñ-jayaḥ,
aśvatthāmā vikarṇaś-ca saumadattis-tathaiva ca.

---

* Chapter I, Stanza 3.

भवान् *bhavān* = yourself; भीष्मः *bhīṣmaḥ* = *Bhīṣma*; च *ca* = and; कर्णः *karṇaḥ* = *Karṇa*; च *ca* = and; कृपः *kṛpaḥ* = *Kṛpa*; च *ca* = and; समितिञ्जयः *samitiñjayaḥ* = victorious (in war); अश्वत्थामा *aṣvatthāmā* = *Aśvathāmā*, the son of *Droṇācārya*; विकर्णः *vikarṇaḥ* = *Vikarṇa*; च *ca* = and; सौमदत्तिः *saumadattiḥ* = the son of *Somadatta i.e., Bhūriśravā*; तथा *tathā* = also; एव *eva* = so; च *ca* = and.

8. *Yourself and* Bhīṣma, *and* Karṇa *and also* Kṛpa, *the victorious in war;* Aśvatthāmā, Vikarṇa *and so also* Bhūriśravā, *the son of* Somadatta. ...

Though *Duryodhana*, in his mental hysteria, got slightly upset at the subjective onslaught of his own brutal motives and past crimes, like the true dictator that he was, he regained his balance in no time. The moment he had spilt out, in his insulting arrogance, the term "twice-born" in addressing his teacher, he realised that he had over-stepped the bounds of discretion. Perhaps the cold silence of the revered *Ācārya* spoke amply to *Duryodhana.*

The tyrant king immediately switches off the topic and starts enumerating the list of heroes in his own army.

In this list, to court the favour of *Droṇa* and to humour him back to a more happy composure, *Duryodhana* mentions *Droṇācārya* himself at the top of the list, even before the name of *Bhīṣma*. Again, it is interesting to note here that he qualifies *Kṛpa*, the brother-in-law of *Droṇa*, with a rather high-sounding qualification as "the victorious in war." Not satisfied even with this, the assiduous diplomat *Duryodhana* named *Aśvatthāmā* who is *Droṇa*'s own son. Out of these seven names mentioned, three are *Droṇa*, his brother-in-law and his son, as though *Droṇa* and his family alone had the monopoly of heroism and chivarly in the vast army of the *Kauravā-s*. The very exaggeration clearly indicates that *Duryodhana* did not mean anything sincerely and his only intention was to bring back the great *Ācārya* to a pleasanter mental mood.

अन्ये च बहवः शूरा मदर्थे त्यक्तजीविताः ।
नानाशस्त्रप्रहरणाः सर्वे युद्धविशारदाः ॥ ९ ॥

Anye ca bahavaḥ śūrā madarthe tyakta-jīvitāḥ,
nānā-śastra-praharaṇāḥ sarve yudha-viśāradāḥ.

अन्ये *anye* = others; च *ca* = and; बहवः *bahavaḥ* = many; शूराः *śūrāḥ* = heroes; मदर्थे *mad-arthe* = for my sake; त्यक्त-जीविताः *tyakta-jīvitāḥ* = who are determined to give up their lives; नाना-शस्त्र-प्रहरणाः *nānā-śastra-praharaṇāḥ* = armed with various weapons and missiles; सर्वे *sarve* = all; युद्ध-विशारदाः *yudha-viśāradāḥ* = well skilled in battle.

9. *And many other heroes also who are determined to give up their lives for my sake, armed with various weapons and missiles, all well-skilled in battle.*

One may wonder why *Duryodhana* was so exhaustive and precise in his list of the great heroes on the *Pāṇḍava* side while he was so negligent in repeating the names of the commandants in his own forces. Even when he counted, as he did in the last stanza, he had repeated but four minor names ignoring the greater personalities in the *Kaurava* forces. Most probably, during the king's talk with *Droṇa*, these were the important army officers who happened to come in his view and *Duryodhana*, in the state of his mental agitation, could only repeat the names of those who were around him at that moment, failing to recapitulate the mightier persons in his army.

He immediately realises the incompleteness of his statement and so, in this stanza, he vaguely covers up his omission by declaring "innumebrable other heroes also are here, determined to lay down their lives for my sake."

The peculiar use of the word "*Tyakta-jīvitaḥ*" can be interpreted in two ways. A softer one by implication is 'determined to lay down their lives' and the other one, more direct is 'those who have already discarded their lives.' In this latter sense, this expression of *Duryodhana* serves as a perfect 'dramatic irony' as all of them within a short time are to die on the battle-field.

The incorrigible vanity of the dictatorial tyrant is amply clear when he arrogates to himself the stupendous honour that such a vast array of heroes had come ready to lay down their lives for "*my sake*." To all careful students of the *Mahābhārata*, it cannot be very difficult to estimate how many of these great veterans would have thrown in their lot with *Duryodhana*, had it not been for the fact that *Bhīṣma*—the grandsire—was fighting in the ranks of the *Kauravā-s*.

अपर्याप्तं तदस्माकं बलं भीष्माभिरक्षितम् ।
पर्याप्तं त्विदमेतेषां बलं भीमाभिरक्षितम् ॥ १० ॥

Aparyāptaṁ tadas-mākaṁ balaṁ bhīṣmā-bhirakṣitam,
paryāptaṁ tvidame-teṣām balaṁ bhīmā-bhirakṣitam.

अपर्याप्तम् *aparyāptaṁ* = insufficient, unlimited; तत् *tat* = that; अस्माकम् *asmākam* = ours; बलम् *balam* = army; भीष्म अभिरक्षितम् *bhīṣma abhirakṣitam* = protected by *Bhīṣma*; पर्याप्तम् *paryāptam* = sufficient, limited; तु *tu* = while; इदम् *idam* = this; एतेषाम् *eteṣām* = their; बलम् *balam* = army; भीम अभिरक्षितम् *bhīma abhirakṣitam* = protected by *Bhīma*.

10. *This army of ours defended by* Bhīṣma *is insufficient, whereas that army of theirs defended by* Bhīma *is sufficient.*

Or

This army of ours protected by Bhīṣma *is unlimited, whereas that army of theirs protected by* Bhīma *is limited.*

In the art of warfare, then known among the ancient *Hindū-s*, each army had, no doubt, a commander-in-chief, but it also had a powerful man of valour, courage and intelligence, who functioned as the "defender." In the *Kaurava* forces, *Bhīṣma* officiated as the "defender," and in the *Pāṇḍava* forces *Bhīma* held the same office.

To play upon the luxurious possibilities of the pregnant vocabulary is a special privilege of all *Saṁskṛta* poets and here we have an example of the same. The word '*Paryāptam*' has two meanings (a) sufficient and (b) measurable. Both these meanings can be read in the stanza and each would illumine for us a different facet of *Duryodhana*'s mental condition.

One is the direct meaning that the army defended by *Bhīṣma* is 'unlimited' while that protected by *Bhīma* is 'limited.' This meaning is suggested by *Ānandagiri*, the elucidator of *Ācārya Śaṅkara's* commentary, but *Śrīdhara Svāmī* gives the other meaning and makes the stanza state that although *Bhīṣma* is the protector of the *Kaurava* forces, *Duryodhana* is feeling that it is 'insufficient' to win a victory; while the *Pāṇḍava* forces, although guarded by a comparatively insignificant warrior like *Bhīma*, it is 'sufficient' in as much as the *Pāṇḍava* fighters are inspired by the high aims of *Dharma* for which they are fighting.

Anyway both the interpretations give us the two different facets of *Duryodhana*'s mind. Perhaps in one way, he is feeling extremely confident because, although his cause is poor and weak, *Bhīṣma* is the protector of his army and, therefore, success is assured. At the same time, his conscience weighs heavy with guilt, because of the crimes that he has consciously done in the past. He, therefore, feels that his army had nothing which would inspire the personnel to their maximum efficiency. The *Pāṇḍava* forces, though less in number, have a righteous cause to fight for. Thus when an army fights for a nobler cause, every soldier fights as an inspired martyr.

We go into such details only to bring out the subtle varieties of meaning which can be expressed when *Saṁskṛta* is used by a literary master as great as *Vyāsa*,

अयनेषु च सर्वेषु यथाभागमवस्थिताः ।
भीष्ममेवाभिरक्षन्तु भवन्तः सर्वे एव हि ॥ ११ ॥

Ayaneṣu ca sarveṣu yathā-bhāvam-avasthitāḥ,
bhiṣma-mevābhi-rakṣantu bhavantaḥ sarve eva hi.

अयनेषु *ayaneṣu* = in the divisions of the army; च *ca* = and; सर्वेषु *sarveṣu* = in all; यथा-भागम् *yathā-bhāgam* = according to division; अवस्थिताः *avasthitāḥ* = being stationed; भीष्मम् *bhīṣmam* = *Bhīṣma*; एव *eva* = alone; अभि-रक्षन्तु *abhi-rakṣantu* = protect; भवन्तः *bhavantaḥ* = you; सर्वे *sarve* = all; एव *eva* = even; हि *hi* = indeed.

11. Therefore do you all, stationed in your respective positions in the several divisions of the army, protect Bhīṣma *alone.*

After thus expressing in a soliloquy, his own estimate of the relative strength and merit of the two forces, now arrayed, ready for a total war, the king in *Duryodhana* rises above his mental clouds of desperation to shoot forth his imperial orders to his army officers. He advises them that each commander must keep to his position and fight in a disciplined order, and all of them should spare no pains to see that the revered *Bhīṣma* is well-protected. Perhaps, *Duryodhana* suspects that the lusty force that he had mobilised is an ill-assorted heterogeneous army constituted of the various tribal chieftains and kings of distant lands and that the strength of such an army could be assured, only when they hold on to a united strategy in all their various manoeuvres. Synchronisation of the different operations is the very backbone of an army's success, and in order to bring this about, as a true strategist, *Duryodhana* is instructing his various commanders working in their different wings to work out the single policy of protecting *Bhīṣma.*

Again, this declaration clearly shows how far *Duryodhana* had realised the unquestionable importance of *Bhīṣma* for his army's efficiency. *Bhīṣma* was considered by *Duryodhana* as the very heat of his army, not only because of the Grandsire's prowess and wisdom, but also because, as the *Kaurava* chief realised, the different kings and warriors had joined his side, because of their reverence for *Bhīṣma*—the most adored and respected warrior of those chivalrous days. If *Bhīṣma* was out of the picture, the so called allies were sure to lose heart and desert the *Kaurava* ranks. Hence, *Duryodhana*'s anxiety for the safety of *Bhīṣma*, and his special instructions that all should, without deserting their posts, always guard *Bhīṣma*.

तस्य संञ्जनयन्हर्षं कुरुवृद्धः पितामहः ।
सिंहनादं विनद्योच्चैः शङ्खं दध्मौ प्रतापवान् ॥ १२ ॥

Tasya sañjanayan-harṣam
kuru-vṛdhdaḥ pitāmahaḥ,
siṁhanādaṁ vinadyoccaiḥ
śaṅkha dadhmau pratāpavān.

तस्य *tasya* = His (*Duryodhana's*); संञ्जनयन् *sañjanayan* = causing; हर्षम् *harṣam* = joy; कुरु वृद्धः *kuru vṛdhdaḥ* = oldest of the *Kurū-s*; पितामहः *pitāmahaḥ* = grandsire; सिंहनादम् *síṁhanādam* = lions's roar; विनद्य *vinadya* = having sounded; उच्चैः *uccaivaḥ* = loudly; शङ्खम् *śaṅkham* = a conch; दध्मौ *dadhmau* = blew; प्रतापवान् *pratāpavān* = the mighty, glorious.

12. *His glorious grandsire (*Bhīṣma*), the oldest of the* Kauravā-s*, *in order to cheer* Duryodhana, *now sounded aloud a lion's roar and blew his conch.*

All the while that *Duryodhana* was busy making a fool of himself and in his excitement putting all the great officers of his army into an uncomfortable mood of desperate unhappiness, *Bhīṣma* was standing, not too far away, observing the pitiable confusions of the tyrant. The revered grandsire noticed, intelligently, in *Droṇācārya*'s silence, the outraged temper of a

* Although *Bāhlīka*, *Bhīṣma's* uncle i.e., *Śāntanu's* younger brother, was the eldest of the *Kaurava* race fighting the war, *Sañjaya* uses the epithet for *Bhīṣma* who possessed better knowledge of righteousness and God. ... Ed.

man of knowledge and action. He realised that the situation could be saved only if all those assembled were jerked out of their mental pre-occupations. The more they were let alone with their revolting thoughts against *Duryodhana*, the more they would become ineffectual for the imminent battle. Understanding this psychology of the officers under his command, the great Marshall *Bhīṣma* took up his war-bugle (conch) and blew it, sending forth roaring waves of confidence into the hearts of the people manning the array.

This action of *Bhīṣma*, though performed by him out of pity for *Duryodhana*'s mental condition; amounted to an act of aggression almost corresponding to the 'first-bullet-shot' in modern warfare. With this lion-roar, the *Mahābhārata* war was actually started, and for all historical purposes the *Kauravā-s* had thereby become the aggressors.

ततः शङ्खाश्च भेर्यश्च पणवानकगोमुखाः ।
सहसैवाभ्यहन्यन्त स शब्दस्तुमुलोऽभवत् ॥ १३ ॥

Tataḥ śaṅkhāś-ca bheryaś-ca paṇavānaka-gomukhāḥ,
sahasaivābhya-hanyanta sa śabdas-tumulo-'bhavat.

ततः *tataḥ* = then; शङ्खाः *śaṅkhāḥ* = conches; च *ca* = and; भेर्यः *bheryaḥ* = kettle-drums; च *ca* = and; पणव आनक-गोमुखाः *paṇva-ānaka-gomukhāḥ* = tabors, military-drums and cow-horns; सहसा एव *sahasā-eva* = quite suddenly; अभ्यहन्यन्त *abhyahanyanta* = blared forth; सः *saḥ* = that; शब्दः *śabdaḥ* = sound; तुमुलः *tumulaḥ* = tremendous; अभवत् *abhavat* = was.

13. *Then (following* Bhīṣma*), conches and kettle-drums, tabors, military-drums and cow-horns blared forth quite suddenly and the sound was tremendous.*

All the commanders were no doubt in high tension, and as soon as they heard the marshall's bugle, individually, each one of them took up his instrument and sounded the battle-cry. Thus, conches and kettle-drums, tabors and trumpets, bugles and cow-horns, all burst forth into a challenging war-call, which *Sañjaya*, half-heartedly, describes as "tremendous." Later on, we shall find that when this challenge was replied to by the *Pāṇḍavā-s*, the sound was described by *Sañjaya* as "terrific," "resounding throughout heaven and earth, and rending the hearts of the *Kauravā-s*." Here is another instance to prove that *Sañjaya* was, evidently, a moral objector to the war-aim of *Duryodhana*. Therefore, we have in him a most sympathetic reporter of the message of the Lord at the battle-front, as given out in His Song Divine.

ततः श्वेतैर्हयैर्युक्ते महति स्यन्दने स्थितौ।
माधवः पाण्डवश्चैव दिव्यौ शङ्खौ प्रदध्मतुः ॥ १४ ॥

Tataḥ śvetair-hayair-yukte
mahati syandane sthithau,
mādhavaḥ pāṇḍavaś-caiva
divyau śaṅkhau pradadh-matuḥ.

ततः *tataḥ* = then; श्वेतैः *śvetaiḥ* = with white; हयैः *hayaiḥ*= horses; युक्ते *yukte* = yoked; महति *mahati* = magnificent; स्यन्दने *syandane* = in the chariot; स्थितौ *sthithau* = seated; माधवः *mādhavaḥ* = *Mādhava*; पाण्डवः *pāṇḍavaḥ* = *Pāṇḍava*, the son of *Pāṇḍu*; च *ca* = and; एव *eva* = also; दिव्यौ *divyau* = divine; शङ्खौ *śaṅkhau*= conchs; प्रदध्मतुः *pradadh-matuḥ* = blew.

14. *Then, also* Mādhava *and the son of* Pāṇḍu, *seated in their magnificent chariot yoked with white horses, blew their divine conchs.*

Continuing the report upon the war-front, *Sañjaya* is taking up now the description of the *Pāṇḍavā-s'* side. The detailed back-ground, so elaborately painted so far by *Vyāsa*, was only to provide a perfect setting against which the two main great characters of the *Gītā* could be brought to play their part. The wealth of detail that has been so lavishly squandered in expressing a simple fact that, from the *Pāṇḍavā*-s' side,

Kṛṣṇa and *Arjuna* answered the battle-cry, clearly shows where *Sañjaya's* sympathies lay. Here, the description—"sitting in the magnificent chariot, harnessed with white horses, *Mādhava* and *Arjuna* blew their conchs divine"—clearly echoes the hope lurking in the heart of *Sañjaya* that due to the apparent contrast in the two descriptions, perhaps, even at this moment *Dhṛtarāṣṭra* may be persuaded to withdraw his sons from the war front.

पाञ्चजन्यं हृषीकेशो देवदत्तं धनञ्जयः ।
पौण्ड्रं दध्मौ महाशङ्खं भीमकर्मा वृकोदरः ॥ १५ ॥

Pāñcajanyaṁ hṛṣīkeśo
devadattaṁ dhanañjayaḥ,
pauṇḍraṁ dadhmau mahā-
śaṅkhaṁ bhīmakarmā vṛkodaraḥ.

पाञ्चजन्यम् *pāñcajanyam* = (the conch named) *Pāñcajanya*; हृषीकेशः *hṛṣīkeśaḥ* = (lit. the Lord of the senses) *Kṛṣṇa*; देवदत्तम् *devadattam* = (the conch named) *Devadatta* (lit. given by God); धनञ्जयः *dhanañjayaḥ* = (the conquerer of wealth) *Arjuna*; पौण्ड्रम् *pauṇḍram* = (the conch named) *Pauṇḍra*; दध्मौ *dadhmau* = blew; महाशङ्खम् *mahāśaṅkham* = great conch; भीम-कर्मा *bhīma-karmā* = doer of terrible deeds (lit. large size/deeds); वृकोदरः *vṛkodaraḥ* = (wolf-bellied) *Bhīma* (lit. having fire in the stomach which can digest anything).

15. Hṛṣīkeśa *blew the* Pāñcajanya *and* Dhanañjaya *(*Arjuna*) blew the* Devadatta *and* Vṛkodara *(*Bhīma*), the doer of terrible deeds, blew the great conch, named* Pauṇḍra.

In his description of the *Pāṇḍava* array, *Sañjaya* is very particular to mention even the name of each warrior's special conch. *Pāñcajanya* was blown by *Kṛṣṇa*.

Hṛṣīkeśa is the name of the Lord and it has often been described as meaning the 'Lord of the Senses.' But this is according to an old derivation: *Hṛṣīka* + *Īśa* = "Lord of the Senses." But the word "*Hṛṣīka*" is an obscure one. Modern commentators prefer to explain it as *Hṛṣī* + *keśa* "Having short hair." This may not fit in with the orthodox description of *Kṛṣṇa* on the charioteer's seat, but it need not be understood that *Kṛṣṇa* had a close crop for the war; it may be interpreted that due to the heavy breeze on the open plains of *Kurukṣetra*, the flowing hairs of the Lord got blown up and ruffled.

Pāñcajanya is a conch made out of a demon called *Pañcajana*. *Dhanañjaya* means a 'conquerer of wealth' and it is a title of *Arjuna* because he went round the country and appropriated the hidden and stagnant wealths of the inactive rulers, and utilised the same for public welfare. *Devadatta* is the name of the conch which was given to *Arjuna* by God-*Indra* who was his divine father.

Vṛkodara means 'wolf-bellied,'— A wolf has a concave belly which does not bulge out even when stuffed-full. This beast is noted for both its great devouring capacity as well as digestive power. Any one with strong digestive power excels in all his doings. *Bhīma* was notorious for possessing these wolf-like qualities. The term *Bhīmakarmā*, as an epithet qualifying *Bhīma*, is a play upon his name and means 'terrible.'

अनन्तविजयं राजा कुन्तीपुत्रो युधिष्ठिरः ।
नकुलः सहदेवश्च सुघोषमणिपुष्पकौ ॥ १६ ॥

Ananta-vijayaṁ rājā kuntī-putro yudhiṣṭhiraḥ,
nakulaḥ sahadevaś-ca sughoṣa-maṇi-puṣpakau.

अनन्त-विजयम् *ananta-vijayam* = (the conch named) *Ananta-vijayam*; राजा *rājā* = the king; कुन्ती-पुत्रः *kuntī-putraḥ* = son of *Kuntī*; युधिष्ठिरः *yudhiṣṭhiraḥ* = *Yudhiṣṭhira*; नकुलः *nakulaḥ* = *Nakula*; सहदेवः *sahadevaḥ* = *Sahadeva*; च *ca* = and; सुघोष-मणि-पुष्पकौ *sughoṣa-maṇi-puṣpakau* = conchs named *Sughoṣa* and *Maṇipuṣpaka*.

16. *King* Yudhiṣṭhira, *the son of* Kuntī, *blew the* Anantavijaya; Nakula *and* Sahadeva *blew their conchs named* Sughoṣa *and* Maṇipuṣpaka.

Anant-vijayam is the conch belonging to the eldest of the *Pāṇḍava* brothers *Yudhiṣṭhira*, and it literally means 'Ever lasting victory.' *Sughoṣa* meaning "Sweet toned" is the conch of *Nakula*, and *Sahadeva's* bugle is called *Maṇipuṣpaka* meaning 'gem-flowered.' These names in themselves need not have any symbolical meaning as some commentators would like to establish. There are some who would like to read in these specific names of the five conchs of the *Pāṇḍavā-s* and the sixth one of *Kṛṣṇa*, a symbolical representation of the six mystical centres (*Cakrā-s*) described by the *Yoga-śastrā-s*. This interpretation, though ingenious, does not appeal to our aestheticism.

काश्यश्च परमेष्वासः शिखण्डी च महारथः ।
धृष्टद्युम्नो विराटश्च सात्यकिश्चापराजितः ॥ १७ ॥

Kāśyaś-ca parame-ṣvāsaḥ śikhaṇḍi ca mahārathaḥ,
dhṛṣṭadhyumno virāṭaś-ca sātyakiś-cāparājitaḥ.

काश्यः *kāśyaḥ* = *Kāśya*, the king of *Kāśi*; च *ca* = and; परम इष्वासः *parama iṣvāsaḥ* = an excellent archer; शिखण्डी *śikhaṇḍī* = *Śikhaṇḍī*; च *ca* = and; महारथः *mahārathaḥ* = mighty chariot-warrior; धृष्टद्युम्नः *dhṛṣṭadhyumnaḥ* = *Dhṛṣṭadyumna*; विराटः *virāṭaḥ* = *Virāṭa*; च *ca* = and; सात्यकिः *sātyakiḥ* = *Sātyaki*; च *ca* = and; अपराजितः *aparājitaḥ* = unconquered, invincible.

17. *The king of* Kāśi, *an excellent archer,* Śikhaṇḍī, *the mighty chariot-warrior,* Dhṛṣṭadyumna *and* Virāṭa *and* Sātyaki, *the unconquered.......*

द्रुपदो द्रौपदेयाश्च सर्वशः पृथिवीपते ।
सौभद्रश्च महाबाहुः शङ्खान्दध्मुः पृथक् पृथक् ॥ १८ ॥

Drupado dropadeyāś-ca
sarvaśaḥ pṛthivī-pate,
saubhadraś-ca mahā-bāhuḥ
śaṅkhān-dadhmuḥ pṛthak pṛthak.

द्रुपद: *drupadaḥ* = *Drupada*; द्रौपदेया: *draupadeyāḥ* = the sons of *Draupadī*; च *ca* = and; सर्वश: *sarvaśaḥ* = all; पृथिवीपते *pṛthivīpate* = O Lord of Earth; सौभद्र: *saubhadraḥ* = son of *Subhadrā* (*Abhimanyu*); च *ca* = and; महाबाहु: *mahābāhuḥ* = the mighty armed; शङ्खान् *śaṅkhān* = conchs; दध्मु: *dadhmuḥ* = blew; पृथक् पृथक *pṛthak-pṛthak.* = respective.

18. Drupada *and the sons of* Draupadī, *O Lord of the Earth, and the son of* Subhadrā, *the mighty armed, blew their respective conchs.*

In the above two verses, we have the enumeration of the great *Mahārathā-s*, battalion-commanders, who, with enthusiasm, loudly blew their conchs, again and again, in an ascending cadence. The arrow that ultimately felled *Bhīṣma* in the *Mahābhārata*-war came from *Śikhaṇḍī*. The charioteer of *Kṛṣṇa*, who was also a battalion-commander in the *Pāṇḍava* army, was called *Sātyakī*.

The report is being addressed to *Dhṛtarāṣṭra* and it is indicated by *Sañjaya's* words, "Oh Lord of the earth."—

स घोषो धार्तराष्ट्राणां हृदयानि व्यदारयत् ।
नभश्च पृथिवीं चैव तुमुलो व्यनुनादयन् ॥ १९ ॥

Sa ghoṣo dhārta-rāṣṭr āṇāṁ hṛdyāni vyadārayat,
nabhaś-ca pṛthivīṁ caiva tumulo vyanu-nādayan.

स: *saḥ* = that; घोष: *ghoṣaḥ* = uproar; धार्तराष्ट्राणाम् *dhārtarāṣṭrāṇām* = *Dhṛtrāṣṭra's* party; हृदयानि *hṛdyāni* = hearts, व्यदारयत् *vyadārayat* = rent; नभ: *nabhaḥ* = sky; च *ca* = and; पृथिवीम् *pṛthivīm* = earth;

च *ca* = and; एव *eva* = also; तुमुल: *tumulah* = tumultuous; व्यनुनादयन *vyanunādayan* = made to reverberate.

19. *That tumultuous sound rent the hearts of (the people of)* Dhṛtarāṣṭra's *party and made both heaven and earth reverberate.*

From the fourteenth stanza onwards *Sañjaya* gives us in all detail an exhaustive description of the *Pāṇḍava* forces, and he spares no pains to bring into the mind of *Dhṛtarāṣṭra* a vivid understanding of the superiority of the *Pāṇḍava* forces. Perhaps, the minister hopes that his blind king will realise the disastrous end and, at least now, will send forth a command to stop the fratricidal war.

In the stanza under discussion, *Sañjaya* says that the sound raised by the *Pāṇḍava* battle-cry resounded in the battle-field and rose up to echo in space. By his super-sensuous vision, *Sañjaya* is detecting in the face of the *Kauravā-s* their reaction to this enthusiastic reply of the *Pāṇḍavā-s*. This stanza can be compared with Verse 13 wherein *Sañjaya* described the *Kaurava* challenge.

अथ व्यवस्थितान्दृष्ट्वा धार्तराष्ट्रान् कपिध्वजः ।
प्रवृत्ते शस्त्रसम्पाते धनुरुद्यम्य पाण्डवः ॥ २० ॥
हृषीकेशं तदा वाक्यमिदमाह महीपते (२१)

Atha vyavasthitān-dṛṣṭvā dhārtarāṣṭrān kapidhvajaḥ,
pravṛtte śastra-sampāte dhanur-udyamya pāṇḍvaḥ.

Hṛṣīkeṣaṁ tadā vākyam-idam-āha mahīpate.

अथ *atha* = now; व्यवस्थितान् *vyavasthitān* = standing arrayed; दृष्ट्वा *dṛṣtvā* = seeing; धार्तराष्ट्रान् *dhārtarāṣṭrān* = *Dhṛtarāṣṭra's* party; कपिध्वज: *kapidhvajaḥ* = monkey ensigned; प्रवृत्ते *pravṛtte* = about to begin; शस्त्र सम्पाते *śastra sampāte* = discharge of weapons; धनु: *dhanuḥ* = bow; उद्यम्य *udyamya* = having taken; पाण्डव:

pāṇḍvaḥ = the son of *Pāṇḍu*; हृषीकेशम् *hṛṣīkeśam* = to *Hṛṣīkeśa*; तदा *tadā* = then; वाक्यम् *vākyam* = words; इदम् *idam* = this; आह = said; महीपते *mahīpate* = O Lord of Earth;

20-21.Then, seeing the people of Dhṛtarāṣṭra's *party standing arrayed and the discharge of weapons about to begin,* Arjuna, *the son of* Pāṇḍu, *whose ensign was a monkey, took up his bow and said these words to* Kṛṣṇa *(*Hṛṣīkeśa*), O Lord of the Earth!*

In these one and a half verses, we have a description of the arrival of the hero of the *Mahābhārata* war, *Arjuna*, on the battle-field. The exact time and nature of his entry are noted here. The shooting had not yet started, but it was imminent. It was the most tense moment; the crisis had risen to its highest pitch. It was at this moment that *Arjuna*, whose ensign was that of *Hanumān*, said the following words to Lord *Kṛṣṇa*.

In those ancient days of chivalrous warfare, each honoured hero had his own personal flag, carrying on it conspicuously, a well-recognised symbol. By the flag flying on the chariot, the enemy could recognise who was the occupant of the chariot. A hero was not generally shot at by an ordinary soldier, but each fought with his equal on the battle-field. This system of carrying a symbol to recognize individuals in the battle-field is faithfully followed even in modern warfare. A high official's vehicle carries insignia of the officer's rank on its very number-plate; on the very uniform enough details are pinned on to recognize the wearer and identify him. *Arjuna*'s ensign was that of a monkey.

The stanza also gives us, in hasty strokes, the information that *Arjuna* was impatient to start the righteous war. He had raised his instrument of war, his bow, indicating his readiness to fight.

अर्जुन उवाच-

सेनयोरुभयोर्मध्ये रथं स्थापय मेऽच्युत ॥ २१ ॥
यावदेतान्निरीक्षेऽहं योद्धुकामानवस्थितान् ।
कैर्मया सह योद्धव्यमस्मिन् रणसमुद्यमे ॥ २२ ॥

Arjuna Uvāca—

Senyor-ubhayor-madhye rathaṁ sthāpaya me'cyuta.
Yāvad-etān-nirīkṣe-'haṁ yoddhu-kāmān-avasthitān,
kairmayā saha yoddhavyam-asmin raṇa-samudyame.

सेनयो: *senyoḥ* = of the armies; उभयो: *ubhayoḥ* = of both; मध्ये *madhye* = in the middle; रथम् *ratham* = chariot; स्थापय *sthyāpaya* = place; मे *me* = my; अच्युत *acyuta* = O *Acyuta* (O unfailing, *Kṛṣṇa*); यावत् *yāvat* = while; एतान् *etān* = these; निरीक्षे *nirīkṣe* = behold; अहम् *aham* = I; योद्धु-कामान् *yoddhu-kāmān* = desirous of fighting; अवस्थितान् *avasthitān* = stand; कै: *kaḥ* = with whom; मया *mayā* = by me; सह *saha* = together; योद्धव्यम् *yoddhavyam* = must be fought; अस्मिन् *asmin* = in this; रण-समुद्यमे *raṇa-samudyame* = eve of battle.

Arjuna said:

21-22. In the midst of the two armies, place my chariot, O Acyuta, *that I may behold those who stand here desirous of fighting and, on the eve of this battle, let me know with whom I must fight.*

Here, we hear *Arjuna*'s soldier-like command to his charioteer to drive and place the vehicle between the two armies so that he might see and recognise the various heroes whom he has to meet and fight in the great war. In expressing thus a wish to review the enemy lines the great hero is showing his daring and chivalry, his great courage and firm determination, his adventurous readiness and indomitable energy. Upto this point in the story, *Arjuna*, the invincible hero of the *Mahābhārata*, was in his own true element unaffected by any mental hysteria.

Kṛṣṇa is addressed here as *Acyuta* meaning "never-failing," "never-falling," "one who knows no slip," "one who does not abandone his stand."

योत्स्यमानानवेक्षेऽहं य एतेऽत्र समागताः ।
धार्तराष्ट्रस्य दुर्बुद्धेर्युद्धे प्रियचिकीर्षवः ॥ २३ ॥

Yotsyamānān-avekṣe-'haṁ ya ete-'tra samāgatāḥ,
dhārtarāṣṭrasya durbuddher-yuddhe priya-cikīrṣavaḥ.

योत्स्यमानान् *yotsyamānān* = with the object of fighting; अवेक्षे *avekṣe* = observe; अहम् *aham* = I; यः *yaḥ* = who; एते *ete* = those; अत्र *atra* = here, (in this *Kurukṣetra*); समागताः *samāgatāḥ* = assembled; धार्तराष्ट्रस्य *dhārtarāṣṭrasya* = of the son of *Dhṛtarāṣṭra*; दुर्बुद्धेः *durbuddheḥ* = of the evil-minded; युद्धे *yuddhe* = in the battle; प्रियचिकीर्षवः *priya-cikīrṣavaḥ* = wishing to please.

23. *For I desire to observe those who are assembled here to fight, wishing to please in battle, the evil-minded son of* Dhṛtarāṣṭra.

This verse only reinforces our impression of *Arjuna* gathered in the previous lines. He is giving the reason why he wants to review the enemy lines. As a man of action, he did not want to take any undue risk and so wanted to see for himself who were the low-minded, power-mad, greed-ridden men who had joined the forces of the *Kauravā-s*, supporting the palpably tyrannical and evidently unjust cause of the unscrupulous *Duryodhana*.

These great men of the time of *Mahābhārata*, who had joined the *Kaurava* forces, were certainly no great champions of any noble cause and their only war aim was to please the most powerful tyrant of that era, *Duryodhana*. They must have had their own expectations of gaining some material benefits, a share in the unrighteous looting of the *Pāṇḍavā-s*. *Arjuna* was anxious to meet those aggressors and immoral men of power, who had assembled on the *Kaurava* lines, greedy to get a share in the spoils of the aggressive war callously waged.

As we read the stanza, we can almost hear the great warrior's teeth grinding, as he spits out these hot words which express his mental estimate of his relentless cousins.

सञ्जय उवाच —

एवमुक्तो हृषीकेशो गुडाकेशेन भारत ।
सेनयोरुभयोर्मध्ये स्थापयित्वा रथोत्तमम् ॥ २४ ॥

Sañjaya Uvāca—

Evam-ukto hṛṣīkeṣo guḍākeśena bhārat,
senayor-ubhayor-madhye sthāpayitvā rathottamam.

एवम् *evam* = thus; उक्तः *uktaḥ* = addressed; हृषीकेशः *hṛṣīkeṣaḥ* = *Hṛṣīkeśa*; गुडाकेशेन *gudhākeśena* = by *Guḍākeśa* (an ephithet of *Arjuna*, lit. the conqueror of sleep); भारत *bhārata* = O *Bhārata* (descendent of king *Bharata*, here refers to *Dhṛtarāṣṭra*); सेनयोः *senayoḥ* = of the armies; उभयोः *ubhayoḥ* = of both; मध्ये *madhye* = in the middle; स्थापयित्वा *sthāpayitvā* = having stationed; रथ उत्तमम् *ratha uttamam* = best of chariots.

Sañjaya said:

24. *Thus addressed by* Guḍākeśa, O Bhārata *(here meaning* Dhṛtarāṣṭra*),* Hṛṣīkeśa, *having stationed the best of chariots between the two armies.....*

भीष्मद्रोणप्रमुखतः सर्वेषां च महीक्षिताम् ।
उवाच पार्थ पश्यैतान् समवेतान्कुरूनिति ॥ २५ ॥

Bhīṣma-droṇa-pramukhataḥ sarveṣām ca mahīkṣitām,
uvāca pārtha paśyaitān-samavetān-kurūn-iti.

भीष्म-द्रोण-प्रमुखतः *bhīṣma-droṇa-pramukhataḥ* = in front of *Bhīṣma* and *Droṇa*; सर्वेषाम् *sarveṣām* = of all; च *ca* = and; महीक्षिताम् *mahīkṣitām* = rulers of the earth; उवाच *uvāca* = said; पार्थ *pārtha* = O *Pārtha*; पश्य *paśya* = behold; एतान् *etān* = these; समवेतान् *samavetān* = gathered; कुरून् *kurūn* = *Kurū-s*; इति *iti* = thus.

25. *In front of* Bhīṣma *and* Droṇa, *and all the rulers of the earth, (the Lord) said,* 'O Pārtha, *behold these* Kurū-s *gathered together.'*

Thus commanded by *Arjuna*, *Kṛṣṇa* drove the splendid chariot and stopped it between the two armies. *Guḍākeśa* was a title by which *Arjuna* was known in the traditions of *Mahābhārata*. It is generally translated as "Lord of sleep" (*Guḍaka* + *Īśa*). But, unfortunately, there is no evidence to justify this name in the exhaustive biography of *Arjuna* given in the great classic.

We may conveniently accept another interpretation offered by a foreign commentator which means 'with hairs twisted into balls' (*Guḍa* + *keśa*). Perhaps, in those days of long-hair fashion during the war, the warriors, by some indigenous processs, got their hair knotted into small bundles so that the heavy breeze of the Punjab plains would not ruffle the hair and send them across the archer's eyes. In a war, vision is very important and even a moment's winking, perhaps, might cost the life of the hero.

This interpretation seems to be quite intelligent and more acceptable than the traditional superstition that *Arjuna* had conquered sleep. To a certain extent, this term can be applied to every man of intense adventurous activities, in as much as all such men of actions, as compared with the generality of idlers, spend less number of hours in sleep.

The term *Bhārata* in the stanza is addressed to *Dhṛtarāṣtra* for whose information *Sañjaya* is reporting the incidents in front of the battle-field.

Even the very chariot described by *Sañjaya* does not escape an ephithet, and he says, 'the splendid chariot.'

The *Kaurava* forces were arrayed in bird-formation and from the previous descriptions, we know that *Bhīṣma* and *Droṇa* along with *Duryodhana* and others were naturally at the headquarters, which were almost at the geometrical centre of the array, representing the "body of the bird." In this Stanza, *Sañjaya*, very beautifully hints the exact position of the chariot between the two armies. At a point "facing *Bhīṣma*, *Droṇa* and all the rulers of the earth," the Divine Charioteer pulled up the reins and brought the royal chariot to a halt. As a dutiful driver, *Kṛṣṇa* says to *Arjuna*, "Behold, O *Pārtha*! all the *Kauravā-s* gathered together."

These are the only words that *Kṛṣṇa* has spoken in the entire first chapter; and these represent the sparks that set fire to and brought down the egoistic edifice of false valuations which the great hero had built for himself as a splendid dwelling place for his personality. Hereafter, we shall find how *Arjuna* reacted to this great challenge and ultimately got his entire "within" wrecked and shattered.

Pārtha means 'Son of *Pṛthā*'—it is a name of *Arjuna*; '*Pṛthā*' was another name of *Kuntī*; the *Saṁskṛta* term *Pārtha* also carries a flavour of the term *Pārthiva* meaning 'clay-made,' 'earth-formed.' The suggestive implication of this term is very striking inasmuch as it connotes that the *Gītā* is the Song of Truth sung by the Immortal to the mortal *Arjuna*, man's all-time representative.

तत्रापश्यत्स्थितान् पार्थः पितॄनथ पितामहान् ।
आचार्यान्मातुलान्भ्रातॄन्पुत्रान्पौत्रान्सखींस्तथा ॥ २६ ॥

Tatrā-paśyat-sthitān pārthaḥ
pitṝn-atha pitā-mahān,
ācāryān-mātulān-bhrātṝn-putrān-
pautrān-sakhīṁs-tathā.

तत्र *tatra* = there; अपश्यत् *apaśyat* = saw; स्थितान् *sthitān* = stationed; पार्थः *pārthaḥ* = *Pārtha;* पितॄन् *pitṝn* = fathers; अथ *atha* = also; पितामहान् *pitāmahān* = grand-fathers; आचार्यान् *ācāryān* = teachers; मातुलान् *mātulān* = maternal uncles; भ्रातॄन् *bhrātṝn* = brothers; पुत्रान् *putrān* = sons; पौत्रान् *pautrān* = grand-sons; सखीम् *sakhīm* = friends; तथा *tathā* = too.

26. *Then* Pārtha *saw stationed there in both the armies, fathers, grand-fathers, teachers, maternal uncles, brothers, sons, grand-sons and friends too.*

श्वशुरान् सुहृदश्चैव सेनयोरुभयोरपि ।
तान्समीक्ष्य स कौन्तेयः सर्वान् बन्धूनवस्थितान् ॥ २७ ॥

कृपया परयाविष्टो विषीदन्निदमब्रवीत् ।(२८)

Śvaśurān-suhṛdaś-caiva senayor-ubhayor-api,
tān-samīkṣya sa kaunteyaḥ sarvān-bandhūn-avasthitān.

Kṛpayā parayā-viṣṭo viṣīdan-nidam-abravīt.

श्वशुरान् *śvaśurān* = fathers in law; सुहृदः *suhṛdaḥ* = friends; च *ca* = and; एव *eva* = also; सेनयोः *senayoḥ* = in the armies; उभयोः *ubhayoḥ* = (in) both; अपि *api* = also; तान् *tān* = these; समीक्ष्य *samīkṣya* = having seen; सः *saḥ* = he; कौन्तेयः *kaunteyaḥ* = son of *Kuntī;* सर्वान् *sarvān* = all; बन्धून् *bandhūn* = relatives; अवस्थितान् *avasthitān* = stationed, standing arrayed; कृपया *kṛpayā* = by pity; परया *parayā* = deep; आविष्टो *āviṣṭo* = filled; विषीदन् *viṣīdan* = sorrowfully; इदम् *idam* = this; अब्रवीत् *abravīt* = said.

27-28. *(He saw) Fathers-in-law and friends also in both the armies. Then the son of* Kuntī, *seeing all these kinsmen standing arrayed, spoke thus sorrowfully, filled with deep pity.*

Thus shown by *Śrī Kṛṣṇa*, *Arjuna* recognised in his enemy lines all his kith and kin, near and dear family members, brothers and cousins, teachers and grandsires, and almost all his acquaintances and friends. He recognized such intimate relations not only in the enemy lines, but even in his own army. This sight, perhaps, brought to his mind, for the first time, the full realisation of the tragedies of a fratricidal war. As a warrior and a man of action, he did not, perhaps till then, fully realize the extent of sacrifice that society would be called upon to make in order that his ambition might be fulfilled and *Duryodhana*'s cruelties avenged.

Whatever might have been the cause, the sight brought into his mind a flood of pity and compassion.

Evidently, this was not an honest emotion. Had it been honest, had his pity and compassion been, *Buddha*-like, natural and instinctive, he would have, even long before the war, behaved quite differently. This emotion which now *Sañjaya* glorifies as "pity" in *Arjuna*, is a misnomer. In the human heart, there is always a great tendency to glorify one's own weaknesses with some convenient angelic name and divine pose. Thus, a rich man's vanity is mis-named as charity when he builds a temple in his own name with the secret aim of immortalising himself. Here also we find that the feeling of desperation that came in *Arjuna*'s mind due to the complete shattering of his mental equilibrium has been mis-named and glorified as 'pity.'

Arjuna had a long life of mental repressions which had created an infinite amount of dynamic energies seeking a field for expression. His mind got split up because of his egoistic evaluation of himself as the greatest hero of his time, and because of his anxious desire for a victorious end of the war. The pre-occupation of his mind, dreaming intensively, about the ultimate end of the war brought about a complete divorce between the 'subjective' and the 'objective' aspects of his mind.*

Later on, in this chapter, we shall discover the various symptoms of this neurotic condition in him and his hysterical

---

* Refer to the General Introduction and the explanation with the help of the charts 'A' and 'B.'

blabberings which are typical of such a mental patient. The endeavour in Chapter I of the *Gītā* is to give the complete "case-history" of a patient suffering from the typical "*Arjuna*-disease." The *Bhagavad Gītā* gives, as said earlier, an extremely efficient "*Kṛṣṇa*-cure" for this soul-killing "*Arjuna*-disease."

अर्जुन उवाच—

दृष्ट्वेमं स्वजनं कृष्ण युयुत्सुं समुपस्थितम् ॥ २८ ॥

Arjuna Uvāca—

Dṛṣṭvemaṁ svajanaṁ kṛṣṇa yuyutsuṁ samupasthitam.

दृष्ट्वा *dṛṣṭā* = having seen; इमम् *imam* = these; स्वजनम् *svajanam* = kinsmen; कृष्ण *kṛṣṇa* = O *Kṛṣṇa*; युयुत्सुम् *yuyutsum* = eager to fight; समुपस्थितम् *samupasthitam* = arrayed.

Arjuna said :

28. *Seeing these my kinsmen,* O Kṛṣṇa, *arrayed, eager to fight......*

सीदन्ति मम गात्राणि मुखं च परिशुष्यति ।
वेपथुश्च शरीरे मे रोमहर्षश्च जायते ॥ २९ ॥

Sīdanti mama gātrāṇi mukhaṁ ca pariśuṣyati,
vepathuś-ca śarīre me roma-harṣaś-ca jāyate.

सीदन्ति *sīdanti* = fail; मम *mama* = my; गात्राणि *gātrāṇi* = limbs; मुखम् *mukham* = mouth; च *ca* = and; परिशुष्यति *pariśuṣyati* = is parching; वेपथुः *vepathuḥ* = shivering; च *ca* = and; शरीरे *śarīre* = in body; मे *me* = my; रोम-हर्षः *roma-harṣaḥ* = horripilation; च *ca* = and; जायते *jāyate* = arise.

29. *My limbs fail and my mouth is parched, my body quivers and my hair stands on end. ...*

In these two stanzas, there is an exhaustive enumeration of the symptoms that the patient could then recognise in his own physical body as a result of his mental confusions. That which *Sanjaya* had glorified as 'pity,' when coming out of *Arjuna*'s own mouth, gains a more realistic expression. *Arjuna* says: "seeing my kinsmen gathered here anxiously determined to fight, my limbs shiver,"... etc.

All these symptoms are described in the text-books of modern psychology as typical symptoms of the mental disease named 'anxiety-state-neurosis.'

गाण्डीवं संस्रते हस्तात्त्वक्चैव परिदह्यते ।
न च शक्नोम्यवस्थातुं भ्रमतीव च मे मनः ॥ ३० ॥

Gāṇḍīvaṁ saṁsrate hastāt-tvak-caiva paridahyate,
na ca śaknomya-vasthātuṁ bhramatīva ca me manaḥ.

गाण्डीवम् *gāṇḍīvam* = *Gāṇḍiva*; संस्रते *saṁsrate* = slips; हस्तात् *hastāt* = from (my) hand; त्वक् *tvak* = (my) skin; च *ca* = and; एव *eva* = also; परिदह्यते *paridahyate* = burns all over; न *na* = not; च *ca* = and; शक्नोमि *śaknomi* = I am able; अवस्थातुम् *avasthātum* = to stand; भ्रमति इव *bhramati iva* = seems whirling; च *ca* = and; मे *me* = my; मनः *manaḥ* = mind.

30. The Gāṇḍīva-*bow slips from my hand, and my skin burns all over; I am also unable to stand and my mind is whirling round, as it were.*

Here *Arjuna* is adding some more details of the symptoms of his disease. Earlier we had a list of symptoms that manifested on the physical body. Now in this stanza, *Arjuna* tries to report recognised symptoms of the maladjustments at his mental level.

Not only is his mind unsteady, agitated and chaotic, but it has lost all its morale. It has come down to the stupid level of accepting and recognising superstitious omens portending disastrous failures and imminent consequences.

Not only does the following stanza vividly picture to us his mental confusions, but it also shows how far his discrimination has been drained off, and his morale destroyed.

निमित्तानि च पश्यामि विपरीतानि केशव ।
न च श्रेयोऽनुपश्यामि हत्वा स्वजनमाहवे ॥ ३१ ॥

Nimittāni ca paśyāmi viparītāni keśava,
na ca śreyo-'nupaśyāmi hatvā svajana-māhave.

निमित्तानि *nimittāni* = omens; च *ca* = and; पश्यामि *paśyāmi* = I see; विपरीतानि *viparītāni* = adverse; केशव *keśava* = O *Keśava*; न *na* = not; च *ca* = and; श्रेय: *śreyaḥ* = good; अनुपश्यामि *anupaśyāmi* = (I) see; हत्वा *hatvā* = killing; स्वजनम् *svajanam* = our people; आहवे *āhave* = in battle.

31. And I see adverse omens, O Keśava. *Nor do I see any good in killing my kinsmen in battle. ...*

In this state of mental confusion, when his emotions have been totally divorced from his intellect, the 'objective-mind,' without the guidance of its 'subjective-aspect,' runs wild and comes to some unintelligent conclusions. He says, 'I desire neither victory, nor empire, nor even pleasure.' It is a recognised fact that a patient of hysteria, when allowed to talk, will, in a negative way, express the very cause for the attack. For example, when a woman, hysterically raving, repeatedly declares with all emphasis, that she is not tired of her husband that she still respects him, that he still loves her, that there is no rupture between them, etc., she, by these very words, clearly indicates the exact cause of her mental chaos.

Similarly, the very denials of *Arjuna* clearly indicate to all careful readers how and why he got into such a state of mental grief. He desired victory. He urgently wanted the kingdom. He anxiously expected to win pleasures for himself and his relations. But the challenging look of the mighty *Kaurava* forces and the great and eminent warriors standing ready to fight, shattered his hopes, blasted his ambitions, and undermined his self-confidence and he slowly developed the well-known "*Arjuna*-disease," the cure for which is the theme of the *Gītā*.

Keśava literally means 'hairy one'; but this description of *Kṛṣṇa* is quite contrary to the elaborate description of the Lord available to us in the entire *Mahābhārata*. Traditionally, *Kṛṣṇa* is represented as sweet in form, soft in flesh, round in shape, smooth in skin. This interpretation of the word can be justified only as indicative of the luxurious dark curly hair on his crown. A description that only indicates that *Kṛṣṇa* was *not* bald headed seems to be quite redundant. and ineffective. Some commentators have pointed out that *Keśava* is a spoilt term for *Kleśva*, meaning he who removes all *Kleśā-s*—one who removes all our sufferings and sorrows.

In a living language, words are often crushed out of shape and some of them long in use get worn off and acquire a new shape altogether. May be *Keśava* is a typical example of such words.

न काङ्क्षे विजयं कृष्ण न च राज्यं सुखानि च ।
किं नो राज्येन गोविन्द किं भोगैर्जीवितेन वा ॥३२॥

Na kāṅkṣe vijayaṁ kṛṣṇa na ca rājyaṁ sukhāni ca,
kiṁ no rājyena govinda kiṁ bhogair-jīvitena vā.

न *na* = not; काङ्क्षे *kāṅkṣe* = (I) desire; विजयम् *vijayam* = victory; कृष्ण *kṛṣṇa* = *O Kṛṣṇa*; न *na* = not; च *ca* = and; राज्यम् *rājyam* = kingdom; सुखानि *sukhāni* = pleasures; च *ca* = and; किम् *kim* = what; नः *nah* = to us; राज्येन *rājyena* = by kingdom; गोविन्द *govinda* = *O Govinda*; किम् *kim* = what; भोगैः *bhogaiḥ* = by pleasures; जीवितेन *jīvitena* = life itself; वा *vā* = or.

32. *For, I desire not victory,* O Kṛṣṇa, *nor kingdom, nor pleasures. Of what avail is dominion to us,*

O Govinda? *Of what avail are pleasures or even life itself? ...*

येषामर्थे काङ्क्षितं नो राज्यं भोगाः सुखानि च ।
त इमेऽवस्थिता युद्धे प्राणांस्त्यक्त्वा धनानि च ॥ ३३ ॥

Yeṣāmarthe kāṅkṣitaṁ no
rājyaṁ bhogāḥ sukhāni ca,
ta ime-'vasthitā yuddhe
prāṇāṁs-tyaktvā dhanāni ca.

येषाम् *yeṣām* = of whose; अर्थे *arthe* = sake; काङ्क्षितम् *kāṅkṣitam* = (is) desired; नः *nah* = by us; राज्यम् *rājyam* = kingdom; भोगाः *bhogāḥ* = enjoyment; सुखानि *sukhāni* = pleasures; च *ca* = and; ते *te* = they; इमे *ime* = these; अवस्थिताः *avasthitāḥ* = stand; युद्धे *yuddhe* = in battle; प्राणान् *prāṇān* = life; त्यक्त्वा *tyaktvā* = having abandoned; धनानि *dhanāni* = wealth; च *ca* = and.

33. They for whose sake we desire kingdom, enjoyment and pleasures stand here in battle, having renounced life and wealth. ...

आचार्याः पितरः पुत्रास्तथैव च पितामहाः ।
मातुलाः श्वशुराः पौत्राः श्यालाः सम्बन्धिनस्तथा ॥ ३४ ॥

Ācāryāḥ pitaraḥ putrās-tathaiva ca pitāmahāḥ,
mātulāḥ śvaśurāḥ pautrāḥ śyālāḥ sambandhinas-tathā.

आचार्याः *ācāryāḥ* = teachers; पितरः *pitaraḥ* = fathers; पुत्राः *putrāḥ* = sons; तथा *tatha* = thus; एव *eva* = also; च *ca* = and; पितामहाः *pitāmahāḥ* = grandfathers; मातुलाः *mātulāḥ* = maternal uncles; श्वशुराः *śvaśurāḥ* = fathers-in-law; पौत्राः *pautrāḥ* = grandsons; श्यालाः *śyālāḥ* = brothers-in-law; सम्बन्धिनः *sambandhinaḥ = relatives;* तथा *tathā = as well as.*

34. Teachers, fathers, sons and also grand-fathers, maternal uncles, fathers-in-law, grand-sons, brothers-in-law and other relatives. ...

Arjuna continues his arguments to *Kṛṣṇa* against the advisability of such a civil war between the two factions of the same royal family. A *Dharma*-hunting *Arjuna* is here mentally manufacturing a case for himself justifying his cowardly retreat from the post of duty where destiny has called upon him to act.

He repeats what he had said earlier because *Kṛṣṇa*, with his pregnant silence, is criticising *Arjuna*'s attitude. The provocatively smiling lips of the Lord are whipping *Arjuna* into a sense of shame. He wants the moral support of his friend and charioteer to come to the conclusion that what he is feeling in his own mind is acceptable and just. But the endorsement and the intellectual sanction are not forthcoming from either the look of *Kṛṣṇa* or the words of the Lord.

एतान्न हन्तुमिच्छामि घ्नतोऽपि मधुसूदन ।
अपि त्रैलोक्यराज्यस्य हेतोः किं नु महीकृते ॥ ३५ ॥

Etān-na hantum-icchāmi ghnato-'pi madhusūdana,
api trai-lokya-rājyasya hetoḥ kiṁ nu mahīkṛte.

एतान् *etān* = these; न *na* = not; हन्तुम् *hantum* = to kill; इच्छामि *icchāmi* = (I) wish; घ्नतः अपि *ghnataḥ api* = even if killed (by them); मधुसूदन *madhusūdana* = O *Madhusūdan* (lit. the slayer of a demon called *Madhu*); अपि *api* = even; त्रैलोक्य राज्यस्य *trailokya rājyasya* = dominion over the three worlds; हेतोः *hetoh* = for the sake of; किम् *kim* = how; नु *nu* = then; महीकृते *mahīkṛte* = for the sake of the earth.

35. *These I do not wish to kill, though they kill me,* O Madhusūdana, *even for the sake of dominion over the three worlds; how much less for the sake of the earth.*

Feeling that he had not expressed his case strongly enough to *Kṛṣṇa* to make him come to this conclusion, and, assuming that it was because of this that the Lord had not given his assent to it, *Arjuna* decided to declare with a mock spirit of renunciation, that he had so much large-heartedness in him that he would not kill his cousins, even if they were to kill him. The climax came when *Arjuna*, with quixotic exaggeration, declared that he would not fight the war, even if he were to win all the three worlds of the Universe, much less so for the mere *Hastināpura*-kingship.

Govinda—This name of *Kṛṣṇa* is explained in the *Sant Parva* according to the legend of *Kṛṣṇa*'s winning back the earth. "The origin of this name may be traced to this legend," writes *Bhandārkar*, "but more probably *Govinda* is a later form of *Govind*," which in *Ṛg Veda* is used as an epithet for *Indra* in the sense of "the finder of the cows."

निहत्य धार्तराष्ट्रान्नः का प्रीतिः स्याज्जनार्दन ।
पापमेवाश्रयेदस्मान् हत्वैतानाततायिनः ॥ ३६ ॥

Nihatya dhārtarāṣṭrān-naḥ kā prītiḥ syāj-janārdana,
pāpa-mevāśraye-dasmān hatvai-tānāta-tāyinaḥ.

निहत्य *nihatya* = having slain; धार्तराष्ट्रान् *dhārtarāṣṭrān* = sons of *Dhṛtarāṣṭra*; नः *naḥ* = to us; का *kā* = what; प्रीतिः *prītiḥ* = pleasures; स्यात् *syāt* = may be; जनार्दन *janārdana* = O *Janārdana* (the destroyer of the *asura* called *Jana*); पापम् *pāpam* = sin; एव *eva* = only; आश्रयेत् *āśrayet* = will accrue, be our gain; अस्मान् *asmān* = to us; हत्वा *hatvā* = having killed; एतान् *etān* = these; आततायिनः *ātatāyinaḥ* = felons (evil doers).

36. *Killing these sons of* Dhṛtarāṣṭra, *what pleasure can be ours,* O Janārdana*? Sin alone will be our gain by killing these felons.*

In spite of all that *Arjuna* said so far, *Kṛṣṇa* is as silentas a sphinx. Therefore, *Arjuna* gives up his melodramatic expression and assumes a softer, a more appealing tone and takes the attitude of explaining in vain, a serious matter to a dull-witted friend. The change of strategy becomes conspicuously ludicrous when we notice *Kṛṣṇa*'s continued silence!

In the first line of the stanza he explains to *Kṛṣṇa* that no good can arise out of killing the sons of *Dhṛtarāṣṭra*... still the wooden-smile of *Kṛṣṇa* does not change and the *Pāṇḍava* hero, his intelligence shattered, tries to find a cause for *Kṛṣṇa*'s attitude. Immediately, he remembers that the *Kaurava* brothers were behaving towards the *Pāṇḍavā-s* as felons. '*Ātatāyinaḥ*' means felons, who deserve to be killed according to the *Artha Śāstra.**

*Śrīdhara Svāmī*** explains that those who have done six kinds of crimes towards others are felons. They are :

(1) set fire to the house of another person;
(2) poison him; or
(3) with sword in hand fall upon him to kill and murder; or
(4) steal his wealth; or
(5) his land; or
(6) his wife.

The *Kaurava*-brothers had committed all these felonies upon the *Pāṇḍavā-s* and therefore, they deserved to be killed. But *Arjuna* says here that according to the *Dharma Śāstrā*, non-killing is the fundamental principle of *Hindū-s*, and, therefore, 'sin alone could be the reward' for killing these felons.

Here we find decadent *Hindūism* polluting its sacred wisdom with the mis-interpretations of hasty students and un-intelligent followers. No doubt, *Sanātana Dharma* rests upon a triple-foundation of *Satyam* (truthful-ness), *Ahiṁsā* (non-voilence) and *Brahmacarya* (Self-restraint), but in the decadence of any religion, its scripture gets mis-construed and mis-interpreted by the un-intelligent folk who have not been guided

* Whether he be *Ācārya*, an old man, or a *Veda*-knowing *brāhmaṇa*, if he comes in front as an *Ātatāyīna* (felon) he should be killed on the spot without a thought. There is no sin involved in killing a felon. (Manu. VIII-350, 351)

** Refer *Vāsiṣṭha Smṛti* III-19.....Ed.

to a proper appreciation of the great and immortal declarations. A philosophy, however great, cannot bless a generation unless its vital and active intelligence comes to wrestle with the ideas and the ideologies propounded by that philosophy. Then and then alone can the intelligentsia of the era get the benefit of the sweet cultural fragrance of that philosophy.

Arjuna is a typical member of the *Hindū* Society of that age and clearly exhibits enough mis-understandings about the right import of the *Śastrā-s*, although he is well-read in the sacred lore. The extent of *Arjuna*'s mis-understanding helps us to understand what motivated *Vyāsa* to re-write the scriptures in the form of the *Gītā* and successfully bring about a *Hindū* renaissance movement in that age. A revolution, as in our own times, Hitler's *Mein Kampf* initiated Germany into National Socialism, Lincoln's declarations ushered Democracy into America and Marx's *Das Capital* paved the way for Communism in Russia, we may say that the *Bhagavat Gītā*, in the *Mahābhārata*, kindled a *Hindū* revival movement in the *Puarāṇik* Age. *Arjuna*'s words here help us to capture a whiff of the poisonous atmosphere in which the sacred truths of our *Upaniṣad-s* had come to rot in the *Vyāsa*-days.

Sin is only a mistake committed by a misunderstood individual ego against its own Divine Nature as the Eternal Soul. To act as the body or the mind or the intellect is not to act up to the responsibilities of a man, but it becomes an attempt to behave under the impulses of an animal. All those acts performed and motives entertained, which create grosser mental impressions and thereby build stronger walls between us and our cognition of the Real Divine Spark in ourselves are called sins.

Arjuna's seemingly learned objection to killing enemies is a mis-interpretation of our sacred texts (*Śastrā-s*), and to have acted upon it would have been suicidal to our very culture. Therefore, *Kṛṣṇa* refuses to show any sign either of appreciation or criticism of *Arjuna*'s stand. The Lord understands that his friend is raving hysterically and the best policy is to allow a mental patient first of all to bring out everything in his mind and thus exhaust himself.

तस्मान्नार्हा वयं हन्तुं धार्तराष्ट्रान् स्वबान्धवान् ।
स्वजनं हि कथं हत्वा सुखिनः स्याम माधव ॥ ३७ ॥

Tasmān-nārhā vayaṁ hantuṁ
dhārtarāṣṭrān-sva-bāndhavān,
svajanaṁ hi kathaṁ hatvā
sukhinaḥ syāma mādhava.

तस्मात् *tasmāt* = therefore; न *na* = (are) not; अर्हाः *arhāḥ* = justified; वयम् *vayam* = we; हन्तुम् *hantum* = to kill; धार्तराष्ट्रान् *dhārtarāṣṭrān* = the sons of *Dhṛtarāṣṭra*; स्व-बान्धवान् *sva-bāndhavān* = our own relatives; स्वजनम् *svajanam* = kinsmen; हि *hi* = indeed; कथम् *katham* = how; हत्वा *hatvā* = having killed; सुखिनः *sukhinaḥ* = happy; स्याम *syāma* = may (we) be; माधव *mādhava* = *Mādhava*.

37. *Therefore we shall not kill the sons of* Dhṛtarāṣṭra, *our relatives; for how can we be happy by killing our own people,* O Mādhava*?*

Here, *Arjuna* concludes his seemingly logical arguments which have got a false look of *Hindū* scriptural sanction. More than deliberate blasphemers of a scripture, the unconscious misinterpreters of a sacred text are the innocent criminals who bring about the wretched downfall of its philosophy. Purring with the satisfaction of a cat in the kitchen, *Arjuna*, in this verse, is licking up his arguments all round and is coming to the dangerous conclusion that he should not kill the aggressors, nor face their heartless challenge! Even then *Kṛṣṇa* is silent.

Arjun's discomfiture makes him really quite conspicuous in his ugliness. In the second line of the stanza, he makes a personal appeal to *Kṛṣṇa* and almost begs of him to think for himself and endorse *Pārtha's* own lunatic conclusions.

With the familiarity born out of his long-standing friendship, *Arjuna* addresses his charioteer with affection as *Mādhava*, and asks him how one can come to any happiness after one has destroyed one's own kinsmen... Still, *Kṛṣṇa* remains silent.

यद्यप्येते न पश्यन्ति लोभोपहतचेतसः ।
कुलक्षयकृतं दोषं मित्रद्रोहे च पातकम् ॥ ३८ ॥

Yadyapyete na paśyanti lobho-pahata-cetasaḥ,
kula-kṣaya-kṛtaṁ dośaṁ mitra-drohe ca pātakam.

यद्यपि: *yadyapiḥ* = though; एते *ete* = these; न *na* = not; पश्यन्ति *paśyanti* = see; लोभ-उपहत-चेतस: *lobha-upahata-cetasaḥ* = with intelligence overpowered by greed; कुलक्षय-कृतम् *kulakṣaya-kṛtam* = the destruction of families; दोषम् *dośam* = evil; मित्र-द्रोहे *mitra-drohe* = cruelty to friends; च *ca* = and; पातकम् *pātakam* = sin.

38. Though these, with their intelligence clouded by greed, see no evil in the destruction of the families in the society and no sin in their cruelty to friends. ...

कथं न ज्ञेयमस्माभिः पापादस्मान्निवर्तितुम् ।
कुलक्षयकृतं दोषं प्रपश्यद्भिर्जनार्दन ॥ ३९ ॥

Kathaṁ na jñeyam-asmābhiḥ pāpā-dasmān-nivartitum,
kula-kṣaya-kṛtaṁ dośaṁ prapaśyad-bhir-janārdana.

कथम् *katham* = why; न *na* = not; ज्ञेयम् *jñeyam* = should be learnt; अस्माभि: *asmābhiḥ* = by us; पापात् *pāpāt* = from sin; अस्मान् *asmān* = this; निवर्तितुम् *nivartitum* = to abstain, to turn away; कुल-क्षय-कृतम् *kula-kṣaya-kṛtam* = in the destruction of family; दोषम् *doṣam* = evil; प्रपश्यद्भि: *prapaśyadbhiḥ* = clearly seeing; जनार्दन *janārdana* = O *Janārdana.*

39. *Why should not we, who clearly see evil in the destruction of the family-units, learn to turn away from this sin,* O Janārdana?

No doubt, the *Kauravā-s*, grown blind in their greed for power and wealth, cannot see the destruction of the entire social structure by this war. Their ambition has so completely clouded their intelligence and sensibility that they fail to appreciate or understand the cruelty in annihilating their own friends.

But *Arjuna* seems to retain his reasoning capacity and can clearly foresee the chaos in which society will get buried by fratricidal war. Now his argument amounts to this: if a friend of ours, in his drunken-ness, behaves nastily, it would be worse than drunken-ness in us, if we were to retaliate; for, we are expected to know that our friend, with his fumed-up intelligence, does not entertain enough discriminative awareness of what he is doing. At such moments, it would be our duty to forgive the mischief and overlook the impudence.

Similarly, here, *Arjuna* argues: "If *Duryodhana* and his friends are behaving as blind aggressors, should the *Pāṇḍavā-s* not retire quietly and suffer the ignominy of a defeat, and consider it their dutiful offering at the altar of peace?" How far this philosophy is dangerous in itself will be seen as we read more and more the passages of the *Gītā* and come to appreciate the pith of its philosophy which is the very kernel of our *Hindū* way-of-living. "Active resistance to evil" is the central idea in the doctrine expounded by *Kṛṣṇa* in the *Gītā*.

कुलक्षये प्रणश्यन्ति कुलधर्माः सनातनाः ।
धर्मे नष्टे कुलं कृत्स्नमधर्मोऽभिभवत्युत ॥ ४० ॥

Kula-kṣaye praṇaśyanti kula-dharmāḥ sanātanāḥ,
dharme naṣṭe kulaṁ kṛtsnama-dharmo-'bhibhavatyuta.

कुलक्षये *kula-kṣaye* = in the destruction of a family; प्रणश्यन्ति *praṇaśyanti* = perish; कुलधर्माः *kula-dharmāḥ* = religious rites of that family; सनातना: *sanātanāḥ* = immemorial, ancient; धर्मे *dharme* = of spirituality; नष्टे *naṣṭe* = on the destruction; कुलम् *kulam* = family, clan; कृत्स्नम् *kṛtsnam* = entire, whole; अधर्म: *adharmaḥ* = inpiety, lawlessness; अभिभवति *abhibhavati* = overcomes; उत *uta* = indeed.

40. In the destruction of a family, the immemorial religious rites of that family perish; on the destruction of spirituality, impiety indeed overcomes the whole family.

Just as a story-teller comes to add new details each time he narrates the same old story, so too, *Arjuna* seems to draw new inspiration from his foolishness, and each time his creative intelligence puts forth fresh arguments in support of his wrong philosophy. As soon as he finishes a stanza, he gets, as it were, a new lease of arguments to prattle, and takes refuge behind their noise.

Continuing his arguments, in the second line of the last stanza, he indicates here that, when individual families are destroyed, along with them the religious traditions of the society will also end, and soon an era of impiety will be ushered in.

In this modern age, we may wonder, at the importance given here to the preservation of family life and its traditions. In the *Hindū* way of living, a family is considered the unit of the society, just as in the modern world, a couple is considered its unit. In a family of the old style, the elder members, fathers, and uncles, maintained strict discipline, and brought about perfect unity among the members and thereby maintained a high standard of life for the family.

Today, on the other hand, a young man, as soon as he peeps into his youth, gets married and starts livings, without the tempering influence of the elders, a life of licence in utter disregard of all social sanctions. Naturally, there is no self-control, nor any self-discipline. Convenience of the moment becomes the rule of life and personal satisfaction, however, debasing it might be, is the only code of ethics which he cares for. In short, the unit of the society, in those days, cared for and tended the *standard of life*, while today it plans and works for raising the *standard of living*. Thus a modern reader finds it rather difficult to appreciate the importance of the family integrity for social happiness and the meaning of what *Arjuna* here calls: "the loss of the family-*dharma*."

In any society, its culture is revived and maintained, not in the same fashion as we bring about some political change in that society. A constitutional change can be easily brought about by a few representatives of the people coming together and agreeing over certain fundamental principles. A democaratic nation today can vote against their existing constitution, when a majority in the country realises the necessity for some reorientation of their political principles. They can bring a new type of government into vogue by re-modelling the constitution. Thereafter, the governed can be forced to respect the constitution through laws and, if need be, forced to obey it through the national police.

A culture, however is not created, changed or maintained by such rough and ready political methods. Just as in the agricultural research farms, we produce, through careful experiments and tender nursing, a better evolved breed; so too, under the shelter of its moral and ethical rules, the society of men can be trained for a higher and diviner way-of-living.

Cultural experiments were the pre-occupations of our fore-fathers and they knew that the culture and tradition of each family was a unit of the total culture and integrity of the whole nation. Hence the importance of the family-*Dharma* so seriously brought forth by *Arjuna* as an argument against this civil war.

अधर्माभिभवात्कृष्ण प्रदुष्यन्ति कुलस्त्रियः ।
स्त्रीषु दुष्टासु वार्ष्णेय जायते वर्णसङ्करः ॥ ४१ ॥

Adharmābhi-bhavāt-kṛṣṇa praduṣyanti kulas-triyaḥ,
strīṣu duṣṭāsu vārṣṇeya jāyate varṇa-saṅkaraḥ.

अधर्म-अभिभवात् *adharma-abhibhavāt* = from the prevalence of impiety; कृष्ण *kṛṣṇa* = O *Kṛṣṇa*; प्रदुष्यन्ति *praduṣyanti* = become corrupt; कुल-स्त्रियः *kula-striyaḥ* = the women of the family; स्त्रीषु *striṣu* = in women; दुष्टासु *duṣṭāsu* = (being) corrupt; वार्ष्णेय *vārṣṇeya* = O! descendent of the *Vṛṣṇi*-clan *(Vārṣṇeya)*; जायते *jāyate* = arises; वर्ण-सङ्करः *varṇa-saṅkaraḥ* = caste admixture.

41. *By the prevalence of impiety,* O Kṛṣṇa, *the women of the family become corrupt; and women being corrupted, O descendent of the* Vṛṣṇi-*clan, there arises "intermingling of castes"* (Varṇa Saṅkara).

Continuing the argument in the previous verse, *Pārtha* declares the consequences that will follow when the true moral integrity of the families is destroyed. Slowly the morality in the society will wane and there will be an "admixture of castes."

Caste is a word, which, in its perverted meaning, has recently come in for a lot of criticism from the educated; and they, no doubt, are all justified, if caste, in reality, meant what we understand it to be in our society today. But what we witness around us, in the name of caste, is the ugly decadence into which the *Hindū* way-of-living has fallen. Caste, in those days, was conceived of as an intelligent division of the available manpower in the community on the basis of intellectual and mental capacities of the individuals.

Those who were intellectuals and had a passion for research and study were styled *brāhmaṇā*-s (*brahmins*); those who had political ambitions for leadership and took upon themselves the risky art of maintaining peace and plenty and saving the country from internal and external aggressions, were called the *Kṣatriyā-s*; those who served the community though agriculture and trade were the *Vaiśyā-s* and, lastly, all those who did not fall in any of the above categories were styled as *Śūdrā-s,* whose duties in society were service and labour. Our modern social workers and officials, agricultural and industrial labourers all must fall under this noble category!

In the largest scope of its implication, when we thus understand the caste-system, it is the same as today's professional groups. Therefore, when they talk so seriously about the inadvisability of "admixture of the castes," they only mean what we already know to be true in our own social pattern: an engineer in charge of a hospital and working in the operation-theatre as a doctor would be a social danger, as much as a doctor would be, if he is appointed as an officer for planning, guiding and executing a hydro-electric scheme!

When the general morality of society has decayed; the young men and women, blinded by uncontrolled passion, start mingling without restraint. And lust knows no logic and cares least for better evolution or better culture. There will be thereafter, unhealthy intermingling of incompatible cultural traits.

सङ्करो नरकायैव कुलघ्नानां कुलस्य च ।
पतन्ति पितरो ह्येषां लुप्तपिण्डोदकक्रियाः ॥ ४२ ॥

Saṅkaro narakāyaiva kula-ghnānāṁ kulasya ca,
patanti pitaro hyeṣāṁ lupta-piṇḍodaka-kriyāḥ.

सङ्करः *saṅkaraḥ* = admixture; नरकाय *narakāya* = for the hell; एव *eva* = also; कुल-घ्नानाम् *kula-ghnānām* = of the slayers of the family; कुलस्य *kulasya* = of the family; च *ca* = and; पतन्ति *patanti* = fall; पितरः *pitaraḥ* = the forefathers; हि *hi* = verily; एषाम् *eṣām* = their; लुप्त-पिण्ड-उदक- क्रियाः *lupta piṇḍa-udaka-kriyāḥ* = deprived of the offering of rice-ball (*piṇḍa*) and water (*udaka*).

42. *'Confusion of castes' leads the slayer of the family to hell; for their forefathers fall, deprived of the offerings of* Piṇḍa *(rice-ball) and water (libations).*

The argument is still continued and *Arjuna* points out the consequences of "caste-admixture." When confusion of the castes has taken place, both outside in the moral life of true discipline and in one's own inner temperament, then the family tradition gets flouted and ruined.

After death, the subtle body, constituted of the mind and intellect, departs from its associations with its physical body. In *Hindūism*, one's direct descendants are expected to perform ritualistic worship with *Piṇḍa* and water for the peace and happiness of the departed. This is the idea of the *śrāddha** ceremony. If we understand this stanza merely as an insistence for continuing strictly the 'ritual in honour of the dead,' we would be missing its real meaning.

In the context of our discourses, we must understand that to the dead it is bread-and-water to see that their survivors maintain and continue the cultural purity that they themselves had so laboriously cultivated and inculcated into the minds of their children. In case the society squanders away its culture, so laboriously built up as a result of the slow blossoming of the social values of life through generations of careful cultivation, necessarily, we will be insulting the very labours of our ancestors. It is attractive and poetic, indeed, to conceive of the dead as watching over their survivors and observing their ways of living from the balcony of their heavenly abode! It would certainly be as painful as the pains of hunger and thirst to them if they were to find that their survivors were deliberately making a jungle of their laboriously laid gardens. Understood thus, the entire stanza appears to be very appropriate.

Each generation passes down the torch of its culture to the next generation, its children, and it is for them to preserve, tend and nourish that torch and hand it over carefully to the succeeding generation, if not more, at least no less bright, than when they got it.

In India, the sages discovered and initiated a culture that is spiritual, and this spiritual culture is maintained and worked out through religious practices, and therefore, culture and religion are, to the *Hindū*, one and the same. Very rarely we find any mention of the term culture, as such, in our ancient

---

* A full account of *Śrāddha* ceremony is found in *Mānava-Dharma*: III-122-286.

literature. More often we meet with the insistence on and the mention of our religious practices.

In fact, the *Hindū* religion is a technique by which this spiritual culture can be maintained and worked out in the community. Therefore, we find in these stanzas, and in similar contexts, always, an enthusiastic emphasis upon the religious life, whether it be in the family or in the society. *Dharma* comprises those divine values-of-life by living which we manifest more and more the essential spiritual being in us. Family-*Dharma* (*Kula-Dharma*) is thus nothing but the rules of living, thinking, and acting in a united, well-planned family. By strictly following these rules we soon come to learn, in the prayer-rooms of our homes, how to live as better citizens of the Aryan-culture.

दोषैरेतैः कुलघ्नानां वर्णसङ्करकारकैः ।
उत्साद्यन्ते जातिधर्माः कुलधर्माश्च शाश्वताः ॥ ४३ ॥

Doṣair-etaiḥ kula-ghnānāṁ varṇa-saṅkara-kārakaiḥ,
utsādyante jāti-dharmāḥ kula-dharmāś-ca śāśvatāḥ.

दोषैः *doṣaiḥ* = by evil deeds; एतैः *etaiḥ* = (by) these; कुल-घ्नानाम् *kula-ghnānām* = of the family destroyers; वर्ण-सङ्कर-कारकैः *varṇa-saṅkar-akārakaiḥ* = causing admixture of caste; उत्साद्यन्ते *utsādyante* = are destroyed; जाति-धर्माः *jāti-dharmāḥ* = caste religious rites; कुल-धर्माः *kula-dharmāḥ* = family religious rites; च *ca* = and; शाश्वताः *śāśvatāḥ* = eternal.

43. *By these evil deeds of the 'destroyers of the family,' which cause confusion of castes, the eternal religious rites of the caste and the family are destroyed.*

What was said in the discourse upon the last stanza will become amply clear by this statement of *Arjuna*. Here also he bemoans that, as a result of the civil war, the religious traditions of the family will all be lost and when he says so, as I have said earlier, if we understand religion as the "spiritual culture of India,' -the training for which was primarily given in the individual homes—then the stanza becomes self-explanatory. We also know that, after a war there is a sudden cracking up of the existing cultural values in any society. Our modern world, panting and sighing under the burden of its own immoralities and deceits, is an example of how war brings about, not only disabled men with amputated limbs, but also deeper ulcers and uglier deformities in their mental make-up.

In these words, we can detect in *Arjuna* almost the world's first conscientious objector to war! In these passages he offers a splendid series of pacifist arguments good for all times!

उत्सन्नकुलधर्माणां मनुष्याणां जनार्दन ।
नरकेऽनियतं वासो भवतीत्यनुशुश्रुम ॥ ४४ ॥

Utsanna-kula-dharmāṇāṁ manuṣyāṇāṁ janārdana,
narake-'niyataṁ vāso bhavatīty-anuśuśruma.

उत्सन्न-कुल-धर्माणाम् *utsanna-kula-dharmāṇām* = whose family religious practices are destroyed, मनुष्याणाम् *manuṣyāṇām* = of the men; जनार्दन *janārdana*= O *Janārdana*; नरके *narake* = in hell; अनियतम् *aniyatam* = for unknown period; वासः *vāsaḥ* = dwelling; भवति *bhavati* = is; इति *iti* = thus; अनुशुश्रुम *anuśuśruma* = we have heard.

44. *We have heard,* O Janārdana, *that it is inevitable for those men, in whose families the religious practices have been destroyed, to dwell in hell for an unknown period of time.*

Kṛṣṇa still refuses to speak. *Arjuna* has come to a point where he can neither stop talking nor find any more arguments. Strangely compelling is the grace of the Lord's dignified silence. Here, in the stanza, *Arjuna* almost concludes his arguments and mentions the tradition which he had heard, that "men, whose family-religion has broken down, will go to hell."

Ordinarily, we find that commentators give a verbatim literal word-meaning of this verse and make the translation almost unitelligible to the modern man. The present day money-conscious man, motivated by his profit-lust and sensuous demands in life, challenges such statements with a self-satisfying argument that "if I go to hell after death, I shall look after myself then, but for the time being, why not I continue my irreligious, unethical way of life, if that would suit my present happiness?"

On the other hand, when we understand the statement in all its scientific implications, even the worst of us will feel the immediate urgency for revolutionising our point of view We have already seen that the family-*dharma* means, in the context of our times, only the cultural purity in the family, which is the unit of the community. We also found that since their culture is essentially spiritual, to the *Hindū-s* "religion is culture."

Therefore, when *Arjuna* says that the leader, who causes the destruction of the family-culture in any generation, will go to hell, he is talking but a political truth, that when a generation gets shattered in its cultural purity, inspite of its secular and material prosperity, it will sink into a hellish existence conceived of and created by its own stupidities. This is a historical truth well recognised and often noticed by all good students of history.

Before the downfall of a national state or an empire, symptoms of internal rupture are generally noticeable, and, in almost all such cases, a fall in the ethical values--such as corruption in office, adulteration in food materials, high-handedness of the government and outrageous indiscipline on the part of the governed—becomes extremely common.

So, *Arjuna* implies that when the unity of home-life is shattered, and when purity of living and sanctity of thought are destroyed in the individual home-life, the generation that has caused such a shattering is ordering for itself and for others a melancholy era of hellish sorrows and sufferings.

अहो बत महत्पापं कर्तुं व्यवसिता वयम् ।
यद्राज्यसुखलोभेन हन्तुं स्वजनमुद्यताः ॥ ४५ ॥

Aho bata mahat-pāpaṁ kartuṁ vyavasitā vayam,
yadrājya-sukha-lobhena hantuṁ svajana-mudyatāḥ.

अहो बत *aho bata* = alas; महत् *mahat* = great; पापम् *pāpam* = sin; कर्तुम् *kartum* = to do; व्यवसिता: *vyavasitāḥ* = resolved, prepared; वयम् *vayam* = we; यत् *yat* = that; राज्य-सुख-लोभेन *rājya-sukha-lobhena* = out of greed for the pleasures of kingdom; हन्तुम् *hantum* = to kill; स्वजनम् *svajanam*= kinsmen; उद्यता: *udyatāḥ* = prepared.

45. *Alas! We are involved in a great sin, in that we are prepared to kill our kinsmen, out of greed for the pleasures of a kingdom.*

Though pitiable, it is indeed pleasantly ludicrous to watch *Arjuna*'s intellectual exhaustion and emotional weariness as expressed in this verse. In his effeminate lack of self-confidence here he bemoans, "Alas! We are involved, etc." These words clearly show that instead of becoming a master of the situation, *Arjuna* is now a victim of it. He has not the virile confidence that he is the master of the circumstances and, therefore, with a creeping sense of growing inner cowardice, he feels almost helplessly persecuted.

This unhealthy mental weakness drains off his heroism and he desperately tries to put a paper-crown upon his cowardice, to make it look divine and angelic, and to parade it as 'pity.' Thus, he deliberately misconstrues* the very aim of the war

* In the *Mahābhārata*, Chapter 21, of *Bhīṣma Parva* opens with half a dozen stanzas in which we find the sense of desparation that assails the mind of *Yudhiṣṭhira*. There, it is *Arjuna* who argues and consoles him; and from those words it is clear that *Arjuna* realised that the war aims of the *Pāṇḍavā-s* were fully fair and noble. "They that are desirous of victory do not so much conquer by might and prowess as by truth, compassion, piety and virtue." Therefore, knowing the difference between piety and impiety, and understanding what is meant by convetousness and having recourse to only exertion, fight without any arrogance; for victory is certain to be had where there is full righteousness"—*Bhīṣma Parva*:-XXI-10 & 11.

and imputes a low motive to the righteous war simply because he wants to justify his pacifist idea, which does not instinctively gurgle out from his known strength, but which oozes out from his ulcerated mind.

यदि मामप्रतीकारमशस्त्रं शस्त्रपाणयः ।
धार्तराष्ट्रा रणे हन्युस्तन्मे क्षेमतरं भवेत् ॥ ४६ ॥

Yadi māma-pratīkāra-maśastraṁ śastra-pāṇayaḥ,
dhārtarāṣṭrā raṇe hanyus-tanme kṣema-taraṁ bhavet.

यदि *yadi* = if; माम् *mām* = me; अप्रतीकारम् *apratīkāram* = unresisting; अशस्त्रम् *aśastram* = unarmed; शस्त्र-पाणयः *śastra-pāṇayaḥ* = weapons-in-hand; धार्तराष्ट्राः *dhārtarāṣṭrāḥ* = the sons *Dhṛtarāṣṭra;* रणे *raṇe* = in the battle; हन्युः *hanyuḥ* = should slay; तत् *tat* = that; मे *me* = of me; क्षेमतरम् *kṣemataram* = far better; भवेत् *bhavet* = would be.

46. If the sons of Dhṛtarāṣṭra, weapons-in-hand, slay me in battle, unresisting and unarmed, that would be far better for me.

In this concluding verse of this chapter, *Arjuna* declares his final opinion that, under the circumstances narrated during his long-drawn limping arguments, it is better for him to die in battle unresisting and unarmed, even if the *Kauravā-s* were to shoot him down, like a hunted deer, with a dozen arrows piercing his royal body!

The word that *Arjuna* uses here is particularly to be noted; the texture of the word used is, in itself, a great commentary upon the thought in the mind of the one who has made the statement. *Kṣema* is the material and physical victory, while *Mokṣa* is the spiritual Self-mastery. Though *Arjuna*'s arguments were all labouring hard to paint the idea that to have fought that war was against the spiritual culture of the country (*Mokṣa*), he himself stated in his conclusions that not to fight this war would be a material blessing (*Kṣema*) inasmuch as an escape from the battle-field now is to gain, perhaps, sure physical security!

The word, therefore, clearly indicates why *Arjuna* felt this false moral compunction on the battle-field. It was not at all due to any religious scruple or spiritual conviction; it was merely because he got mentally demoralised at the sight of the great army of the *Kauravā-s* standing in array, so determined to fight, and so confident to gain a sure victory. In short, anxiety for the fruit-of-his-action (victory in battle) demoralised *Arjuna* and he got himself into an 'anxiety-state-neurosis.'

सञ्जय उवाच-

एवमुक्त्वार्जुनः संख्ये रथोपस्थ उपाविशत् ।
विसृज्य सशरं चापं शोकसंविग्नमानसः ॥ ४७ ॥

Sañjaya Uvāca—

Evam-uktvārjunaḥ saṁkhye ratho-pastha upāviśat,
visṛjya saśaraṁ cāpaṁ śoka-saṁvigna-mānasaḥ.

एवम् *evam* = thus; उक्त्वा *uktvā* = having said; अर्जुनः *arjunaḥ* = *Arjuna*; संख्ये *saṁkhye* = in the battle-field; रथोपस्थः *rathopasthaḥ* = on the seat of the chariot; उपाविशत् *upāviśat* = sat down; विसृज्य *visṛjya* = having cast away; सशरम् *saśaram* = along with arrows; चापम् *cāpam* = bow; शोक-संविग्न-मानसः *śoka-saṁvigna-mānasaḥ* = with a mind overwhelmed with sorrow.

Sañjaya said :

47. Having thus spoken in the midst of the battle-field, Arjuna sat down on the seat of the chariot, casting away his bow and arrow, with a mind distressed with sorrow.

The concluding stanza of this chapter contains the words of *Sañjaya* in which he gave the running commentary of what he saw on the battle-field. Exhausted by his weary arguments, *Arjuna*, completely shattered within, sank back on the flag-staff in the open chariot, throwing down his kingly weapons.

This is the scene at which we shall leave *Arjuna* in the First Chapter of the *Gītā*.

ॐ तत्सदिति श्रीमद् भगवद् गीतासु उपनिषत्सु
ब्रह्मविद्यायां योगशास्त्रे श्रीकृष्णार्जुन संवादे
'अर्जुनविषादयोगो' नाम
प्रथमोऽध्यायः ॥ १ ॥

Oṁ tat-sat-iti Śrīmad Bhagavad Gitāsu Upaniṣatsu
brahma-vidyāyaṁ yogaśāstre Śrī-Kṛṣṇārjuṇa saṁvāde
'arjuna-viṣādayogo' nāma
prathamo'dhyāyaḥ.

Thus, in the Upaniṣad-s of the glorious Bhagavad-Gītā, in the Science of the Eternal, in the scripture of yoga, in the dialogue between Śrī Kṛṣṇa and Arjuna, the first discourse ends entitled:

THE YOGA OF THE ARJUNA-GRIEF

In the scriptural text-books of ancient times, the end of a chapter was indicated by some sign or symbol. In modern days, this is not necessary, inasmuch as, we have the passages in print before us and we can see that one section or chapter has ended and another has begun. Even here, the printers have to mark the end of one chapter and, by a separate title, indicate the beginning of the next.

In olden days, it was much more difficult, since books were not printed, and each student got during his study a new edition of the scripture printed on the memory-slabs of his own mind. Since scripture-study was in those days from mouth to mouth, the students had to memorise whole text-books and chant them daily. In such a case it was necessary to have some word or words to inform both the reciter and the listeners as to the ending of a section and the fresh beginning of another. This was done by some conventional symbol.

In the *Upaniṣad-s*, the accepted method was to recite the last *Mantra* or the concluding portion of the last *Mantra* of the chapter twice. In the *Gītā*, however, we have the repetition of a statement, which may be considered as an epilogue, in *Saṁskṛta* called as a *Saṅkalpa Vākya*. The same *Saṅkalpa* is repeated at the end of each chapter, the difference being only that at the end of each chapter, that chapter-number is mentioned along with the special title of that chapter.

The *Gītā Saṅkalpa Vākya* is a beautiful statement of pregnant words coveying a wealth of details regarding the very text-book. *Śrimad Bhagavad Gītā* has been considered here as an *Upaniṣad* nay—each chapter in the *Gītā* is considered as an *Upaniṣad*, and among the eighteen *Upaniṣad-s*, together constituting the Divine Song, here we end the first of them, entitled "The *Yoga* of *Arjuna's* Despondency."

These chapters are called *Upaniṣad-s* because these are declarations concealing such deep significances that a hasty reader will miss their full import, unless he does long and intense meditation over the wealth of suggestive meaning that lies concealed behind the simple looking stanzas of the *Gītā*. Just as in the *Upaniṣad-s*, here also we need the help of a sympathetic teacher who can train us in the art of opening the seven-hundred lockers in the treasure chamber of *Gītā*.

Upaniṣad is a word indicating a literature that is to be studied by sitting (*ṣad*), near (*Upa*) a teacher, in a spirit of receptive meekness and surrender (*ni*). The contents of the scriptural text-books are, all over the world, the same. They teach us that there is a changeless Reality behind the ever-changing phenomenal world of perceptions, feelings and understandings.

This great *Advaitik* Truth, as declared in the *Hindū* scriptural text-books, is termed by the name *Brahman* and therefore, the text-book that teaches us the nature of the *Brahman* and shows us the means of realising it, is called *Brahman*-knowledge (*Brahma Vidyā*).

Unlike Western philosophy, among the Aryans, a theory is accepted as a philosophy only when the philosopher prescribes for us a practical technique by which all seekers can discover and experience for themselves the Goal indicated in that philosophy. Thus, in all *Hindū* philosphies there are two distinct sections: one explaining the theory and the other describing the technique of practice. The portion that explain the technique of living the philosophy and coming to close subjective experience is called *Yoga Śāstra.*

The word *Yoga* comes from the root '*Yuj*' meaning to join. Any conscious attempt on the part of an individual, to lift his present available personality and attune it to a higher and more perfect ideal, is called *Yoga* and the science of *Yoga* is called *Yoga Śāstra*. Since in this Epilogue, the *Gītā* is called a *Yoga Śāstra*, we must expect to discover in the *Song of the Lord*, not only airy philosophical expositions of a Truth too subtle for the ordinary man to grasp, but also instructions by which every one of us can from this present state of imperfection, hope to reach, step by step, the giddy heights of the Divine pinnacles, that stand eternally swathed in the transcendental glory of Absolute Perfection.

The theme of philosophy and *Yoga* cannot be very attractive to the ordinary men of the world because it is so scientific and it deals with imperceptible ideologies. Mathematics cannot be thrilling reading except for a mathematician; and mathematics can very well afford to ignore those who have no taste for it. But religion tries to serve all and the anxiety of all prophets is to serve every one in all generations. Thus, in order to tame a difficult theme and to contain it within the ambit of a text-book of universal acceptance, the teachers of old had to discover methods by which the subjective ideologies could be given an appealing look of substantial objectivity. This was done by giving a detailed picture of the teacher, so that in our mental image he is so much familiarised that we feel his words also as something very familiar to us.

In the tradition of the *Hindū* text-books, the great *Ṛṣī-s* worked out the subtle ideas containing the crystallised truths into an easily digestible capsule called *Dharma*. In the *Upaniṣad-s*, we have a complete picture of a teacher and a taught, painted with hasty strokes, unfinished and rough. In the *Gītā*, on the other hand, it being a philosophical discourse embedded in the mythology of the nation, we find a finished picture, palpitating with life, against a scintillating situation, wherein the very same ancient truths have been re-asserted.

Lord *Kṛṣṇa* is now made to repeat the *Upaniṣadik* truths in the context of a great conflict to serve his life-long friend *Arjuna*, who is shown as seriously suffering from a total mental rupture. Therefore, we shall expect in the *Gītā* a much more sympathetic explanation and guidance than when the same truths came out from the inspired saints, who were not as much in contact with the weaknesses of ordinary mortals. This glory of the *Gītā* has been indicated here when the *Saṅkalpa Vākya* says that it is a conversation between the Lord and a mortal.

This chapter is called by a self-contradicting title. It is named as the *Yoga of Arjuna's Grief*. If 'grief' could be *Yoga*, almost all of us, without a choice, are already *Yogin-s*. In the commentary of this chapter, it is indicated that the *Arjuna*-condition of utter despair is the auspicious mental attitude wherein the *Gītā*-seeds are to be sown, and the flowers of *Kṛṣṇa*-perfection gathered. Be it in an individual or a society, in a community or a nation, religion and philosophy will be in demand only when the heart has come to experience the *Arjuna*-grief.

To the extent that the world of today has felt its incompetence to face the battle of life, not daring to destroy their near and dear values of economic expansion and industrial lust, to that extent it is fit for listening to the message of the *Gītā*. Just as the act of cooking, by itself, is not fulfilled without the eating that follows, so also, in spite of the best that may be available in life, a sense of incompleteness is felt and a deep hunger to gain a better awareness and fuller existence in the world is experienced. The scriptural texts cannot in themselves help any one. Since this mental condition is so unavoidable before the actual *Yoga* is started, even the initial mental condition is called, by a wishful anticipation, as *Yoga*. For learning and living the *Gītā*, the *Arjuna*-condition is the initial *Sādhanā*.

Oṁ Oṁ Oṁ Oṁ Oṁ

Shreemad Bhagawad Geeta

Chapter – II

INTRODUCTION

OUR SIX SCHOOLS OF PHILOSOPHY

About five thousand years before the birth of Christ, Hinduism came to face a great crisis in its spiritual and cultural history created by a decadent society and its own misinterpretations of its great culture. A restatement of the scriptural truths in a language and spirit understandable to the people was the demand of the age, and *Vyasa* came to answer this call.

The eternal truths of the Vedas are no doubt complete and exhaustive. But when I say it, the English-educated folk in India may not take it without a pinch of (that truth-distorting) salt. I would rather quote the western writers themselves. Sydenham says : "You, Hindus, are the heirs of all ages, if you will but accept your inheritance! And you can be true and worthy leaders of thought in India if you will learn to study your great faith for yourself and, overcoming mental inertia of taking your beliefs readymade, think out your religion for yourself and form concepts and cherish convictions which, while illuminating the abiding meaning of life, have a more vital present day significance."

The half-educated are the most difficult to be dealt with.

The exhaustiveness of the Vedas are to us an idle legendary description. We should not easily believe them nor will we try to experiment upon them and come to a direct understanding of the same. Vedanta as found in the Vedic literature is an exhaustive and scientific theory, compared with which the modern science, both in treatment and con-

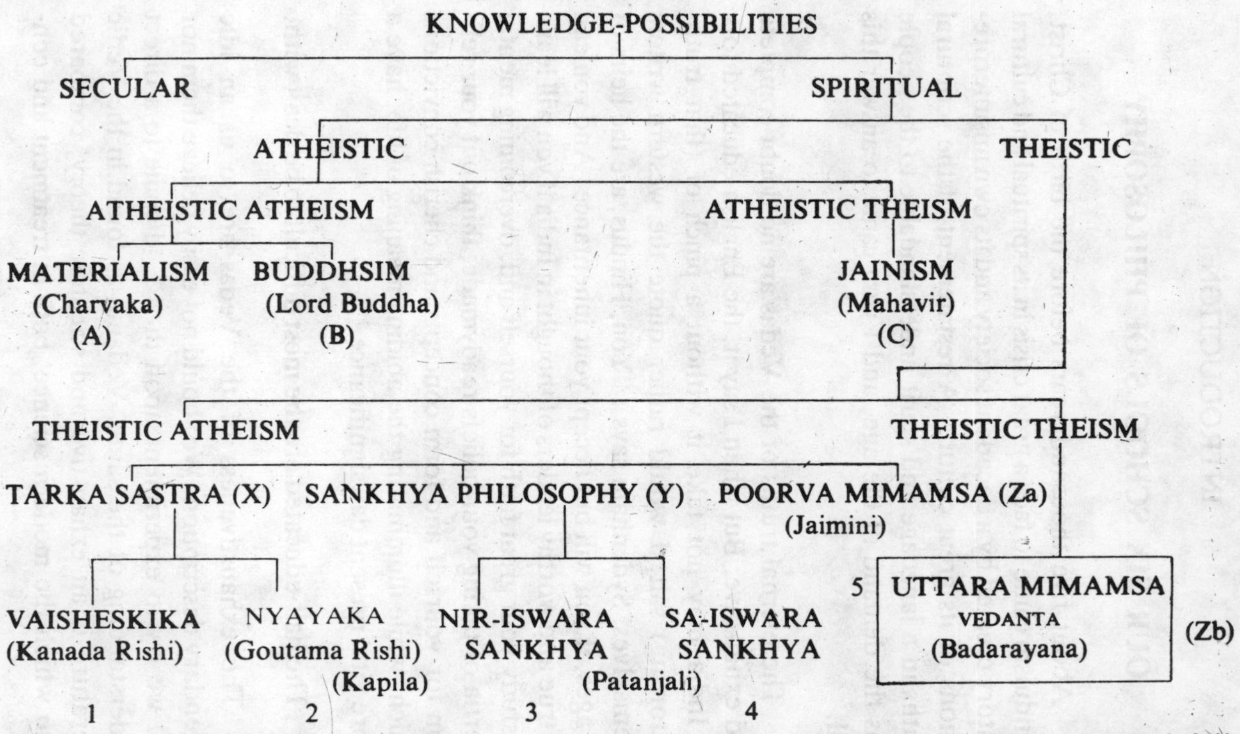

The *Shad-darsanas*, or the Six Schools of Philosophy, are considered by some as 1, 2, 3, 4, 5 and 6, and by others as constituted of (A), (C), (X), (Y) and (Za Zb).

tent, is almost childishly incomplete and vague. John Woodroffe in this connection declares : "An examination of the Vedic thesis shows that it is in conformity with the most advanced philosophic and scientific thought of the West, and that where this is not so, it is the scientist who will go to the Vedants and not the Vedants to the scientist."

Such a completely scientific thesis cannot be evolved without the self-dedicated and intense intellectual activity of generations of great men. Thus, by the time the Geeta appeared on the scene of the Hindu intellectual life, we had had many schools of philosophy. Many of them, undeveloped then, continued their individual growth to become fully evolved systems of thought in later days.

We have thus in philosophy today altogether six recognised main schools of thought. All of them, arguing differently, arrive at seemingly independent conclusions which, when digested by a sincere student, would indicate the same Truth. To help us gain a comparative estimate of the relative merits of these different systems of thought, scholars have provided us with a beautiful classification of all these schools of thought.

In the chart on p. 2 you will find the different philosophies classified under a system of Hindu tradition. Knowledge available for man in the world, whatever be the source, falls under two distinct groups. According to the Veda, knowledge can either take us to an understanding and appreciation of the objects outside, or of our own Real Nature. All bits of knowledge that contribute to our better understanding of the world fall under the category of SECULAR knowledge, as distinct from SPIRITUAL knowledge which is that branch of wisdom which, in its fulfilment, takes us towards a subjective experience of the Reality behind the phenomenal world, which is the life-spark in us. We are not concerned with 'Secular' knowledge here, as our theme is the enquiry into the 'Spiritual'.

The spiritual knowledge available to man is broadly divided into two groups : ATHEISTIC and THEISTIC. This division should not be understood to have only the usual base significances for Atheism and Theism indicating, respectively, lack of faith or faith in a divine Truth or prophet. Here, in this classification, Atheists are those who neither believe in any fundamental truth other than the body and the world outside nor have any faith in the Vedic declarations and scriptural truths. In short, they believe only in knowledge gained through direct perception; since Atman cannot be seen or perceived by any known means they refuse to accept the Vedic declarations or believe in the divine possibilities in man.

Even among the atheistic we can perceive two types : those who are full-fledged atheists indicated in the chart as ATHEISTIC ATHEISM, and those who, though they do not believe in the Vedas, certainly do believe in a subtle truth other than the gross body and the objects of the world. They fall under ATHEISTIC THEISM. ATHEISTIC ATHEISM was preached by two philosophers, Charvaka and Buddha.

The Charvaks believe that there is no goal to be achieved in life other than a happy living in complete sensuousness unrestrained even by any sentimental scruples, ethical or moral. They believe that we come from nowhere and go nowhere, but we just *are*. And the only bliss of living here is the joy of eating and indulging — and this is all the goal that need be considered, need be endeavoured for, in life. If

Epicureanism is enunciated with tight and exhaustive philosophy, highly logical and exhaustive, it would be, we may say, the Charvaka philosophy. Necessarily, therefore, they fall under the category of out and out atheists indicated by us in the Chart as ATHEISTIC ATHEISM.

When we say that the Buddhists also fall under the same classification, we do not mean the sting in the word 'atheism' which the theists have now come to associate it with. It only indicates that the Buddha, as a revolt against the excessive Vedic ritualism of his age, had to deny the Veda all authority, and the Eternal that the Buddhists believe in is declared by one group, the *Asatvadins,* as 'Non-existent', and by another group the *Ksanika-vijnana-vadins,* as an ever-changing series of conscience-flickerings in the intelligence.

The Jains fall under the classification of *Atheistic Theism,* inasmuch as Sri Mahavir also denied to the Veda any sanction of a truth; but he believed in *the* eternal Truth which is constant and permanent, perfect and all blissful. Thus the philosophy of Mahavir falls in this scheme of classification, under the heading ATHEISTIC THEISM.

Taking the *Theistic* school of philosophers, we find that they too fall under two groups : THEISTIC ATHEISM and THEISTIC THEISM. *Theistic Atheists* are those schools which believe in the Vedic declarations, but do not believe in the One Eternal Divine Factor indicated by the word *Brahman* in the Vedic lore, and *Theistic Theists* represent the philosophy that not only believes in the Vedas as a great source of true knowledge, but also believes in the non-dual *Brahman* which is the One Eternal Truth indicated by the Upanishadic declarations.

Theistic Atheism, which does not believe that Truth can be realised only by the study of, reflection in and deep meditations upon, the Upanishadic declarations, falls under three main groups : *Tarka, Sankhya* and *Purva-Mimamsa. Tarka Sastra* is a term indicating the points of view reached by Kanada Rishi and Gautama Rishi. Kanada's philosophy, *Vaisheshika,* differs now and then from the philosophy of Gautama, called *Nyaya. Nyaya* and *Vaisheshika* are two parallel streams of thought, now and then parting — to flow on the two sides of some insurmountable mountain of objections — only to meet again and flow hand in hand until they meet another difference in conception; yet they both reach the same Infinite ocean of Bliss.

The *Sankhya* philosophy is the most scientific in treatment and, perhaps, the most appealing to the modern mind or our scientific age. The Sankhyas are extremely analytical and indeed highly faithful in their intellectual appeal. Extremely rational, their scientific approach has the flavour of modernity. The Sankhyas again fall under two groups, marshalled behind the two great expounders of this school of thought : Kapila and Patanjali. Kapila's philosophy does not take into consideration the God-principle, while Patanjali adds to the fundamental factors of his doctrine the concept of Iswara also. On this basis, these philosophies are termed *Nir-Isvara Sankhya* and *Sa-Isvara Sankhya.*

The third school of philosophy that falls under the *Theistic Atheism* is the *Purva-Mimamsa. Purva* means 'earlier', and *Mimamsa* means 'sequence in logical thinking'. The Vedas proclaim their bulk of declarations in two distinct layers; in the earlier sections *(Karma-kanda),* seemingly dualistic, and in the later portion *(Gyana-kanda)* positively nondualistic. The earlier Vedic thought and the logic of their conclusions had been compiled together to form a perfect philosophy of Maharshi Jaimini. *Jaimini Sutras* constitute the Bible of the *Purva-Mimamsa*.

According to Jaimini's philosophy, man has to follow faithfully the ritualistic portion of the Vedas, as a result of which infinite merits will accrue. To enjoy the fruits of such merits the individual souls will get a chance to live for a fixed period of time in a realm of Consciousness where they could experience subtler and more intense sensuous enjoyments. This temporary, periodical resort in the Heavens is conceived by the followers of *Purva-Mimamsa* as the Goal of Existence. In our own days, the Arya Samajists fall under this category.

Pure *Theistic Theism* is preached in the *Brahma-Sutras* by Badarayana, who has been identified as Vyasa — the author of the Geeta. The philosophy enunciated in the *Brahma-Sutras* is a crystallisation of the points of view preached in the Upanishads, and is known as *Uttara-Mimamsa*. Later on, this school was brought out of its obscurity to prominence as *Advaita Vedanta* by Sri Sankaracharya.

Thus, as it stands today, Hindu philosophy falls under six schools. To enumerate the names of these six schools is not so easy, since in India there is an orthodox pronouncement and a heterodox insistence on this topic. The orthodox believe that the declarations of philosophers who recognise the Vedas alone are to be accepted as Hindu Philosophy, while there are others who are broad-minded enough to believe that all philosophies declared by Indians born and living in *Aryavarta* are to be considered as representing the varieties of views expressed upon the Unknown.

According to the orthodox, the schools of philosophy

are : (1) *Vaiseshika,* (2) *Nyaya,* (3) *Nir-Isvara Sankhya,* (4) *Sa-Isvara Sankhya,* (5) *Purva-Mimamsa,* and (6) *Uttara-Mimamsa (Vedanta).* However, the broad-minded pundits of our country also recognise another enumeration in which they give an equal status to the *Atheistic* school also. Thus they enumerate the six schools as (1) *Charvaka,* (2) *Bauddha,* (3) *Jaina,* (4) *Tarka,* (5) *Sankhya,* and (6) *Veda**.

My attempt herein is more to give you a bird's-eye view of the entire extent of thought and to indicate that in the Geeta there is an attemt on the part of the Father of Vedanta to synthesize, vitalise and reorientate all the points of views of the *Theistic* group with the business of life as we live it. The difference between *Theistic Atheism* and *Theistic Theism,* as I said earlier, is in that all great teachers in life, Kanada, Gautama, Kapila, Patanjali and Jaimini, declared dualism while the only school of thought that had dared to declare that spiritual man is the eternal Truth is *Vedanta,* theistic in faith and spirit.

The Geeta is an attempt at bringing together all the salient factors in all schools of thought in a happy synthesis. In the Geeta we are shown the merits and demerits of all the schools. It teaches us how to make use of them all without prejudice, so that ultimately we may reach the acme of Perfection as described in the immortal doctrine of Vedanta.

* Both *Purva-Mimamsa* and *Uttara-Mimamsa* being earlier and later portions of the Vedas.

GEETA CHAPTER II

YOGA OF KNOWLEDGE

INTRODUCTION

In this chapter entitled *Sankhya Yoga,* we get an exhaustive summary, as it were, of the whole philosophical contents of the Geeta. Roughly, we may say that the first ten stanzas explain the circumstances under which Arjuna totally surrenders to the 'Krishna-influence'.

From stanza 11 to 46 we have a digest of the *Sankhya,* meaning here not so much a repetition of the Sankhya philosophy, but a word denoting 'the logic of thought in a philosophy'. From stanza 47 to 60 we have an exhaustive, though hasty, sketch of the 'Yoga of Action' as adumbrated in the entire Geeta. From stanza 61 to 70 the Path of Love *(Bhakti Yoga)* has been indicated, and in stanzas 71 and 72 the Path of Renunciation *(Sannyasa Yoga)* has been slightly suggested. Thus the Second Chapter of the Geeta can be taken as an epitome of the entire Geeta.

We find in the Geeta all the known Paths to Perfection sketched in the Vedas — *Gyana, Bhakti,* and *Karma* — by which the Upanishadic Realization is reached when one has fully purified himself by the pursuit of ritualism *(Karmakanda)* and has spent a period of time in living the *Upasanakanda.* People believed that these three are irreconcilable factors and so many schools rose up, and each started quarelling with all others. This was the chaotic condition in which Vyasa found Hinduism of the Puranic Age. In the Geeta he had tried to find for the Aryan children of the Vedas a reconciliation and a synthesis in which all can walk hand in hand.

Many are the modern reviewers of the Geeta who fail to realise this idea and claim, as in *Geeta Rahasya,* that "*Jnana* accompanied by *bhakti* and dominated by *karma* is the Geeta Way for Perfection." Others say, "*Bhakti* is the most emphatic creed in the Geeta-teachings." There are still others who say that *jnana* alone is the theme, and that Geeta is an exclusive textbook for *sannyasins*. In fact, all these are explained in the Geeta and much more — the synthesis of them all, as indicated in the body of Chapter II.

TEXT II

अथ द्वितीयोऽध्यायः

तं तथा कृपयाविष्टमश्रुपूर्णाकुलेक्षणम् ।
विषीदन्तमिदं वाक्यमुवाच मधुसूदन ॥ १ ॥

SANJAYA UVACA

1. *taṁ tathā kṛpayāviṣṭam áśrupūrṇākulekṣaṇam*
viṣīdantaṁ idam vākyam uvāca madhusūdanaḥ

तम् — to him, तथा — thus, कृपया — with pity, आविष्टम् — overcome, अश्रुपूर्णाकुलेक्षणम् — with eyes filled with tears and agitated, विषीदन्तम् — despondent, इदम् — this, वाक्यम् — speech, उवाच — spoke, मधुसूदनः — Madhusudana.

Sanjaya said

1. *To him who was thus overcome with pity and despondency, with eyes full of tears and agitated, Madhusudana (the destroyer of Madhu) spoke these words.*

The second chapter opens with an announcement from Sanjaya which, with a few rightly chosen words, gives a complete picture of Arjuna's sad condition in his mental state of desperation. His mind has become overwhelmed with pity and sorrow. The very expression as it stands clearly indicates that Arjuna was not the master of the situation at that time, but on the contrary the situation had taken charge of Arjuna as its victim ! To get ourselves overridden by our life's circum-

stances is to ensure disastrous failures on all occasions. Only a weakling, who allows himself to be saddled with the occasions, can be victimised by the outer happening. Arjuna in his present neurotic condition has become a slave to the outer challenge.

The estimate of Sanjaya not only gives us the mental condition of Arjuna but also pointedly gives us a hint that the cracking in the inner personality of Arjuna has made deep fissures into the character of the great hero. The greatest archer of his time — Arjuna — has been so totally impoverished within that he has come to weep like a simple maiden!

To Arjuna thus overwhelmed with an emotion of misplaced pity and weeping silently in his inward desperations, Madhusudana (slayer of the demon, Madhu), Lord Krishna, spoke the following words. Here, it is to be noted that modern psychology has also noted and recorded that the climax in the attack of hysteria is a tearless weeping.

श्रीभगवानुवाच

कुतस्त्वा कश्मलमिदं विषमे समुपस्थितम् ।
अनार्यजुष्टमस्वर्ग्यमकीर्तिकरमर्जुन ॥ २ ॥

SRI BHAGVAN UVACA

2. *kutas tvā kaśmalam idaṁ viṣame samupasthitam*
anārya-juṣṭam asvargyam akirti-karam arjuna

कुतः — whence, त्वा — upon thee, कश्मलम् — dejection, इदम् — this, विषमे — in perilous straits, समुपस्थितम् — comes,

अनार्य unworthy, जुष्टम् — practised by, अस्वर्ग्यम् — heaven-excluding, अकीर्तिकरम् — disgraceful, अर्जुन — O Arjuna.

The Blessed Lord said

2. *Whence is this perilous condition come upon thee, this dejection, un-Aryan like, heaven-excluding, disgraceful, O Arjuna?*

The Lord of the Hindus is surprised to see that a king, claiming himself to be an Aryan, is feeling so flabbergasted on the battle-field. The instinct of a true Aryan is to feel balanced and equipoised in all conditions of life and to face situations diligently compelling them to change their threatening attitude and to make them favourable to himself. When life is courted properly, even the ugliest situation can burst out into a charming smile of success. It all depends upon the intelligent man's dexterity in steering himself across the bumping roads in life. Thus Lord Krishna characterises Arjuna's behaviour as *un-Aryan*. The Aryans are extremely sensitive to the higher calls of life, righteousness and nobility, both in thought and action.

The Divine Charioteer is extremely surprised at discovering such an attitude in his friend whom he has known for years by then, through thick and thin. The mood of dejection was, in fact, quite alien to the mental habit and intellectual nature of Arjuna. Thus we have an expression of wonderment here, and the Lord asks, "Whence comes upon thee this dejection . . ." etc.

It is believed by the Hindus that to die fighting for righteousness is the duty of one born in the family of kings, and by so sacrificing his life on the battle-field for a noble cause, he would reach and enjoy the Heaven of the Heroes *(Veera-swargam).*

क्लैब्यं मा स्म गमः पार्थ नैतत्त्वय्युपपद्यते ।
क्षुद्रं हृदयदौर्बल्यं त्यक्त्वोत्तिष्ठ परंतप ॥ ३ ॥

3. *Klaibyaṁ mā sma gamaḥ pārtha naitat tvayy upapadyate*
kṣudraṁ hṛdaya-daurbalyaṁ tyaktvottiṣṭha paramtapa

क्लैब्यम् — impotence, मा स्म गमः— do not get, पार्थ — O Partha, न — not, एतत् — this, त्वयि — in thee, उपपद्यते — is fitting, क्षुद्रम् — mean, हृदयदौर्बल्यम् — weakness of the heart, त्यक्त्वा — having abandoned, उत्तिष्ठ — stand up, परंतप — O Scorcher of foes.

3. ***Yield not to impotence, O Partha! It does not befit thee. Cast off this mean weakness of heart! Stand up, O scorcher of foes!***

In stinging reproachful words Krishna is deliberately lashing the anxiety-state-neurotic in Arjuna. Krishna who was all this time silent, now bursts forth into an excessive eloquence in which every word is a chosen missile, a hissing hammer-stroke, that can flatten any victim.

The word *klaibyam* means the mental attitude of one who is neither masculine enough to feel a passionate courage and daring, nor womanly enough to feel the soft emotions of hesitant desperations. In modern parlance, sometimes friends wonder at the impotency of another friend and express their surprise with such an exclamation as, "Is he a man or a woman?" meaning that from his behaviour it is not very easy to decide which characteristic is predominant in him. Emotionally, therefore, Arjuna is behaving now as a contradiction, effeminately-manly, and manly-effeminate, just as a eunuch of the Indian royal courts looks like a man but dresses as a woman, talks like a man but feels like a woman, is physically strong but mentally weak.

So far Krishna was silent and the silence had a deep meaning. Arjuna, cowed down by compassion, had taken the decision not to fight and was all along mustering arguments in support of it. As a diplomat, Krishna knew that it was useless to contradict his friend earlier when he was inspired to argue eloquently in support of his own wrong estimate of things. But the tears in the eyes of Arjuna indicated that the inward confusion had reached a climax.

In the tradition of religious devotion, it is very truly said and firmly believed all over the world, that the Lord, in His high seat, keeps mum and almost deaf so long as we are arguing and asserting our maturity as intellectual beings. But when we come down to live and act as an emotional being, when tears of desperation trickle down the cheeks of a true soul, the Lord of Compassion even unasked, rushes forward to reach the lost soul and guide him out of his inward darkness to the resplendent light of wisdom. A soul identifying itself with the intellect can seek and discover itself; but when it is identifying itself with the mind, it needs help and guidance.

When the Lord's grace comes, as it comes here in the Geeta, it first reaches man with a stern vehemence almost shattering in its impact. The fiery touch of the Lord's grace when it descends upon his devotees is invariably felt by the seeker more as an avalanche than as the refreshing shower of divine mercy. The spiritual grace must necessarily re-orientate the heart and burn away its negativities before the spirit can radiate its sway upon matter. True to this great principle observed everywhere and experienced by every true seeker, in the Geeta too we find that when the silent Lord from the charioteer's box started speaking, His words gleamed and landed on Arjuna like lightning, to burn his wrong mental tendencies in the fire of shame.

Soft words of sympathy could not have revived Arjuna's drooping mind to vigour. Thus Krishna rightly lashed his friend with these stinging words of ridicule dipped in the acid of satire ! Krishna ends his word-treatment with an appeal to Arjuna to "Get up and act".*

अर्जुन उवाच

कथं भीष्ममहं संख्ये द्रोणं च मधुसूदन ।
इषुभिः प्रतियोत्स्यामि पूजार्हावरिसूदन ॥ ४ ॥

ARJUNA UVĀCA

4. *kathaṁ bhīṣmaṁ ahaṁ saṁkhye*
droṇām ca madhusūdana
isubhīḥ pratiyotsyami pūjārhāv arisūdana

कथम् — how, भीष्मम् — Bhishma, अहम् — I, संख्ये — in battle, द्रोणम् – Drona, च — and, मधुसूदन– O Madhusudana, इषुभिः — with arrows, प्रतियोत्स्यामि– shall fight, पूजार्हौ – worthy to be worshipped, अरिसूदन — O Destroyer of enemies.

Arjuna said

4. *How, O Madhusudana, shall I in battle fight with arrows, against Bhishma and Drona, who are fit to be worshipped, O Destroyer of enemies!*

---

* In similar circumstances the Lord said to Job "Gird up now the lions like a man." *Bible* : Job 38 : 3.

In spite of the scorching words of Krishna, the warrior seems to be not too ready to reconsider his decision 'not to fight'. On the other hand, he is here found to repeat a few more arguments as to why he should not fight the battle against his adored grandsire, Bhishma, and revered gurudev, Dronacharya. They are fit to be worshipped with flowers and sandal-paste, and Arjuna asks if he can stand up against such great men and fight them with arrows.

The motive-hunting cowardice in Arjuna has come to pick up a great argument seemingly quite convincing to the undiscriminating. On the other hand, to one who has not lost his balance and who knows perfectly the art of evaluating such a situation, this is no problem at all and Arjuna's arguments are quite hollow. The war that is imminent is not between individuals due to any personal rivalry. Arjuna has no personality apart from the Pandava forces, and the pair, Drona and Bhishma, are also not mere individual entities; in their identifications, they are the Kaurava forces. The two forces are arrayed to fight for certain principles : the Kauravas are fighting for their policy of *adharma*; the Pandavas are fighting for the principles of *dharma* as enunciated in the ancient lore of the Hindus.

So glorious being the cause, when the two armies representing the will of the people have marshalled themselves, Arjuna, the hero, had no individual right to accept any personal honour or dishonour or to insist on any respect or disrespect in meeting the individuals who are champions of the wrong side. Without taking this total viewpoint of the situation, Arjuna made the mistake of arrogating to himself an individual egoism and observed the problems through the glasses of his ego. He recognised himself to be disciple of

Drona and the grandson of Bhishma. The very same teacher and grandsire were also seeing Arjuna on the opposite camp, but they felt no compunction because they had no such egoistic misconceptions. They drowned their individuality in the forces that they were championing. In short, Arjuna's egoism was the terrible cause for his moral confusions and misconceptions.

I have discussed this portion often with some of the best men of our country and I have found all of them justifying Arjuna's argument. That is to say, this is a very subtle point to be decided and, perhaps, Vyasa thought that this riddle of the society must be solved with the very principles of Hinduism for the guidance of the Hindu generation. The more we identify ourselves with the little 'I' in us, the more will be our problems and confusions in life. When we expand ourselves through our larger identifications — with an army, a cause or a principle or a nation or an age — we shall find our moral confusions dwindling themselves into almost nothingness. Perfect morality can be declared and lived only by him who has sought to live and discover his real identity with the Self which is One-without-a-second, everywhere, in all beings and forms. Later on, we shall find Krishna advising this Truth as a philosophical treatment for Arjuna's mental rehabilitation.

गुरुनहत्वा हि महानुभावान्
श्रेयो भोक्तुं भैक्ष्यमपीह लोके ।
हत्वार्थकामांस्तु गुरुनिहैव
भुञ्जीय भोगान् रुधिरप्रदिग्धान् ॥ ५ ॥

5. *gurūn ahatva hi mahānubhāvān*
śreyo bhoktuṁ bhaikṣyam apiha loke
hatvārtha-kāmāṁs tu gūrūn ihaiva
bhuñjīya bhogān rudhira-pradigdhān

गुरून् — teachers, अहत्वा– instead of slaying, हि — indeed, महानुभावान् — most noble, श्रेयः — better, भोक्तुम् — to eat, भैक्ष्यम् — alms, अपि — even, इह — here, लोके — in the world, हत्वा — having slain, अर्थकामान् — wealth and desire, तु — indeed, गुरून् — guru, इह — here, एव — also, भुञ्जीय — enjoy, भोगान्— enjoyments, रुधिरप्रदिग्धान् — stained with blood.

5. *Better indeed in this world to eat even the bread of 'beggary' than to slay the most noble of teachers. But if I kill them, even in this world all my enjoyments of wealth and desires will be stained with blood.*

Continuing his high sounding but futile arguments, due to his false estimate of himself and his problem, Arjuna poses himself here as a martyr of his own morality and ethical goodness.

His gurus, meaning both Drona and Bhishma, are characterised here as *Mahanubhavan* — men who are the ideal of their age, symbolising the best in our culture, who in their broadmindedness and courage of conviction had themselves offered many a sacrifice at the altars of the *Sanatana Dharma,* the Hindu science of perfect living. Such noble men who form the very touchstone of our culture in that era, are not to be eliminated from life merely for the fulfilment of an individual's appetite for power and position. Not only in their own age, but for milleniums the world shall be impoverished by the heartless squandering of such precious lives.

Thus Arjuna says that it would be nobler for himself and the Pandava brothers to live upon the bread of beggary than come to kingship after destroying all the glorious flowers in the garden of our culture. After annihilating them all, elders and teachers, supposing the Pandavas were to get kingdom back, Arjuna points out how his noble Aryan heart will not be able to enjoy either the kingdom or its wealth, for everything would be smeared by the bitter memories of the glorious blood that would have been split in the war.

Once we misread a situation, sentiments would cloud our understanding and that we too would learn to act as an Arjuna in our own life, is clearly indicated here in the detailed narration of the incident by Vyasa.

न चैतद्विद्मः कतरन्नो गरीयो
यद्वा जयेम यदि वा नो जयेयुः ।
यानेव हत्वा न जिजीविषामस्तेऽ-
वस्थिताः प्रमुखे धार्तराष्ट्राः ॥ ६ ॥

6. *na caitad vidmaḥ kataran no gariyo*
yad vā jayema yadi vā no jayeyuḥ
yān eva hatvā na jījīviṣāmas
te 'vasthitāḥ pramukhe dhārtaraṣṭrāḥ

न — not, च — and, एतत् – this, विद्म – we know, कतरत् – which, नः — for us, गरीयः – better, यत् – that, वा — or, जयेम – we should conquer, यदि – if, वा — or, नः — us, जयेयुः — they should conquer, यान् — whom, एव — even, हत्वा — having slain, न — not, जिजीविषामः — we wish to live, ते — those, अवस्थिताः — (are) standing, प्रमुखे — in face, धार्तराष्ट्राः – son of Dhritarashtra.

6. *I can scarcely say which will be better, that we should conquer them or that they should conquer us. Even the sons of Dhritarashtra, after slaying whom we do not wish to live, stand facing us.*

The earlier two stanzas from Arjuna, no doubt, indicate to us the state of perplexity and confusion in his objective mind. That the state of hysteria within has now developed to attack even his intellectual composure is indicated in the stanza. The stimuli coming from the array of the enemy lines as they touch his objective mind created therein a problem to solve which he needed the guidance of the rational capacities of his intellect — the subjective mind. Split as he was within, his mental personality, divorced from his intellect, could not easily come to any definite decision. His egoistic self-evaluation and the ego-created intense anxieties for the fruits of the great war intervened between his mind and intellect, separating them on the two sides of an almost unbridgeable gulf. Hence, Arjuna's confusions here.

Mind, generally functioning as an efficient receiving and despatching clerk, receives the information of the perceptions conveyed to it by the sense-organs, and after arranging these perceptions in order, conveys them to the intellect for its judgement. The intellect, with reference to its own stored up memories of similar experiences in the past, comes to a final decision which is conveyed to the mind for execution; and the mind in its turn issues the necessary orders for the organs of action to act upon. All these are happening at every moment, all through our waking state in our intelligent existence in the midst of the objects of the world.

Where these equipments are not functioning co-operatively with a perfect team spirit, there the individual is shattered in contents and becomes inefficient in meeting life as a victorious mortal. The rehabilitation of that individual is the re-adjustment and re-education of his inner world, and where his personality has become once again tuned up and adjusted, the individual shall come to exhibit better efficiency in life.

Poor Arjuna, victimised not so much by the external world as by his own mental condition, is seen here as incapable of judging whether he should conquer his enemy or by an ignoble retreat allow them to conquer him. By this stanza, Vyasa is indicating to us that the hysteria in Arjuna was not only mental, but at the level of the intellect also he has got himself shattered and unhinged.

कार्पण्यदोषोपहतस्वभावः
पृच्छामि त्वां धर्मसंमूढचेताः ।
यच्छ्रेयः स्यान्निश्चितं ब्रूहि तन्मे
शिष्यस्तेऽहं शाधि मां त्वां प्रपन्नम् ॥ ७ ॥

7. *karpanya-doṣopahata-svabhavah*
pṛcchāmi tvām ḍharma-sammudha-cetāḥ
yacchreyah syān niścitaṁ brūhi tan me
śisyaste 'haṁ śādhi mām tvāṁ prapannam

कार्पण्यदोषोपहतस्वभावः — with nature overpowered by the taint of pity, पृच्छामि — I ask, त्वाम् — to thee, धर्मसंमूढचेताः — with a mind in confusion about duty, यः — which, श्रेयः — good, स्यात् — may be, निश्चितम् — decisively, ब्रूहि — say, तत् — that, मे — for me, शिष्यः — disciple, ते — thy, अहम् — I, शाधि — teach, माम् — me, त्वाम् — to thee, प्रपन्नम् — taken refuge.

7. *My heart is overpowered by the taint of pity; my mind is confused as to duty. I ask Thee, tell me decisively what is good for me. I am Thy disciple. Instruct me who has taken refuge in Thee.*

In this stanza, when Arjuna has completely realised the

helpless impotency in himself to come to any decision, he surrenders totally to Krishna. He in his own words admits the psychological shattering felt and lived by him in his bosom. Even the cause of it he has instinctively diagnosed correctly to be an uncontrollable amount of overwhelming pity. Of course, Arjuna does not realise that it is his misplaced compassion. Whatever it be, the patient is now under the mental stress of extreme confusion and bewilderment.

Arjuna confesses that his intellect *(chetas)* has gone behind a cloud of confusions regarding what is *dharma* and *adharma* at this moment for him. The problem — whether to fight and win over the enemies or not to fight and allow the enemies to win over him — which is urgently seeking a solution, cannot be rationally judged with the present depleted mental capacities of Arjuna.

We have already explained* *dharma* and found that the *dharma* of a thing 'is the law of its being.' A thing cannot remain itself without faithfully maintaining its own nature, and *that nature which makes a thing what it is* is called its *dharma*. Hinduism insists on the *Manava dharma*, meaning, it insists that men should live true to their own essential nature as godly and divine and, therefore, all efforts in life should be directed towards maintaining themselves in the dignity of the soul and not plod on through life like helpless animals.

Here, the question in Arjuna's mind is on how best he should make use of his situation and act according to that which is expected of him according to his own nature. But his intellect was so much confused that it could not come to a decision upon what is *dharma* and what is *adharma*. In this inward confusion, the great archer declares his total surrender

* In the concluding portion of the introduction to Chapter I.

to Krishna as a disciple and requests the Lord to explain to him definitely what path of action would be conducive to his own inward growth. The word *sreyas* not only indicates material prosperity but also includes the cultural aspiration which, in India for the Hindus, is nothing but the spiritual blossoming of the mortal man to the cognition of Reality within himself.

In the confession that *'I am thy disciple'*, there are volumes of suggestions summarised. The relationship between the teacher and the taught in India is unique. The student, of course, has an attitude of total surrender to his master whom he had tested and found fit for total reverence as nothing short of a living and speaking God. The teacher also, having accepted a disciple, considers it his duty to guide the boy always with kindness, love and affection a thousand times more than any father could ever feel for his own son. If the student is expected to follow faithfully every bit of instruction given out by the teacher, the teacher has also the responsibility of removing all the doubts of the student, even for a hundredth time, if need be.

Here Arjuna indicates that he is quite ready to follow all the instructions of the Lord and maintain perfect faith in the wisdom of his Divine Charioteer. The Pandava must also be considered to indicate that if he, in his foolishness, were to raise doubts even for the thousandth time, Krishna must have the large-heartedness, compassion and kindness to explain again to the disciple vividly his message. In the entire bulk of the Geeta we definitely read how often Arjuna had punctuated Krishna's message with his own doubts. Never has Krishna, even once, been seen growing impatient to his disciple, but, on the other hand, each question, as it were, is seen to add more enthusiasm and interest to the discourses on the battle-field.

न हि प्रपश्यामि ममापनुद्याद्
यच्छोकमुच्छोषणमिन्द्रियाणाम् ।
अवाप्य भूमावसपत्नमृद्धं
राज्यं सुराणामपि चाधिपत्यम् ॥ ८ ॥

8. *na hi prapaśyāmi mamāpanudyad*
yac chokam ucchoṣaṇam indriyāṇām
avāpya bhūmāv asapatnam ṛddhaṁ
rājyāṁ surāṇām api cādhipatyam

नहि — not, प्रपश्यामि — I see, मम — my, अपनुद्यात् — would remove, यत् — that, शोकम् — grief, उच्छोषणम् — dried up, इन्द्रियाणाम् — of my senses, अवाप्य — having obtained, भूमौ — on the earth, असपत्नम् — unrivalled, ऋद्धम् — Prosperous, राज्यम् — dominion, सुराणाम् — over the Gods, अपि — even, च — and, अधिपत्यम् — lordship.

8. *I do not see that it would remove this sorrow that burns up my senses, even if I should attain prosperous and unrivalled dominion on earth, or even lordship over the Gods.*

Arjuna here is indicating to Krishna the urgency of guidance but for which he will be left to suffer the voiceless agonies of an inward pain. The patient is unable to explain or even indicate vaguely the source from which the pain is rising in him. This mental sorrow in Arjuna is affecting even his sense organs : even his *indriyas* are being blasted by the overheated sorrows within him : he finds it very difficult even to see or hear things properly.

It is natural for any reasonable human creature to feel an intellectual impatience to solve a problem of the mind and make it quiet and peaceful. Poor Arjuna also has tried his best to bring some consolation to himself through his own intellectual discrimination. The sorrow that he has felt is not for the acquisition and possession of any sensuous object in the outer world, because, as his own words indicate, he has already thought them over and found that even an empire over the whole earth, flourishing under his kingship — nay, a lordship over even the gods — would not wipe off his present sense of sorrow.

Some reviewers have concluded that these words indicate the amount of detachment *(vairagya)* which Arjuna had discovered in himself. Moreover, according to some, the pang that he is feeling within himself is the 'silent call of the spirit' from within and not the roaring sobs of a heart persecuted by his own sensuous desires. We must be extremely imaginative to see these traits in the Arjuna of Kurukshetra.

According to the tradition of Vedanta, Vyasa, the father of Vedanta, has brought here in his masterpiece a disciple who is seeking a life of cultural perfection, godly and divine *(Sreyas)*, with perfect and complete detachment from the sensuous urges natural to all undeveloped animal-men. The urgency felt by Arjuna, as is evident from his own words, may be considered as amounting to the burning aspiration for liberating himself from the limitations of a mortal. All that he needed to make himself perfect is the right discrimination *(viveka)* which the Lord of the Senses, Hrishikesa, will be giving him throughout the length of the Divine Song.

संजय उवाच

एवमुक्त्वा हृषीकेशं गुडाकेशः परंतपः ।
न योत्स्य इति गोविन्दमुक्त्वा तूष्णीं बभूव ह ॥ ९ ॥

Sanjay uvaca

9. *evam uktva hrṣīkeśaṁ gudākeśah paramtapah*
na yotsya iti govindam uktva tuṣnīṁ babhūva ha

एवम् — thus, उक्त्वा — having spoken, हृषीकेशम् — to Hrishikesha (master of the senses), गुडाकेशः – the conqueror of sleep, परन्तपः — destroyer of foes, न योत्स्य – I will not fight, इति — thus, गोविन्दम् — to Govinda, उक्त्वा — having said, तूष्णीम् — silent, बभूव — became, ह — certainly.

Sanjay said

9. *Having spoken thus to Krishikesa, Gudakesa, destroyer of foes, said to Govinda : "I will not fight", and became silent.*

This stanza and the following together constitute the running commentary of Sanjaya, the faithful reporter of the Geeta. He says that after surrendering himself to Krishna, seeking the Lord's guidance, the great Conqueror of Sleep and the Scorcher of his foes, Arjuna, declared to the Lord of the Senses, Krishna; that the Pandavas shall not fight. Saying this to Govinda, Arjuna became silent and quiet.

'*Tushnim bhava*' is an attitude of mental and physical quietness in an individual who has been suddenly stunned by a situation and who has lost all control over his senses and awareness of what is happening around him. This sort of stunned silence and total blackout that one feels at the sudden impact of the news of a great tragedy can be very conveniently considered as very nearly the condition of *tushnim bhava*.

In this description, Sanjaya is making use of a wealth of terms; all of which together give us the general impression that the irresistible warrior, Arjuna, has surrendered to the right guide since Lord Krishna, is the Lord of the Senses. Again it is to Him who once regained the whole world (Govind) that Partha has surrendered himself. Sanjaya is using all these extra wealth of details in his report to the blind old king, because he has still hopes that the king might avert the calamity.

No single individual alive at that period had the authority to call back the armies from the field of Kurukshetra except the blind old uncle of the Pandavas. He has the status and the weight of opinion necessary for ordering a truce even at such a time of crisis when it looked as though the time had slipped out of the hands of everybody. Sanjaya hoped that Dhritarashtra would understand the futility of their fighting against Arjuna, the Sleepless Harasser of his enemies, who would certainly come to win over the Kaurava forces since the Knotted-haired warrior (Gudakesa) had surrendered himself to the Lord of the Senses (Hrishikesa), the Winner of the World (Govinda). But Dhritarashtra was born blind and had grown deaf to the words of warning uttered by the good, due to his infinite attachment of his children.

तमुवाच हृषीकेशः प्रहसन्निव भारत ।
सेनयोरुभयोर्मध्ये विषीदन्तमिदं वचः ॥ १० ॥

10. *tam uvāca hṛṣīkeśaḥ prahasann iva bhārata*
senayor ubhayor madhye viṣīdantam idam vacaḥ

तम् — to him, उवाच — spoke, हृषीकेशः — Hrishikesa (the master of the senses), प्रहसन् — smiling, इव — as it were, भारत — descendant of Bharata, सेनयोः — of the armies,

उभयोः— of both, मध्ये — in the middle, विषीदन्तम् — despondent, इदम् — this, वचः — word.

10. *To him who was despondent in the midst of the two armies, Hrishikesa, as if smiling, O Bharata, spoke these words.*

Thus standing between the two forces, the good and the bad, arrayed for a battle to death, Arjuna (the jiva) surrendered completely to the Lord, the subtler discriminative intellect, the charioteer who held the five senses back and halted the body in a perfect standstill. When the stunned and confused ego — Arjuna — totally surrenders to Krishna, the Lord, with a smile, reassures the jiva of its final victory, and declares the entire message of spiritual redemption, the Geeta. In this sense we analyse the picture painted in Sanjaya's words, borrowing sanction from the Upanishads.*

It is quite clear that *Kathopanishad* must have inspired Vyasa to bring in the realistic picture as a fitting background to the greatest philosophical-poem of the world, the Geeta, for we find that many stanzas in the Geeta are literal borrowings from or have the flavour of the *Katha*-verses.

Once we accept to read this Upanishad-sense into the picture painted here with the words of Sanjaya, we can discover in it an eternal truth. When the ego (Arjuna) in its dejections sits back in the body (chariot), throwing up all instruments of activities *(Gandiva)*, and when the sense-organs (the white horses) are held back well under control by the pulled reins (the mind), then the charioteer (the Pure

* Refer Swamiji's *Discourses on Kathopanishad* — the analogy of the chariot : I, iii. 3-9.

Intellect) shall guide the ego to divine strength and to ultimate success over the forces of *adharma* with the help of those of *dharma*, even though the former may be greater than the latter.

श्रीभगवानुवाच

अशोच्यानन्वशोचस्त्वं प्रज्ञावादांश्च भाषसे ।
गतासूनगतासूंश्च नानुशोचन्ति पण्डिताः ॥ ११ ॥

Sri Bhagavan uvaca

11. *ásocyān anvásocas tvam prajnā-vādāms ca bhāṣase*
gatāsūn agatāsūms ca nanusocanti panditah

अशोच्यान् — those who should not be grieved for, अन्वशोचः— hast grieved, त्वम् — thou, प्रज्ञावादान् — words of wisdom, च — and, भाषसे — speakest, गतासून् — the dead, अगतासून् — the living, न — and, नानुशोचन्ति — grieve not, पण्डिताः — the wise.

The Blessed Lord said

11. *You have grieved for those that should not be grieved for; yet you speak words of wisdom. The wise grieve neither for the living nor for the dead.*

Though Sankara starts his philosophical commentary of the Geeta only with this stanza, he has an introduction to his own commentary wherein he explains his philosophical stand. This introductory portion concludes with a statement by which he explains the why and wherefore of Lord Krishna's opening lines in the discourse. To quote Sankara : *'Now finding no means other than Self-knowledge for the deliverance of Arjuna, who was thus confounded as to his duty and was deeply plunged into the mighty ocean of grief, Lord Vasudeva, who wished to help his friend out of it, introduced him to Self-knowledge in the following words.'* From this stanza onwards, the pure philosophy in Geeta starts. The above-quoted passage from Sankara clearly indicates that our earlier explanation of Arjuna's neurotic condition is in line with the great Acharya's own opinion.

When we rightly diagnose Arjuna's dejection, though its immediate cause is the challenge of the war, it is not very difficult for us to realise that his condition of mental torture is only a symptom of a deeper disease. Just as a true doctor will try to eradicate a disease not by curing the symptoms but by removing the cause of the disease, so too, here Lord Krishna is trying to remove the very source of Arjuna's delusion.

The ego rises when the Pure Self is not recognised, and this deep-seated ignorance in man not only veils his divine nature from himself, but also projects on the Reality a positive misconception. The 'egocentric idea' that he is conditioned by his own body, mind and intellect, is the true seed of Arjuna's delusory attachments with his own relations and the consequent deep compassion that has reached his bosom to make him so impotent and helpless. Grief and dejection are the prizes that delusion demands from its victim, man. So, to rediscover ourselves to be really something higher than our own ego is to end all the fancy sorrows that have come to us through false identifications.

Thus, the eternal spirit in man, asserting its false relationships with his body, comes to feel bound by a thousand relationships with the world of things and beings among the outer objects. The same perfect principle-in-life, playing on the field of the mind, comes to experience the imperfections of the emotional world as its own. The divine spark of life, again, as it often does, assuming a false identity with the intellect, comes to sob and suffer for its hopes and desires, its ambitions and ideologies, which are the characteristic pre-occupations of the intellect.

The Self thus getting reflected in the intellect, body and senses is the ego which is the victim of the world of objects, feelings and ideas. To this ego belongs all the sad destinies of life and the fleeting thrills of acquisition and possession. It is the ego in Arjuna that came to suffer its neurotic condition, goaded by its own delusions and its instinctive misapprehensions. Krishna knew in his infinite wisdom that *misapprehension of Reality* can take place only when it is preceded by a pitiable *nonapprehension of Reality*. Therefore, in order to cure the very source of Arjuna's delusion, Krishna is here advising him the very cream of knowledge as declared in the immortal books of the Hindus : the Upanishads.

A re-education of the mind through metaphysical and psychic methods is the last word in psychotherapy which the West has yet to discover and accept, but which the East has declared and justified to the world. Krishna is starting his entire Geeta lessons with this attempt at the re-education of Arjuna. In India this has been accepted, experimented upon and found so successful for generations that it was the very basis of the national educational policy of this country long before the Western specialists dictated how Indians should be educated for the foreigners' benefit. Before Macaulay's educational experiment was performed upon the Indian and had produced out of them the hapless breed of the day, the golden era of the Hindu culture was fed, directed and maintained by the indigenous system of education wherein everyone in the *gurukulas* was initiated from their very childhood into the humanistic science : it explained to the children their essential Divine Nature.

After their scholastic or professional training, therefore, they walked into the world knowing perfectly well where to place themselves in the scheme of things in life. They were not hoodwinked by life; nor did they expect life to be a mysterious cave where infinite riches lie scattered waiting for them to claim it. The contrast becomes ludicrously spectacular when we compare these fully educated men of those days with the partially instructed and misguided students of the present age who walk out of the university to realise that they have education but no knowledge.

True to that traditional cultural conception of education, here the great master, Krishna, starts His instructions to Arjuna with a direct discourse upon the eternal Reality. 'You are mourning for them who should not be mourned for : Bhishma and Drona are not merely the body-encasement in which they are now functioning. Drona is appreciated not because of his birth or for his colour, but because of the knowledge of archery and the wisdom which the Brahmin teacher possesses. His knowledge and wisdom are not of the body, but they are in his mind and intellect. So too with Bhishma; he is revered not because his body is aged, nor because he can still wield a bow and arrow, but he is respected and adorned as a glorious flower of Hindu culture in that age. The cultural eminence that characterised Bhishma are the qualities of his mind and intellect.

The inner equipments of both Bhishma and Drona allowed through them a glorious expression of the life-principle or the soul in them, and these great men were incomparable due to this divine shine that beamed out through them. In this war of clashing weapons, to consider that the cultural soul of Bhishma will be wounded, and the life of Drona, the master and military genius, will be ended is a mere delusory concept of an uninitiated understanding. By this statement Krishna has indicated to Arjuna a greater self then the ego in every embodiment.

At every level of our personality we view life and come to our own conclusions over things. Thus, we have a physical estimate of the world outside from our body level, apart and quite distinct from our emotional picture of the life from our mental level; and also an intellectual concept of life from the level of our intellect, which differs from both the above estimates. Physically, what I see to be a woman is mentally my mother, and intellectually, the same sacred feminine form is a bundle of cells, each having in its protoplastic contents a nucleus to preside over its functions. The imperfections that I see in a physical object can fail to give me misery if I successfully gild the object with my emotional appreciation of it. Similarly, an object which is physically abhorrent and mentally shameful can still fail to provide me with any sorrow if I can appreciate it from my intellectual level.

Similarly, that which gives me despondency and dejection at the physical, mental, and intellectual levels can yield a thrilling inspiration if I perceive it from the spiritual level. Krishna is advising Arjuna to renounce his physical, emotional and intellectual estimates of his teacher and his grandsire and the whole battlefield problem and to re-evaluate the situation from his spiritual understanding.

This great and transcendental Truth has been so suddenly expounded in the Geeta that it has the stunning effect of a sudden blast unexpectedly occurring in front of Arjuna. We shall later on understand how this subtle psycho-physical shock therapy had effected immeasurable good to the hysterical constitution of Arjuna. To add some extra physical strength to his statement, as it were, Krishna harnesses the power of his irony to the dynamic momentum of the philosophy when he says : 'Yet you speak words of wisdom.' In the first chapter, Arjuna had, almost in a spirit of teaching Krishna, quoted the *artha-sastra* and contradicted it on the strength of the greater authority of *dharma-sastra*.

'*Pragya vadan*' has now been interpreted in this commentary as 'words of wisdom'. However, a German commentator has given a unique interpretation for the same word : *pragya* + *avadan* : he laboriously squeezes out of this word a meaning, 'arguments contrary to the views of the wise'. Though this meaning has been pressed out of the word, still an intimate student of Geeta cannot but feel entertained by this interpretation. The suggestion is that Arjuna's hesitation to kill his enemies at the warfront is against the declarations of all our great *rishis* of old. *Dharma-sastra* misunderstood and misinterpreted has been the cause of the dreary Hindu decadence.

Krishna explains his earlier statement by indicating how men of true wisdom never feel miserable and never moan either for things that are or for things that are no more. They understand that the outer world of objects is essentially finite and, therefore, things in it must perish and be born again. Continuity of change is the nature of finitude and it is this change that we understand as death. To moan for change is not to understand the nature of finitude, and it is as unintelligent as to complain of light in the sun! Therefore, wise men who understand life do not moan for things that exist nor for things that depart.

In Sri Sankara's commentary we have been guided by the great Acharya with his indications which explain the connection of thought in each verse with its following one. We propose to indicate these connections wherever possible.

"Why do they deserve no grief? Because they are eternal. How? — The Lord says" :

न त्वेवाहं जातु नासं न त्वं नेमे जनाधिपाः ।
न चैव न भविष्यामः सर्वे वयमतः परम् ॥ १२ ॥

12. *na tv evāham jātu nāsaṁ na tvaṁ neme janādhipāḥ*
na caiva na bhaviṣyāmaḥ sarve vayam ataḥ param

न — not, तु — indeed, एव – also, अहम् — I, जातु — at any time, न — not, आसम् – was, न — not, त्वम् — thou, न — not, इमे — these, जनाधिपाः – rulers of men, न — not, च — and, एव — also, न — not, भविष्यामः – shall be, सर्वे — all, वयम् — we, अतः – from this time, परम् — after.

12. *It is not that at any time (in the past) indeed, was I not, nor were you, nor these rulers of men. Nor, verily, shall we ever cease to be hereafter.*

The continuity of the existence of the soul is emphatically brought out here and Arjuna who is hearing from Krishna these stunning declarations must have certainly felt a joyous consolation in himself. The Vedantic literature that he must have studied earlier must have been somewhere in his mind, but very rarely students of philosophy are adepts in employing their knowledge in practically meeting the situations in life.

Krishna here declares in unequivocal terms that the embodied soul in everyone is set on a great pilgrimage in which it comes to identify itself with varied forms temporarily to gain fixed specimens of experiences. He says that neither Himself nor Arjuna nor the great kings of the age who have assembled in both the armies are mere accidental happenings; they do not come from nowhere and at their death do not become mere non-existent nothingness. It is the Charvaka philosophy which refuses to consider anything beyond the knowledge gained through direct perception, and, therefore, it is the Charvakas who believe that we have come from nowhere and go nowhere. But philosophical thinking guides man's intellect to the apprehension of a continuity from the past, through the present, to the endless future. The Spirit remaining the same, it gets itself seemingly conditioned by different body-equipments and comes to live through its self-ordained environments.

It is this conclusion of the Hindu philosopher that gave them the most satisfactory theory of reincarnation. The most powerful opponents of this idea are the fanatic Christians of the East who themselves seem not to have studiously followed their own scriptures. Christ Himself has, if not directly, at least indirectly, proclaimed this doctrine when He told His disciples that John the Baptist was Elijah. The most learned of the Christian fathers, Origen had clearly declared : "Every man received a body for himself according to his deserts in former lives."

There is no great thinker in the past nor any in the present who had not accepted, expressly or tacitly, these logical conclusions in the doctrine of reincarnation. The Buddha constantly made references to his previous births. Virgil and Ovid regarded the doctrine as perfectly self-evident. Josephus observed that the belief in reincarnation was widely accepted among the Jews of his age. Solomon's *Book of Wisdom* says : "To be born in sound body with limbs is a reward of the virtues of the past lives." And who does not remember the famous saying of the learned son of Islam who declared, "I died out of the stone and I became a plant : I died out of the plant and became an animal. I died out of animal and became a man. Why then should I fear to die ? When did I grow less by dying ? I shall die out of man and shall become an angel !"

In the later times this most intelligent philosophical belief was accepted as a doctrine by the German philosophers, Goethe, Fichte, Schelling and Lessing. Among the recent philosophers, Hume, Spencer and Max Muller have recognised this doctrine as incontrovertible. Among the poets of the West also we find many a burnished intellect soaring into the cloudless sky of imagination, and within their poetic flights they too have intuitively felt the sanction behind this immortal doctrine — Browning, Rossetti, Tennyson and Wordsworth, to mention but a few names.

The reincarnation theory is not a mere dream of the philosophers, and the day is not far off when the fast developing science of psychology in the West will come to rewrite their scripture under the sheer weight of observed phenomena. An uncompromising intellectual quest for understanding life cannot satisfy itself if it is thwarted at every corner by 'observed irregularities'. We cannot ignore them all for long as mere 'chances'. The infant prodigy, Mozart, is a spectacular instance which cannot be explained away : to be logical we must accept the idea of the continuity of the embodied souls. This genius wrote sonatas at the age of four, played in public at the age of five, composed his first opera at the age of seven. Without the reincarnation theory, we will have to label this wondrous incident as an accident and throw it into the dustbin of chance and bury it there to be forgotten.

In India, too, we have observed many such instances. "An amazing story came from the village of Shadinagar in Farrukhabad district where a girl aged seven stated that she remembered her previous birth, her village, home, and her relations in her earlier life. This girl, Ram Kali, daugher of Pandit Ganga Vishnu, a Brahmin, when she was only three years old, told her father of her previous life in a village named Maglabagh. She had three sons and she said that one was born shortly before her death! She insisted on meeting her sons, Shiya Ram and Ram Swaroop. The report went that when she reached the place she could recognise the place and her sons. When cross-examined she described the alterations and repairs which were effected to the house some years ago! In the end, her parents left for their home, the child still crying bitterly in the arms of her mother, sobbing at the forced separation she had to suffer from her past life's children!"

Thus examples are often noticed but rarely compiled as evidences to prove this great theory of reincarnation. The modern world, as I said, is yet to discover this great and self-evident law of life. And, to an uninitiated student this theory may seem too staggering for quiet appreciation. When Krishna declared that none of them, including Himself, Arjuna and the great kings, even after their death on the battle-field, "shall cease to exist in future", Arjuna, a typical man-of-the-world, could not grasp it as self-evident. His questioning eyes made the Lord explain again the idea through an example in the following stanza.

"Why do they deserve no grief? For, they are eternal in essence. How? — The Lord says" :

देहिनोऽस्मिन्यथा देहे कौमारं यौवनं जरा ।
तथा देहान्तरप्राप्तिर्धीरस्तत्र न मुह्यति ॥ १३ ॥

13. *dehino 'smin yathā dehe kaumāraṁ yauvanam jarā*
tathā dehāntara-prāptir dhīras tatra na muhyati

देहिनः — of the embodied (soul), अस्मिन् — in this, यथा — as, देहे — in body, कौमारम् — childhood, यौवनम् — youth, जरा — old age, तथा — so also, देहान्तरप्राप्तिः — at attaining of another body, धीरः — the firm, तत्र — thereat, न — not, मुह्यति — grieves.

13. *Just as in this body the embodied (soul) passes into childhood, youth and old age, so also does he pass into another body; the firm man does not grieve at it.*

It is the law of memory that the experiencer and the memoriser must both be the same entity; then alone can memory power function. *I* cannot remember any of *your* experiences nor can *you* remember any of *my* experiences : I can remember my experiences as readily and easily as you can remember your experiences.

In our old age, every one of us can remember the main incidents of our own childhood and youth. In the progress of growth, childhood dies away and youth appears, and youth dies before old age can come to assert itself. In the old man, it is self-evident that neither his childhood nor his youth is with him, and yet, he can remember his own early days. Applying the principle of memory, it becomes quite clear then that 'something' in us is common in all the different stages of our growth, so that the same entity could remember its own experiences gained by it in the past through the chidish body and, later, through the youthful structure.

Thus youthfulness may be considered as a birth when childhood has met with its death. So too, old age is born when youthfulness is dead. And yet, none of us feel the least disturbed by these changes; on the other hand we, in fact, feel happier due to the wealth of experiences we have come to gain as the status of the body rises from the innocent childhood to its mature old age. Using this subjective experience of everyone in the world as a standard of comparison, Krishna is trying to bring home to Arjuna that the wise men do not worry when they leave one body for purposes of taking another one.

This stanza is again asserting in unequivocal terms the truth behind the reincarnation theory. And viewed in this understanding, death can be no more a threat to a wise man. We do not moan at the death of childhood following which alone can we come to experience youth; we are confident in our knowledge that by entering the age of youth, though the childhood has ended, there is a continuity of existence of the one in the child into the one in the youth. Soo too, at the moment of death, there is no extinction of the individual, but the embodied ego of the dead body leaves its previous structure and, according to the *vasanas* (mental impressions) that it had developed during its embodiment, gets itself identified with a physical equipment where it can express itself completely and seek it perfect fulfilment.

Sankara gives here a beautiful sequence connecting the present stanza with that which is to follow. *"If by the realisation of the Eternal Self one may not come to the delusory sorrow at the thought that the Self is dead, yet, quite common among the people, as we see, is the painful delusion that the Self is subjected to heat and cold, pleasure and pain, as also to the grief due to the loss of pleasure of it or due to the arrival of pain." Answering this probable doubt the Lord explains the following :*

मात्रास्पर्शास्तु कौन्तेय शीतोष्णसुखदुःखदाः ।
आगमापायिनोऽनित्यास्तांस्तितिक्षस्व भारत ॥ १४ ॥

14. *mātrā-sparsās tu kaunṭeya śītoṣṇa-sukha-duḥkha-dāḥ*
āgamāpāyino nityāḥ tāṁs titiksasva bhārata

मात्रास्पर्शाः — contacts of senses with objects, तु — indeed, कौन्तेय — O Kaunteya, शीतोष्णसुखदुःखदाः – producers of cold and heat, pleasure and pain, आगमापायिनः - with beginning and end, अनित्याः — impermanent, तान् — them, तितिक्षस्व — bear (thou), भारत — O descendant of Bharata.

14. *The contacts of senses with objects, O son of Kunti, which cause heat and cold, pleasure and pain, have a beginning and an end; they are impermanent; endure them bravely, O Descendant of Bharata.*

In this stanza we will notice that the Lord is addressing Arjuna with two different epithets — as 'son of Kunti' *(Kaunteya)* and as 'descendant of Bharata' *(Bharata).* According to Anandagiri, it is meant to indicate that Arjuna is fit for this great instruction into the spiritual Truth since he is born of a noble mother and has a nobler lineage on his father's side.

According to the accepted theory of perception in Vedanta an object is perceived not *by* the sense-organs but *through* them. The *indriyas* are instruments through which the perceiving-ego gathers the knowledge of the various objects. If the perceiver is not actually contacting the objects through the sense-organs, the objects as such cannot bring any individual under its perception.

That the same object can give two different types of experiences to two different individuals is very well known.

The object remaining the same, if it can give different experiences, it is evidently clear that it is because of the difference in the mental composition in the individuals. It is also observed that objects of one's intense fancy during a certain stage in our life, by themselves become a nuisance to the same individual after a time; for, as time passes on, the mental constitution of the individual also gets changed. In short, it is very clear that the external objects can convey their stimuli to the level of our experience only when our minds come in contact with the objects through the sense-organs.

He who can understand that the objects-of-the-world, in the flux of change, should 'come and go' — should come to exist and disappear to perish — shall not allow himself to be tossed about by the existence or non-existence of the finite things of the world. In the flood of time, things and incidents, circumstances and environments, flow up to our *present* from the unknown *future* to give us vivid experiences of varied intensity, and they, in their very nature, cannot remain permanently but must of necessity pass on to become one with the entire *past*. Nothing can remain the same, even for a short period, in the world-of-objects where change alone is the changeless law.

Having understood this finite nature of the changeable objects-of-the-world wherein everyone of them has a beginning and an end, at no occasion need a wise man despair at the things that *are* or at the things that *are not*. Heat or cold, success or failure, pain or joy — none of them can be permanent. Since every situation, of its own nature, must keep on changing, it would be foolish to get ourselves upset at every change noticed. The wise thing would necessarily be to suffer them meekly with the comfort and consolation of the knowledge of their finite nature. It is the attitude of the wise to go through life, both in joy and sorrow, success and failure, pain and joy, with the constant awareness that "even this will pass away."

The external world of challenges is finite inasmuch as they have a beginning and an end. Not only that, Krishna adds : "they are impermanent by their very nature." By the term 'impermanent' used here, the Lord means that the sense-objects, apart from being finite, are impermanent inasmuch as the same object which gives pleasure at one moment starts yielding pain at another moment to the enjoyer. This inconsistency is indicated by the term *anitya* used in the stanza.

"What good will accrue to him who bears heat and cold in life? — Listen" :

यं हि न व्यथयन्त्येते पुरुषं पुरुषर्षभ ।
समदुःखसुखं धीरं सोऽमृतत्वाय कल्पते ॥ १५ ॥

15. *yaṁ hi na vyathayanty ete puruṣaṁ puruṣarṣabha*
sama-duḥkha-sukhaṁ dhīraṁ so 'mṛtatvāya kalpate

यम् — whom, हि — surely, न व्यथयन्ति — afflict not, एते — these, पुरुषम् — man, पुरुषर्षभ — chief among men, समदुःखसुखम् — same in pleasure and pain, धीरम् — firm, सः — he, अमृतत्वाय — for immortality, कल्पते — is fit.

15. *O chief among men, that firm man whom, surely, these afflict not, to whom pleasure and pain are same, is fit for realising Immortality of the Self.*

Calm endurance in both pleasure and pain is a condition necessary for the right knowledge of the true Self, according to the technique of Self-realisation as explained in the Upanishadic lore. Based upon that fact, here Lord Krishna explains that one who has found in himself a mental equipoise, wherein he is not afflicted or disturbed by circumstances of pain and pleasure, alone 'is fit for attaining Immortality.'

Mortality is the most dreadful of pains known to all living creatures. Instinctively, even the most courageous hero will feel unnerved when he is under the threat of unavoidable death. It is a challenging spectre that can throw a dreadful shadow of fear and sorrow across everyone's life. The one seeking perfection strives hard to transcend these realms of threat and fear. Naturally, in the early Upanishads the supreme achievement has been indicated by the term Immortality, meaning, 'deathlessness' *(amritattvam),* although it may be interesting to note that in the later Upanishads the same has come to be indicated by the term 'birthlessness'.

When the Transcendental Truth or the Eternal Perfection has been indicated by the term Immortality, it is not used in its limited sense of 'deathlessness' of the body. Here the term 'death' not only indicates the destruction of the physical embodiment but also includes and incorporates within its embrace of significance the entire range of finite experience, where, in each one of them, there is an extinction-experience. No experience gained through either the body, or the mind, or the intellect is permanent. In other words, each experience is born to live with us for a short period and then to die away in us. These chains of finite experiences stretch out in front of us as the paths of sorrow and pain in our life. The term Immortality, used by the Rishis to indicate the 'supermanhood' envisages how the individual ego walking the thorny path of finite sorrows gets itself transcended to the Infinite experience of the eternal and the permanent.

This topic of 'Immortality' is the very theme of the Vedic literature, but by the time of Vyasa the Hindu generation had come to believe that this divine God-life can be achieved only through some special training fit only for some rare few to pursue. Through the Geeta, our poet-seer, Vyasa, is making Lord Krishna declare that the purpose of life for everyone is the attainment of perfection, and to evolve oneself to it one must make use of every little chance in one's own allotted life. To train ourselves to endure meekly the little pin-pricks of life, and with magnanimous joy, heat and cold, success and failure, pain and pleasure, is itself the highest training that life can provide to all of us.

Ordinarily, man gets himself overwhelmed by the little exasperations in his life, which are essentially life's very nature, life being constituted of endless, ever-changing schemes of things, each in itself finite. To waste our life complaining against, brooding over and despairing for the happenings around us, is to shamelessly lay waste our life. Endure them calmly, is the advice given in the previous stanza.

The commercial outlook in the ordinary man will not easily accept a scriptural injunction unless it explains the practical benefit that might accrue to him by his obedience to the law. This stanza is dedicated to an explanation of the practical benefits of living life with true understanding.

An incompetent idler's hapless endurance in life is not in itself what is indicated here. It is especially said that the equipoise of the mind, in both pleasure and sorrow, entertained by a 'wise man' *(dheera)* makes him fit for the highest cultural self-development. That is to say, the equanimity should not flow out from the dark caves of one's stupidity and inertia, but must gurgle out from the open sunny fields of one's own wisdom and understanding. When one understands the essential nature of the objects of the world to be finite, out of that realised knowledge one gains enough balance for calm endurance; then he would not feel exalted in pleasure or dejected in pain.

So long as we live in the body as the body, we will not be able to ignore or calmly endure sorrows of the body. But when we are fired by a sentiment of love or hatred, we invariably make ready sacrifices of the bodily pleasures. In my love for my son, I am ready to make any sacrifice of my physical needs so that I may give him a good education, etc. When intellectually one gets fired up by some idea or ideology, for the satisfaction of it he readily ignores and overlooks the comforts and pleasures of his body and mind. The martyrs and revolutionaries in the world could, with pleasure, face physical persecution and mental agonies for the satisfaction of their intellectual life and for the fulfilment of their ideas and ideologies.

Thus, if an ordinary man is to struggle hard constantly, with his mind held in perfect equanimity, through his share of pleasure and pains in life, he can successfully do so only to that extent to which he is capable of standing apart from his own physical, mental and intellectual identifications. When a mortal does thus detach himself from his usual personality layers and, from apart, watch them as a witness, he is at that moment in the realm spiritual and, therefore becomes fit for the attainment of Immortality — the ultimate spiritual goal.

"For the following reasons also it is proper that you should abandon your grief and distressing delusion and should calmly endure heat and cold, etc." For :

नासतो विद्यते भावो नाभावो विद्यते सतः ।
उभयोरपि दृष्टोऽन्तस्त्वनयोस्तत्त्वदर्शिभिः ॥ १६ ॥

16. *nāsato vidyate bhāvo nābhāvo vidyate sataḥ*
ubhayor api dṛṣṭo 'ntas tv anayos tattva-darśibhiḥ

न — not, असतः — of the unreal, विद्यते — is, भावः– being, न — not, अभावः — non being, विद्यते — is, सतः — of the real, उभयोः — of the two, अपि – also, दृष्टः— (has been) seen, अन्तः– the final truth, तु — indeed, अनयोः – of these, तत्त्वदर्शिभिः — by knowers of the truth.

16. *The unreal has no being; there is no non-being of the Real; the truth about both these has been seen by the knowers of the Truth (or the seers of the Essence).*

Here is another reason why the vagaries of life and the varieties of experience should not upset but, on the other hand, must be cheerfully endured by a wise man. This stanza, while giving the philosophical reasons championing the cause of mental tranquility, indicates that it can rise only out of an intellectual grasp of the interpretation of life.

In Vedantic literature, the *Real* and the *un-Real* are very scientifically distinguished. These two categories are not considered as undefinables in our ancient literature, though they do not declare these to be definables. The rishis have clearly indicated what constitutes the Real and what are the features of the unreal. That which is not in the beginning and which will not be in the end, but, at the same time, seemingly that which exists in the present is called the unreal. In the language of the *Karika,** "That which is non-existent in the beginning

* Refer Swamiji's *Discourses on Mandukya and Karika*, Chapter II, Verse 6.

and in the end, is necessarily non-existent in the intermediary stages also; obejcts we see are illusory, still they are regarded as if real."

Naturally, the Real is that which defies all change and remains the same in all periods of time : past, present and future. Thus, in an ordinary example of one misunderstanding a post in the dark to be a ghost, the ghost-vision is considered unreal as compared with the post because the hallucination cannot be permanent, and it does not remain after the re-discovery of the post. Similarly, on waking up from our dream we do not get anxious to provide for our dream-children because as soon as we wake up we realise that the dream was unreal. Before we went to bed, the dream-children were not with us, and after waking up, our dream-children are no more with us; and thus we understand and realise that our dream-children whom we loved and tended as *real* during our dream are in fact unreal only.

By significance, therefore, the Real is that which exists at all occasions : in the past, present and future. The past is relatively real, it was, it is and it will be. Now the stanza becomes clear : "the unreal never is; the Real never is not." Objectively spoken, every philosophy becomes, to the practical intelligence of an ordinary man, an elaborate, airy nothingness. But when, the same philosophical concept is applied in the subjective world and individually realized, at least at the level of the intellect it becomes perfectly lucid. When thus this idea of the Real and the unreal in our philosophy is digested in our subjective understanding with reference to our own life, it will become very clear to us.

The life in our matter envelopments, we know, is finite inasmuch as every little experience at all the three levels of our existence — among the objects, with our sentiments, in the company of our ideas — is finite. The body changes at every moment, the mind evolves and the intellect grows. In all changes, all evolutionary movements and growth, each is indicated by a constant death to its previous state in order that the thing concerned may change, evolve or grow. Body, mind and intellect constitute the flux of change in us, and all of them, therefore, according to our definition, cannot be real.

But is there a Real entity behind it ? In order that change may take place, no doubt, a changeless substratum is necessary. For the waters of the river to flow, a motionless riverbed must be there. Similarly, in order to hold together the millions of experiences at the levels of our body, mind and intellect, and to give us the experience of a synchronised whole — which we call life — we must necessarily have some substratum, changeless and real, which is common to all the three.

Something in us remains unchanged, as it were, all through our changes, holding the vivid experiences together as a thread in a necklace. On closer analysis, it becomes clear that it can be nothing other than the Self in us, the Pure Awareness. Experiences that have come under one's awareness do not constitute any vital aspect of one's own Self; life is the sum-total of experiences that have been devised by the touch of one's illuminating Consciousness. In childhood I was conscious of my childhood life; in my youth I was conscious of my youthful life; and in my old age I am again conscious of my present experiences. The Consciousness remaining the same, endless experiences came under it, got illumined and died away. This Awareness by which I become conscious of things in my life, because of which I am considered as alive, but for which I will have no more existence in this given emobodiment, that spiritual entity, eternal and all pervading, unborn and undying, the one changeless factor, is the Infinite in me. And this Atman is the Real.

Men of knowledge and wisdom have known the essence, meaning and implication of both these, the Self and the non-Self, the Real and the unreal which, in their mysterious combinations, constitute the strange phenomenon called the world.

"What then is that which is ever Real? Listen":

अविनाशि तु तद्विद्धि येन सर्वमिदं ततम् ।
विनाशमव्ययस्यास्य न कश्चित्कर्तुमर्हति ॥ १७ ॥

17. *avināśi tu tad viddhi yena sarvam idaṁ tatam*
vināśam avyayasyāsya na kaścit kartum arhati

अविनाशि — indestructible, तु — indeed, तत् – that, विद्धि – know (thou), येन — by whom, सर्वम् — all, इदम् – this, ततम् – is pervaded, विनाशम् – destruction, अव्ययस्यास्य – of the imperishable, न — not, कश्चित् — anyone, कर्तुम् – to do, अर्हति – is able.

17. *Know That to be indestructible by which all this is pervaded. None can cause the destruction of That — the Imperishable.*

In the last stanza we were told by the Lord what exactly is the difference between the Real and the unreal. According to the definition, if unreal be that which is dying and, therefore, finite, then to any average intelligent man, life is only full of finite things and, naturally he must fail to understand what exactly is that which is the Imperishable, the Immutable. The ever-real is described here in the strict language of a scientific definition by the Lord for the benefit of Arjuna, an average intelligent man.

The real is that which envelops everything that exists and which is the very stuff and substance of all the worlds of perceptions which we experience. Different mud pots, each different in form, shape and colour, may have different names according to the things they contain or according to the purpose for which they are used. Though each one of them has thus a different name, yet, all of them are, we may say, enveloped by — or permeated with — one and the same stuff, the mud, without which none of the pots can exist. From mud they came, in mud they exist, and when they are destroyed, their names and forms shall merge back to become mud. All the mud pots are enveloped by mud which is the Reality holding the world of mud pots together.

Similarly, the world of finite changes is entirely permeated through and enveloped by the Real the Changeless. And Bhagavan adds that there is no possibility even for a moment, of this Real, getting destroyed, even by a fraction, The Lord's declaration, "None can cause the destruction of That", is so emphatic and conclusive that Sankara in his commentary says : "Nobody — not even the Iswara, the Supreme Lord — can destroy the Self." *(Iswaro-pi)*.

"What then is the unreal (asat) whose existence is not constant? Listen" :

अन्तवन्त इमे देहा नित्यस्योक्ताः शरीरिणः ।
अनाशिनोऽप्रमेयस्य तस्माद्युध्यस्व भारत ॥ १८ ॥

18. *antavanta ime deha nityasyoktāḥ śaririṇaḥ*
anāśino 'prameyasya tasmād yudhyasva bhārata

अन्तवन्तः — having an end, इमे — these, देहाः — bodies, नित्यस्य — of the everlasting, उक्ताः — are said, शरीरिणः — of the embodied, अनाशिनः — of the indestructible, अप्रमेयस्य — of the incomprehensible, तस्मात् — therefore, युध्यस्व – fight, भारत — O descendant of Bharata.

18. *They have an end, it is said, these bodies of the embodied Self. The Self is eternal, indestructible, incomprehensible. Therefore, fight, O Bharata.*

The physical forms constituted by the matter envelopments are all perishable equipments for the indwelling Self which is the eternal factor, ever in its nature changeless, indestructible and incomprehensible. By the term *ever-changeless,* the Supreme is indicated to be eternal because the non-eternals by their nature must be ever-changing, since change is the insignia of the finite. The term *indestructible* is not an unnecessary tautology when it is used in conjunction with the term 'ever-changeless', meaning, eternal. Here the term 'indestructible' is to indicate, as Sankara says, both the types of destructions that are possible in a structure which we usually observe in life. The body may be said to have come to destruction on the funeral pyre where it indicates a total annihilation; and it may be that a fat man due to illness may get himself reduced in girth, wherein also we say his health is destroyed. Thus either a total destruction or partial destruction is possible in finite objects. Here, by using the two terms, eternal *(nitya)* and indestructible *(anasin),* the Lord is indicating that neither a total nor a partial destruction is possible in the Supreme.

By qualifying the eternal as *unknowable* is not in any sense to indicate that the Supreme is 'unknown'. The term 'unknowable' is only meant to express here that it is not knowable through the usual organs of perception. The sense-organs are the instruments through which Consciousness beams out and, in Its awareness, objects get illumined. These instruments of cognition, whether they be sense-organs, or the mind, or the intellect, in themselves are inert and can have their knowledge of perception only when they are dynamised by the conscious spark of life. As such, these organs cannot make the very Consciousness an object of their apprehension.* Therefore in terms of our most common source of knowledge — direct perception — the Sastra says here that the Supreme is 'unknowable', It being self-determined *(swatahsiddha)*.

"Therefore, fight O descendant of Bharata." — This is really not a command to fight. A religion that is built upon the concept of extreme forgiveness and large-hearted tolerance as envisaged in the principle of non-violence could not raise a slogan of chaos or revolutionary bloodthirstiness in its very scripture. Such an interpretation is the unintentioned mischief of a commentator who would not read the Geeta in the context of the *Mahabharata*.

The Bhagawad Geeta is not a dry philosophical text-book; it draws its nourishment from the very story in which it is rooted so well. Krishna is addressing not 'man' as such from the quiet caves of the Himalayas, but he is talking to his friend, prince Arjuna, on the battlefield where duty has called him to arms for a fight with an army that stands for certain un-Aryan principles. The world has come to overhear His

---

* Refer Swamiji's *Discourses on Kenopanishad.*

words to Arjuna. Naturally, therefore, the great teacher at the driver's seat has to call upon his disciple, Arjuna, not to renounce *Gandhiva,* his weapon of activity, but to pick it up again and act diligently in the field wherein duty has called him. Thus viewed, the words "Fight O Son of India," means that it is a religious call on every Hindu to discard his defeatist mentality and face wholeheartedly and sincerely the situations in every given field of his life at every given moment in his existence. Active resistance to evil is the Krishna creed in the Geeta.

"The Lord now quotes two Vedic mantras to confirm the view that Geeta Sastra is intended to remove the cause of samsar, such as grief and delusion. It is only a false notion of yours, says the Lord, that you think thus : "Bhishma and others will be killed by me in the battle : I will be their slayer' . . .How?"

य एनं वेत्ति हन्तारं यश्चैनं मन्यते हतम् ।
उभौ तौ न विजानीतो नायं हन्ति न हन्यते ॥ १९ ॥

19. *ya enaṁ vetti hantāraṁ yaś cainaṁ manyate hatam*
ubhau tau na vijānīto nāyaṁ hanti na hanyate

यः — he who एनम् — this (self), वेत्ति — knows, हन्तारम् — slayer, यः — he who, च — and, एनम् — this, मन्यते — thinks, हतम् — slain, उभौ — both, तौ — those, न — not, विजानीतः — know, न — not, अयम् — this, हन्ति — slays, न — not, हन्यते — is slain.

19. *He who takes the Self to be the slayer, and he who thinks He is slain, neither of these knows. He slays not, nor is He slain.*

It is a Hindu tradition that the children of *Aryavarta,* though they may appreciate intellectualism, do not accept any theory as a spiritual or philosophical idea unless the new theory or restatement has been exhaustively proved to be fully supported by the existing immortal scriptures : the Upanishads. This idea was so strictly followed in the past that even Lord Krishna, considered by the Hindus as the greatest manifestation of Reality that ever came upon the earth as an incarnation, had to substantiate his declarations with quotations from the Upanishads. Herein we have the meaning of a well-noted mantra in Kathopanishad* summarised.

The Self being Immutable, It is neither slain nor can It be the slayer. Those who think that they have been slain when the body is slain and those who feel that they are the slayers, know not the real nature of the Self and hence they pattle such meaningless assertions. That which is killed is the perishable body and the delusory arrogation 'I am slain' belongs to the ego-centre. The Self is that which is beyond the body and the ego since the Pure Consciousness is the illuminator of both these factors — the body and the ego. In short, being immutable, the Self is neither the agent nor the object of the action of slaying.

"How is the Self immutable? This is answered by the next verse?" :

न जायते म्रियते वा कदाचि-
न्नायं भूत्वा भविता वा न भूयः ।
अजो नित्यः शाश्वतोऽयं पुराणो
न हन्यते हन्यमाने शरीरे ॥ २० ॥

* Read Swamiji's *Discourses on Kathopanishad,* I. ii. 19.

20. *na jāyate mriyate vā kadācin*
nāyaṁ bhūtvā bhavitā vā na bhūyaḥ
ajo nityaḥ śaśvato 'yam purāṇo
na hanyate hanyamāne śarīre

न — not, जायते — is born, म्रियते — dies, वा — or, कदाचित् — at any time, न — not, अयम् — this, (self), भूत्वा — having been, भविता — will be, वा — or, न — not, भूयः — (any) more, अजः — unborn, नित्यः — eternal, शाश्वतः — changeless, अयम् — this, पुराणः — ancient, न — not, हन्यते — is killed, हन्यमाने — being killed, शरीरे — in body.

20. *He is not born, nor does He ever die; after having been, He again ceases not to be; unborn, eternal, changeless and ancient, he is not killed when the body is killed.*

This stanza labours to deny in the Self all the symptoms of mutability recognised and experienced by the body. The body is prone to different changes and these modifications are the sources of all sorrows in every embodiment. These six changes are common to all and they may be enumerated as birth, existence, growth, decay, disease and death. These changes are the common wombs of all pains in a mortal's life. All these are denied in the Self in this stanza to prove the immutability of the Self. This verse is also a substantial and faithful reproduction of the words of Yama in Kathopanishad.*

Unlike the physical body, the Self is not born, It being the eternal factor that exists at all times. Waves are born and they die away, but the ocean is not born with the waves, nor does it die away when the wave disappears. Since there is no birth, there is no death; things that have a beginning alone can end;

* Refer Swamiji's *Discourses on Kathopanishad*, I. ii. 18.

the rising waves alone can moan their dying conditions. Again, it is explained that like the birth of a child who was not existing before, and who has come to exist after the birth, the Atman is not something that has come to be born due to or because of the body. Thus, the Self is unborn and eternal birthless and deathless, *(ajah, nitya)*.

By the term unchangeable *(saswatha)* all other modifications such as existence, growth, decay and disease are denied in the Self. When the body is slain, the Self is not slain, just as when a wave is destroyed the ocean is not destroyed; when a pot is broken, the mud is not broken. The verse insists that the Self cannot be killed. This is an assertion which amounts to a repetition since it has already been said that it is deathless. Sankara, therefore, interprets the idea in 'It is not slain' as 'It has no transformation' : the Self is not subject to any transformation or transmigration.

"Having thus started the proposition that the Self is neither an agent nor an object of the action of slaying and having established the arguments for the immutability of the Self, Lord Krishna here concludes the proposition as follows" :

वेदाविनाशिनं नित्यं य एनमजमव्ययम् ।
कथं स पुरुषः पार्थ कं घातयति हन्ति कम् ॥ २१ ॥

21. *vedāvināsinam nityaṁ ya enam ajam avyayam*
katham sa puruṣaḥ pārtha kaṁ ghātayati hanti kam

वेद — knows, अविनाशिनम् — indestructible, नित्यम् — eternal, यः — who, एनम् — this (self), अजय — unborn, अव्ययम् — inexhaustible, कथम् — how, सः — he, पुरुषः — man, पार्थ — O Partha (son of Pritha), कं — whom, घातयति — cause to be slain, हन्ति — kills, कम् — whom.

21. *Whosoever knows Him to be indestructible, eternal, unborn, and inexhaustible, how can that man slay, O Partha, or cause others to be slain?*

Summarising what he had said so far, as the Law of Being *(dharma)* of the Self, which indicated rather than defined the eternal, immutable Reality, in this stanza we have in the form of an interrogation a denial that those who know this shall have no dejection or sorrow afterwards in the face of life's realities.

Having known the Self to be indestructible, eternal, unborn and inexhaustible, Krishna asks Arjuna, "How can one arrogate to oneself the stupid idea of agency?" The Lord says that neither can such an individual be a man causing someone to slay nor be himself a slayer. In the context of the given situation, Krishna advises thus. It is interesting to note that He means both Himself and Arjuna by His words. If this knowledge of the Reality has come to the intellectual recognition and acceptance of Arjuna, he will have no more justification to feel himself the killer of the unborn. If he cannot be the killer, Krishna means, "How am I the one who prompts you to slay your relations?"

"To return to the immediate subject. It has been stated that the Self is indestructible. In what way is it indestructible?" Here, in the following, is an explanatory example.

वासांसि जीर्णानि यथा विहाय
नवानि गृह्णाति नरोऽपराणि ।
तथा शरीराणि विहाय जीर्णा-
न्यन्यानि संयाति नवानि देही ॥ २२ ॥

22. *vāsāṁsi jīrṇāni yathā vihāya*
navāni gṛhṇāti naro' parāṇi
tathā śarirāṇi vihāya jīrṇāny
anyāni samyāti navani dehī

वासांसि — clothes, जीर्णानि — worn out, यथा — as, विहाय — having cast away, नवानि — new, गृह्णाति — taken, नरः — man, अपराणि — others, तथा — so, शरीराणि — bodies, विहाय — having cast away, जीर्णानि — worn out, अन्यानि — others, संयाति — enters, नवानि — new, देही — the embodied.

22. *Just as a man casts off his worn-out clothes and puts on new ones, so also the embodied Self casts of its worn-out bodies and enters others which are new.*

This is one of the oft-quoted famous stanzas in the Geeta which, in a very striking example, explains to us how the ego-centric entity in an individual readily leaves its associations with one set of equipments and arrogates to itself another conducive envelopment for living a new set of its required experiences. The example that Vyasa uses is so universal that in the Lord's own mouth they ring with a note of irresistible appeal.

This striking example which comes within the comprehension of everyone is made use of by the Lord so that not only Arjuna but even those who are overhearing these 18 discourses, even at this distance of time, may come to understand the idea clearly.

Just as an individual changes his clothes to suit the convenience of the occasion, so too the ego-centre discards one physical form and takes to another which will be most suited for it to gain the next required type of experiences. In his nightgown no one will plan to go to his office, nor will the same person in his stiff-collar feel happy in the evenings while playing tennis. He changes his dress according to the field where he is intending to work for the time being. Similar is the why and wherefore of death and thereafter.

Changing of clothes that have become worn-out on our own shoulders cannot be a pain to anyone of us, especially when that undressing is for the purpose of putting on a new set of clothes. Similarly, when the mind-intellect-equipment finds that its embodiment in a given form can no longer help it to earn any more experience from its available environments which would facilitate its evolutionary pilgrimage, it feels its present form to be worn-out *(jeerna)*. This 'worn-out' condition of a body is to be decided neither by its age nor by its biological condition; nor can anybody other than its wearer, the ego, decide it.

Critics rise up in hosts, however, against the truth of this stanza and their main platform of argument is built upon the observed facts of young people dying away in the bloom of their life. It is only the observers' opinion that the individual was young and his body was not worn-out, but from the standpoint of the evolutionary necessity of the ego concerned, that body was already useless for it. A rich man feels like changing his house or vehicle almost every year, and he invariably finds ready purchasers. As far as the rich owner is concerned, the thing has become useless for him, while for the purchaser it is 'as good as new!' Similarly, here nobody else can decide whether a given body is worn-out or not except its own wearer.

In short, the stanza emphasizes the doctrine of reincarnation which we had already explained in an earlier stanza.*

* Stanza 12.

On the whole, it must have definitely conveyed to Arjuna the idea that death grins only at those who have no understanding and that it has no pain for those who understand its implications and working. Just as changing dress is no pain to the body, so too, when the dweller in the body leaves the envelopment, no pain is possible; and, by undressing, it does not mean that thereafter we are ever to live naked. So too, this embodied Self ere-long discovers an appropriate equipment from which to function so as to earn for itself new sets of experiences. Evolution and change are all for the mind and intellect, and not for the Self. The Self is perfect and changeless, and needs no evolution in Itself.

"Why is the Self changeless? The Lord says" :

नैनं छिन्दन्ति शस्त्राणि नैनं दहति पावकः ।
न चैनं क्लेदयन्त्यापो न शोषयति मारुतः ॥ २३ ॥

23. *nainam chindanti śastrāṇi nainam dahati pāvakaḥ*
na cainam kledayanty āpo na śoṣayati mārutaḥ

न — not, एनम् — this (self), छिन्दन्ति — cleave, शस्त्राणि – weapons, न — not, एनम् — this, दहति — burns, पावकः – fire, न — not, च — and, एनम् — this, क्लेदयन्ति — wet, आपः — waters, न — not, शोषयति – dries, मारुतः— wind.

23. *Weapons cleave It not, fire burns It not, water wets It not, wind dries It not.*

The Transcendental Truth can be explained only in terms of the limited and the finite, or else the students, who have no experience of the Beyond, will not be able to conceive or apprehend the Absolute and the Eternal. When a traveller in a distant clime, having discovered a beautiful bird of wondrous plumage, comes back to his own native land and explains the beauty which he saw, he will have to talk to his friends in terms of the bird's plumage, that are native to folks on his native land. The *unseen* is explained always in terms of the *seen,* and thereby the unknown becomes fully indicated rather than defined; for any unknown quantum merely defined in itself is as unknown without the definition.

Similarly here the changeless, immutable Self is being described by Lord Krishna in terms of the mutable and ever-changing world which is very familiar to Arjuna and all people like us. In the world of change objects come to their annihilation through instruments of death, or they are consumed by fire or destroyed by water or dried up by air. These are the various means and methods by which the objects of the world come to their destruction. All these means are declared as impotent in bringing about the destruction of the Self.

"Weapons cleave It not." — It is very well-known that with an axe one can cut down a thing, and with a bullet one can shoot some other object, but neither can one would water, fire, air or space with a sword, however sharp it may be. The principle is that no instrument can hit or destroy a subtler element than itself. Naturally, therefore, Atman, the Self, the very cause of the subtlest element space and, necessarily therefore, subtler than space, cannot be cut asunder by the gross instruments.

"Fire cannot burn It." — Fire generally can burn things other than fire, but fire cannot burn itself. The burning capacity in fire is the very Essence, the Truth in it and, therefore, fire cannot burn its own essence, namely, the firy nature. Wherever there is fire, it can consume things only in space, and yet, space is never consumed by fire. Things are con-

sumed by fire in space. If space itself cannot be consumed by fire, how impotent it must feel when it tries to consume the cause of space, the Self.

"Water cannot wet It." — Things get soaked only when they have got interspaces in themselves. A piece of bread can be soaked in water or milk but a piece of iron cannot be soaked, as iron has no interspace in it. When the substance is one homogeneous mass containing nothing other than itself to condition it, water cannot enter the substance and therefore cannot soak it. Another method of destruction observed is either through the quick effects of water, that is, drowning, etc., or through the slow effects of moisture, such as, corroding, etc. Even these are not available in destroying the Truth.

When we read these declarations of Lord Krishna that the Self cannot even be touched much less destroyed by fire, water, etc., we are reminded of the significant allegorical story in *Kenopanishad.** It has been beautifully indicated in the wondrous suggestive language of the inimitable Rishi, that Lord Agni, Vayu, etc., have no power of their own, except that which is allowed to them by the Eternal, Absolute.

"Wind dries It not." — Dehydration process is possible only when there are some minute traces of water in the substance dehydrated. And it has been proved by experiments that every crystal has got its own water of crystallisation which, when removed, causes the crystals to lose their distinct shapes and forms and get themselves pulverised into a fine powder. These are days when vegetables and food materials are dehydrated for purposes of preservation. This is possible because substances contain moisture molecules within them.

---

* Read Swamiji's *Discourses on Kenopanishad*, Khanda IV.

The Supreme Consciousness contains nothing other than Itself and, therefore, annihilation through the process of dehydration is not possible.

Apart from this direct word-meaning, on the whole the stanza indicates a deeper significance wherein we read a fuller estimate of the Eternal. These significances are better brought out in the next stanza where Lord Krishna gives out how and why the Truth is eternal.

"For what reason? Why should we and how can we recognise the Self to be eternal?"

अच्छेद्योऽयमदाह्योऽयमक्लेद्योऽशोष्य एव च ।
नित्यः सर्वगतः स्थाणुरचलोऽयं सनातनः ॥ २४ ॥

24. *acchedyo'yam adāhyo'yam akledyo syosya eva ca*
nityaḥ sarva-gataḥ sthāṇur acalo 'yam sanātanaḥ

अच्छेद्यः — cannot be cut, अयम् — this (self), अदाह्यः — cannot be burnt, अयम् — this, अक्लेद्यः— cannot be wetted, अशोष्यः— cannot be dried, एव — also, च — and, नित्यः — eternal, सर्वगतः — all-pervading, स्थाणु — stable, अचलः—immovable, अयम् — this, सनातनः — ancient.

24. *This Self cannot be cut, nor burnt, nor wetted, nor dried up. It is eternal, all-pervading, stable, immovable and ancient.*

Summarising the previous stanza, the Lord says that the Self cannot be cut, nor burnt, nor wetted, nor dried up, and therefore, he concludes it must be 'everlasting'. It is amply clear that if a thing cannot be annihilated by any of the known methods of destruction discovered and perfected by man, then that given object must be everlasting.

Here, in the second line, we have a series of qualities listed out indicating the Truth, and they are not a haphazard collection of terminologies picked up at random and used in haste. Each word is chosen to be in a sequence with the previous one. That which has indestructibility, as indicated in the first line, should necessarily be everlasting *(nitya)*. That which is thus eternal must be necessarily all-pervading *(sarvagatah)*.

'All-pervading' is a short word of inconceivable depth of significance. All-pervading is that which pervades everywhere and, therefore, there is nothing that is not pervaded by the All-pervasive. Eternal Truth envelops all and the All-pervading has no shape nor can have one, since that which has a shape is conditioned all along its outline by something other than itself.

A man with a head, trunk and limbs has got a shape because all around him, along the margin of his outline, is space which is something other than the carbon material of his skull and bones. A thing conditioned should necessarily have a form of its own. By the term 'all-pervading' it is meant that it has only Itself all around It and at all places, and that It is unconditioned by anything other than Itself.

A truth that is thus eternal *(nitya),* homogeneous and all-pervading *(sarvagatah)* must necessarily be stable *(sthanu)* because no change can ever happen in it. That which is thus stable must be firm *(achala),* for it cannot shake or move since moving implies the transfer of a thing from one set of time and place to another set of time and place where it was not already before. Since the Self is all-pervading, there is no spot, in space or period in time, where It is not already and, therefore, just as I cannot move myself in myself, the Self cannot move anywhere. A motionless thing is indeed firm.

Here the two terms, stable *(sthanu)* and firm *(achala)*, may seem a tautology : they both having almost the same meaning. But the former means the stability at the base, just as in the case of a banyan tree. At the base of the trunk it is stable and yet at its top it is moving. Truth is 'stable' at the base, and 'firm' at the top. It has no movement anywhere in Its Infinite glory.

'*Sanatana*' — that which is ancient. The implication of this term can fall under two categories : the obvious and the suggestive. The former indicates that the Self is not new *(nuthana)* but it is ancient and, therefore, we, as students of *Brahma Vidya,* need not hesitate to accept it as we should necessarily if the theory were a modern ideology yet to be verified by observed experimental data. Following the latter in its suggestiveness, it implies that the Self is unconditioned by time and place. Perfection gained, whether it be in India or at the North Pole, in the present generation or in the chaste periods of the Vedic culture, in all places and at all times, by all seers in all religions of the world, the Self experienced at the time of their God-realization can only be one and the same.

"*Moreover, Bhagavan adds*" :

अव्यक्तोऽयमचिन्त्योऽयमविकार्योऽयमुच्यते ।
तस्मादेवं विदित्वैनं नानुशोचितुमर्हसि ॥ २५ ॥

25. *avyakto 'yam acintyo 'yam avikāryo 'yam ucyate*
tasmād evam viditvainaṁ nānuśocitum arhasi

अव्यक्तः — unmanifested, अयम् — this (self), अचिन्त्यः — unthinkable, अयम् — this, अविकार्यः – unchangeable, अयम् —

this, उच्यते — is said, तस्मात् — therefore, एवम् — thus, विदित्वा — having known, एनम् — this, न — not, अनुशोचितुम् — to grieve, अर्हसि — (you) deserve to.

25. *This (Self) is said to be unmanifested, unthinkable and unchangeable. Therefore, knowing This to be such, you should not grieve.*

During the eloquent arguments of Arjuna in the first chapter, we were tempted to believe that the Pandava is a great advocate of logical thinking and forceful presentation. But, observing the unearthly eloquence and depth of significance in Krishna's delivery, championing the cause of action from the bulwark of Knowledge, we are soon disillusioned in our estimation and we readily offer the best place for the Lord Himself.

This eternal, all-pervading Self is certainly unmanifest, unthinkable and unchangeable and, therefore, having known this Truth in its essential nature, Krishna argues that it is neither possible to kill nor get really killed! Each of these terms used here is quite expressive of certain logical truths.

'*Unmanifest*' — The five great elements that we know, when they become subtler, lose their capacity to impinge themselves upon our sense perceptions; and when we go up from earth to air, we find our perception of them fading away. However, the five great elements can, to some extent, be perceived through our sense-organs. But the cause of ether, the subtlest of the five elements, becomes too subtle for our perception and, therefore, we will have to assume that it is unmanifest.

A thing is called manifest when we can perceive it through one or the other of our sense-organs. That which is beyond all these five sense-organs is called unmanifest. I cannot see, smell, hear, taste or touch a full-grown mango tree in a mango seed. And yet, I know that the seed is the cause of the tree. Under the circumstances, the tree is said to be in an 'unmanifest' condition in the seed. Similarly, when they say that Truth is unmanifest they only mean that It cannot be perceived through the sense-organs. We, in our Upanishads, have exhaustive explanations why our senses cannot bring the Eternal as an object for their sense-perceptions.* It is the very subject because of which the sense-organs can perceive.

'*Unthinkable*' — After denying the sense-organs any play in the field of Truth, we are told here that the human mind also cannot think, nor can the human intellect rationalise over and comprehend the Infinite. The Self being the very life that energies the mind and the intellect which are in themselves inert and insentient, it becomes obviously clear that the mind and intellect cannot make the Self an object of their comprehension and continue comprehending all for themselves. A telescope-gazer cannot see himself with his telescope : he cannot be at once the *seer* and the *seen*. Thus here, the Lord's word, 'unthinkable', is to be understood as meaning 'incomprehensible' by the mind and the intellect of the seeker.

'*Unchangeable*' — This term indicates that the Self is without parts because things that have parts in themselves are things which have form, and those that have form must necessarily come under the category of the finite and express in themselves various modifications and changes.

By these terms, Truth is declared as immutable, un-

---

* Read Swamiji's *Discourses on Kenopanishad*.

manifest, unthinkable and unchangeable. Therefore, understanding thus the Self, Krishna advises Arjuna to end his grief. One who understands the eternal nature of the Self can have neither the occasion to perceive himself as the slayer nor to recognise others as slain.

"Granting that the Self is not ever-lasting, the Lord proceeds" :

अथ चैनं नित्यजातं नित्यं वा मन्यसे मृतम् ।
तथापि त्वं महाबाहो नैवं शोचितुमर्हसि ॥ २६ ॥

26. *atha cai'nam nityajātam nityam vā manyase mrtam*
tathā'pi tvam mahābāho nai'vām śocitum arhasi

अथ — now, च — and, एनम् — this (self), नित्यजातम् — constantly born, नित्यम् — constantly, वा — or, मन्यसे — thinkest, मृतम् — dead, तथापि — even then, त्वम् — thou, महाबाहो — mighty armed, न — not, एवम् — thus, शोचितुम् — to grieve, अर्हसि — (thou) deserve to.

26. ***But even if you think of Him as being constantly born and constantly dying, even then, O mighty-armed, you should not grieve.***

This and the following stanzas are arguments in which the materialist's point of view has been, for the purpose of argument, accepted by Krishna. According to the materialists, direct perception alone is an authority for belief. With this standard for their knowledge, when they try to measure life, they have to accept life as a constant flux of infinite births and infinite deaths. Things are born, and they die away. This whirl of birth and death is constant. And this constant change is life to them. Krishna argues that if life is but a constant repetition of births and deaths, then also, hero *(mahabahu)* as you are, you do not deserve to grieve at this occasion.

The thousands that are manning the Kaurava forces 'come from nowhere, but they were just born, and they must die away leaving no trace of themselves here or in the hereafter', would be the materialistic viewpoint of life. Naturally, therefore, there is no occasion for Arjuna to moan for them. Bubbles on a rainy day in our courtyard must come, play for a moment to dazzle in the light, and die away; there is neither a hereafter nor a past. As such, the occasion that is now facing Arjuna is not an occasion to weep.

"Accordingly" :

जातस्य हि ध्रुवो मृत्युर्ध्रुवं जन्म मृतस्य च ।
तस्मादपरिहार्येऽर्थे न त्वं शोचितुमर्हसि ॥ २७ ॥

27. *jātasya hi dhruvo mṛtyur dhruvaṁ janma mṛtasya ca*
tasmād aparihārye 'rthe na tvaṁ śocitum arhasi

जातस्य — of the born, हि — for, ध्रुवः — certain, मृत्युः — death ध्रुवम् – certain, जन्म — birth, मृतस्य — of the dead, च — and, तस्मात् — therefore, अपरिहार्ये — inevitable, अर्थे — in matter, न — not, त्वम् — thou, शोचितुम — to grieve, अर्हसि — you ought.

27. *For, certain is death for the born, and certain is birth for the dead; therefore, over the inevitable you should not grieve.*

That which is born must die, and after death things are born again. Here Krishna is continuing to view the whole situation from the materialistic angle again. The Materialists take life to be a constant flood of appearances of forms, arising from nowhere and themselves disappearing into nowhere. The theists believe that the embodiments are taken up by the individual ego in order that it may eke out its experiences and learn to grow in its understanding of life and ultimately realise the Truth behind it all. Thus, this is a common meeting point of both the theists and the atheists : both of them believe life to be a continuous chain of birth and death.

If life be thus, in its very nature, a stream of births and deaths, against this unavoidable and inevitable arrangement no intelligent man should moan. Standing in the sun in summer, one must be indeed stupid to moan for and complain against the heat and the glare. Similarly, having come to life, to complain against the very nature of life is indeed an inexcusable delusion. On this score also, to weep is to admit one's own ignorance and stupidity. Krishna's life is on the whole a message of cheer and joy. His doctrine of life is an insistence that 'to weep is folly and to smile is wisdom'. 'Keep smiling', seems to be Krishna's philosophy put in two words, and that is why, seeing his dear friend weeping in life, the Lord got whipped up, as it were, to an enthusiasm to save Arjuna from his delusions and raise him back to the true fields of life.

Connecting this stanza with the following, Sankara says: *"Neither is it proper to grieve over beings which are mere combinations of (material) causes and effects; for"* :

अव्यक्तादीनि भूतानि व्यक्तमध्यानि भारत ।
अव्यक्तनिधनान्येव तत्र का परिदेवना ॥ २८ ॥

28. *avyaktādīnī bhūtāni vyakta madhyāni bhārata*
avyakta nidhanāny eva tatra kā paridevanā

अव्यक्तादीनि — unmanifest in the beginning, भूतानि — beings, व्यक्तमध्यानि — manifested in their middle state भारत — O descendant of Bharata, अव्यक्तनिधनानि — unmanifested again in the end, एव — also, तत्र — there, का — what, परिदेवना grief.

28. *Beings are experienced to be unmanifest in their beginning, are seen to be manifest in their middle state, O Bharata, and are noticed to be unmanifest again in their end. What is there then to grieve about?*

From this stanza onwards we have a beautiful presentation of the whole problem of Arjuna from the standpoint of the man-of-the-world. Krishna's scheme was such that he started a purely philosophical discussion, the point of view of *Theistic Theism.** After this, he argued from the standpoint of *Atheistic Atheism* in the last two verses. Now, in these ten verses he is trying to explain the problem as viewed through the goggles of a common man of the world and his intellectual judgement.

The material world of objects strictly follows the law of causation. The world of 'effects' rises from the world of 'causes'. In a majority of cases, the effects are manifest and the causes are unmanifest. To project from the unmanifest to manifestation is the creation of a thing, when it happens strictly following the law of causation.

Thus, the manifest world of today was in an unmanifest condition before its creation. And now, it is temporarily available for cognition as fully manifest, and it shall fade away into the unmanifest again. It amounts to saying that the pre-

* Refer Introduction, the classification of the six schools of philosophy.

sent came from the unknown and shall return to the unknown. Even if viewed thus, why should one moan, for the spokes of a wheel that turn eternally must come *down* only to *rise* up again.

Again, the dream-children, unmanifest before and which came into manifestation during the dream, had become unmanifest again on waking up. Why moan, you bachelor, for the wife unmarried who had disappeared along with your dream; the children unborn who dissolved with your dream!

If there be, as Krishna says, an Infinite, Eternal, Truth which is changeless and deathless, in which alone this drama of change occurs, this whirl of birth and death spins, how is it that we are not able to realise It even though explained to us repeatedly. According to Sankara, Bhagawan feels that he should not blame Arjuna for his incapacity to understand the obvious Self.

Sankara says : *"The Self just spoken of is very difficult to realise. Why should I blame you alone while the cause, ignorance, is common to all? One may ask : How is it that the Self is so difficult to realise? The Lord says"* :

आश्चर्यवत्पश्यति कश्चिदेन-
माश्चर्यवद्वदति तथैव चान्यः ।
आश्चर्यवच्चैनमन्यः श्रृणोति
श्रुत्वाप्येनं वेद न चैव कश्चित् ॥ २९ ॥

29. *āscaryavat pāśyati kaścit enam-*
āścaryavad vadati tathaiva cānyaḥ
āścaryavac cainam anyaḥ śṛṇoti
śrutvāpy enam veda na cai'va kaścit

आश्चर्यवत् — as a wonder, पश्यति — sees, कश्चित् — someone, एनम् — this (Self), आश्चर्यवत् — as a wonder, वदति — speaks of, तथा — so, एव — also, च — and, अन्यः — another, आश्चर्यवत् — as a wonder, च — and, एनम् — this, अन्यः — another, शृणोति — hears, श्रुत्वा — having heard, अपि — even, एनम् — this, वेद — knows, न — not, च — and, एव — also, कश्चित् — anyone.

29. *One sees This as a wonder; another speaks of This as a wonder; another hears of This as a wonder; yet, having heard, none understands This at all.*

Substantially of the same tempo in spirit and words as in *Kathopanishad,** here is a statement which implies and indicates the rarity of *Brahma-vidya.*

The Eternal Absolute is explained to us a Infinite, all-knowing and all-blissful. But our experience of ourselves, as far as we know, is that we are finite, ignorant and miserable. Thus, between the Reality which is our Self and what we experience ourselves to be, there seems to be as much difference as between heat and cold, light and darkness. Why is it we are not able to recognise the Self which is our Real Nature?

In our ignorance, when we try to perceive the Truth, it seems to be a goal to be reached at some distant place, in a distant period of time. But, in fact, if we are to believe our Lord's words, the Self being the essential nature, we are never far from it. A mortal is as far away from Immortality, the sinner is as far removed from a saint — the imperfect is as far removed from Perfection — as the dreamer is from the waker! Man awakened to this Self's glory is God; God forgetful of His own glory is the deluded man.

---

* Read Swamiji's *Discourses on Kathopanishad,* Chapter I, Section ii, Mantra 7.

To the body, mind and intellect, the very existence of the subtler Self beyond these envelopments is an idea that cannot be even conceived, and when a mortal, through the techniques of self-perfection, comes to recognise himself to be the Self, he is struck with a wondrous ecstasy of that supersensuous experience.

The emotion of wonder, when it rises in the mind, has got the capacity to black out, for the time being, all cognitions, and the individual who has been struck with wonder comes to forget himself and becomes, for the moment, one with the very emotion. As an experiment try to surprise fully somebody and quietly watch his attitude. With his mouth open and unseeing eyes protruding out, every nerve in him stretched to the highest tension, the victim of wonderment stands fixed to the spot as a statue carved in moist, cold, flesh! The same is the thrilled hush of lived joy in the temple of experience when the Self, all alone with the Self, comes to live as the Self! And, therefore, the great rishis of old borrowed the term 'wonderment' to indicate to the student what exactly would be the condition of his personality layers at the moment when his ego drops off from the resplendent Infinite form of the Self.

The construction is such that it can be interpreted as 'men who realise the Self in all Its resplendent, unconditioned beauty and gorgeous might, are the marvellous few' — rare, rare, indeed! Of them, except for a rare few, others become mum when they try to express in finite words the Joy Infinite in their bosom. But the rare few talk and find in themselves not only a capacity to express in their own language of symbolism all about their new discovery, but they bring this Infinite wisdom within the limited intellectual comprehension of the deluded men of their generation. Masters, such as,

Buddha, Christ, Zoroaster, Mahabir and others are wonderful geniuses inasmuch as they are indeed very rare.

When these are few appear in the world to bless us with their words of right direction, divine encouragement and undying call to us to rise to our divine stature, the ungrateful brute in all of us rises in revolt against the prophet and provides him with an untimely grave. Even to listen to such masters and their divine expositions, very few gather. And the wonder of wonders is that even after hearing, the unprepared and the uninitiated cannot understand and comprehend the Truth.*

True knowledge makes a man realise that he is a 'soul with a body', but now, in his ignorance, he thinks that he is a 'body with a soul'. By the exclamation of wonder at the realisation, at the declaration and at the very proper listening to Truth, it is not meant to discourage the seekers. On the other hand, it is mainly intended to encourage those seekers who listen well, and also those who cannot listen properly. Those who *listen* well are encourged to *reflect* on what they have heard and to *meditate* until they realise the Self in them. The unintelligent listeners also feel encouraged by the very same statement expressing the rarity of this knowledge, to make repeated attempts at listening *(sravanam)* continuous reflection *(mananam)*, and long contemplation *(nididhyasanam)*.

Here the Lord concludes the subject of this section thus :

---

* For a more exhaustive treatment of this stanza, read Swamiji's *Discourses on Kathopanishad*.

देही नित्यमवध्योऽयं देहे सर्वस्य भारत ।
तस्मात्सर्वाणि भूतानि न त्वं शोचितुमर्हसि ॥ ३० ॥

30. *dehī nityaṁ avadhyo' yaṁ dehe sarvāsya bhāratā*
tasmāt sarvāṇi bhūtāṇi na tvaṁ śocitum arhasi

देही — indweller, नित्यम् — always, अवध्यः — indestructible, अयम् — this, देहे — in the body, सर्वस्य — of all, भारतः— O descendant of Bharata. तस्मात् — therefore, सर्वाणि — (for) all, भूतानि — creatures, न — not, त्वम् — thou, शोचितुम् — to grieve, अर्हसि — you should.

30. *This, the Indweller in the body of everyone is ever indestructible. O Bharata; and therefore, you should not grieve for any creature.*

The subtle Reality in each body, the indwelling Spirit in every living creature, is eternal and indestructible. All that is destroyed is only the container : the finite matter envelopment. Therefore, Arjuna has been advised that he should not grieve at facing his enemies and, in the great battle, even killing them if need be. In bringing out this idea, the entire earlier section has been used by Krishna wherein he argued so well to establish the eternal nature of the soul and the finite nature of the bodies.

Rightly Sankara concludes that this stanza winds up the entire section opened in Verse 11.

"Here in this verse it has been shown that from the standpoint of Absolute Truth, there is no occasion for grief and attachment. Not only from the standpoint of Absolute Truth, but also" :

स्वधर्ममपि चावेक्ष्य न विकम्पितुमर्हसि ।
धर्म्याद्धि युद्धाच्छ्रेयोऽन्यत्क्षत्रियस्य न विद्यते ॥ ३१ ॥

31. *svadharmam api cāvekṣya na vikampitum arhasi*
dharmyāddhi yuddhāc chreyo'nyat
kṣatriyasya na vidyate

स्वधर्मम् — own duty, अपि— also, च— and, अवेक्ष्य — looking at, न — not, विकम्पितुम् — to waver, अर्हसि — you should, धर्म्यात् — righteous, हि — indeed, युद्धात् — than war, श्रेयः — higher, अन्यत् — other, क्षत्रियस्य — of a Kshatriya, न — not, विद्यते — is.

31. *Further, looking at thine own duty thou oughtest not to waver, for there is nothing higher for a* Kshatriya *than a righteous war.*

It is the duty of a Hindu Prince *(Kshatriya)* to fight in the interest of his country, people and culture. Arjuna belonged to the group of *Kshatriyas* not only by an accident of birth but also by the quality of his inner mental constitution. He has the required physical enthusiasm, moral fire, intellectual alacrity and heroic daring that make it impossible for him to rest contented in quiet study and contemplation without getting himself agitated tremendously when he finds the unhappy lot of his country or people, or when he detects that the sacred Aryan culture has been threatened by imperceptible un-Aryan invasions. In short, all political leaders, social workers, enthusiastic upholders of our national purity and culture, all of them fall under the classification of *Kshatriya* according to the *Sanatana* culture of this ancient land. But in the slow decadence of our culture, we have come to accept by mistake that these caste classifications are the hereditary birthrights that come upon the children born of their respective fathers.

Thus, Arjuna's personal call of character *(swadharma)* is that of a leader of his generation *(Kshatriya)* and, as such, when his generation is called upon to answer a challenge of an organised un-Aryan force *(adharma)*, it is his duty not to waver but to fight on and defend his sacred national culture. To the leaders of the people, there can be nothing nobler than to get a glorious chance to fight for their noble cause. Here Arjuna has been called upon to fight a righteous war wherein his enemies are true aggressors. Therefore, it is said that such a chance comes indeed only to a lucky few. That a king must fight on such an occasion is vividly brought out in the *Mahabharata.**

"And regarding other reasons why the battle should be fought, the Lord says" :

यदृच्छया चोपपन्नं स्वर्गद्वारमपावृतम् ।
सुखिनः क्षत्रियाः पार्थ लभन्ते युद्धमीदृशम् ॥ ३२ ॥

32. *yadrcchayā copapannaṁ svarga dvāram apāvṛtam*
sukhinah ksatriyāh pārtha labhante yuddham īdrśam

यदृच्छया — of itself, च — and, उपपन्नम् — come, स्वर्गद्वारम् — the gate of heaven, अपावृतम् — opened, सुखिनः — happy, क्षत्रियाः — Kshatriyas, पार्थ — O Partha, लभन्ते — obtain, युद्धम् — battle, ईदृशम् — such.

32. *Happy indeed are the Kshatriyas, O Partha, who are called to fight in such a battle that comes of itself as an open door to heaven.*

* Udyoga Parva, Chapter 72, Verse 18 says : The sin that is committed, by killing one who does not deserve to be killed is as great as the sin of *not* killing one who deserves to be killed.

As used here, Kshatriya is not the name of a caste; it merely indicates a certain quality of the mental *vasanas* in the individual. Those who have an ever bubbling enthusiasm to defend the weak and the poor besides their own national culture from all threats of aggressions are called Kshatriyas. Such leaders of men are not allowed to be themselves tyrants and aggressors, according to the code of morality of the Hindus. But at the same time, a cold, feminine and almost cowardly non-resistance is not the spirit of the Hindu tradition. In all cases where, unasked, the Hindu nation is edged on to wage a war on principles of righteousness *(upapannam)*, the leaders of India are ordered here to fight in defence of their culture and to consider themselves fortunate to get the chance to serve the country. Such battlefield opens up the gates of Heaven wide for the defending heroes who fight diligently on the side of *dharma*.

It is interesting to note how Lord Krishna in the scheme of his exhortations comes down slowly from the highest pinnacles of Vedantic ideologies to a lower plane of material philosophy and still lower down to a mere point of view of an average worldy man. From all these different strata he views the problem and presents Arjuna with the same satisfactory conclusion that the war must be fought. When thus, in the logical sequence of his argument, Bhagavan reaches the plane of the common man's point of view, he detects that his argument has slightly gone home to Arjuna. Just as a dexterous pugilist would press hard once a weak point is discovered in his rival, in his intellectual duel, having detected a weak point in Arjuna, Lord Krishna is vehemently thrusting forward to play upon that discovered weakness.

Here we find one more verse dedicated in expressing another argument in which there is nothing much philosophical. The traditional belief that to a Hindu king there cannot be a greater occasion in life than that in which he gets a chance to justify himself in a war to defend his culture must have been very well known to Arjuna. On the whole, Lord Krishna is emphasising the idea upon his friend that it is an unavoidable duty towards the country and the culture that Arjuna should fight for this righteous cause.

"It is indeed a fact that it is your duty, and now in case you renounce it and run away from the battlefield, then":

अथ चेत्त्वमिमं धर्म्यं संग्रामं न करिष्यसि ।
ततः स्वधर्मं कीर्तिं च हित्वा पापमवाप्स्यसि ॥ ३३ ॥

33. *atha cet tvam imuṁ dharmyaṁ*
saṁgrāmaṁ na kariṣyasi
tatah svadharmaṁ kīrtiṁ ca
hitvā pāpam avāpsyasi

अथ चेत् — but if, त्वम् — thou, इमम् — this, धर्म्यम् — righteous, संग्रामम् — warfare, न — not, करिष्यसि — will do, ततः — then, स्वधर्मम् — own duty, कीर्तिम् — fame, च — and, हित्वा — having abandoned, पापम् — sin, अवाप्स्यसि — shall incur.

33. *But if you will not fight this righteous war, then, having abandoned your own duty and fame, you shall incur sin.*

In case you refuse to engage yourself in this glorious war then not only will you be renouncing your own *swadharma* and honour, but you will also come to incur positive sin in not having fulfilled your noble duty. Not to face this army of un-Aryan forces is as much sinful as to murder and kill those who deserve not such a treatment.

Dharma, we have already explained, is the 'law of being'. Every living creature has taken up its form and has come into the world of objects for one great purpose, which is to gain an exhaustion of its existing mental impressions. The bundle of *vasanas* with which an individual has arrived in this life in his incarnation is called his *swadharma.* When classified thus, Arjuna falls under the group of the 'kingly' who are characterised by adventurous heroism and insatiable thirst for honour and fame.

Not to make use of the evolutionary chances provided by life is to reject and refuse the chances provided for a vasana-catharsis. By not exhausting the old *vasanas,* one will be living under a high *vasana*-pressure when the existing tendencies are crowded up by the influx of new tendencies. Not fighting the war Arjuna may run away from the field, but he will certainly come to regret his lost chances since his mind is so composed that he can find complete relief and solace only by living the intensely dangerous life of the battlefield. A boy with tendencies for art cannot be successfully trained to become a businessman or an economist since these are contrary to his nature. If an overanxious parent in the name of mistaken love, projects upon a growing child his own intentions and plans, invariably we will find that the young boy grows up into a crushed personality.

Example of the type are seen everywhere in the world, especially in the spiritual field. With over enthusiasm for spiritual development, there are many seekers who, at the mere appearance of a misery or at the threat of a sorrow, decide to run away into the jungles 'seeking God', and invariably end in a lifelong tragic disaster! They have in them sensuous *vasanas* which can be satisfied only in the encumbrance of a family under the roof of their own houses. Rejecting them all, they reach the Himalayan caves and then all the day through they can neither meditate upon the Lord nor find a field for sensuous enjoyment. Naturally, they will be entertaining more and more agitations in their mind. These agitations of the mind are otherwise called sin *(papam)*.

Sin in Hinduism is considered a mistake of the mind in which it acts contrary to its essential nature as the Self. Any act of sensuousness in which the mind pants forward into the world of objects, hoping to get thereby a joy and satisfaction, necessarily creates within its bosom more and more agitations; and this type of a mistake of the mind is called a sin.

In short, the Lord indicates to Arjuna a psychological truth known and recognised vaguely now by the modern world. With this understanding of the stanza, when one reads the reports of modern State-education to the children according to the observed psychological traits in them, in Russia and other countries, one feels surprised how much the Hindus of that age had progressed in the field of psychology. All these niceties and subtle beauties in this verse are lost when we merely translate the word to mean that Arjuna will incur sin if he does not fight.

"Not only will you have given up your duty and fame but also".

अकीर्तिं चापि भूतानि कथयिष्यन्ति तेऽव्ययाम् ।
संभावितस्य चाकीर्तिर्मरणादतिरिच्यते ॥ ३४ ॥

34. *akīrtiṁ cāpi bhūtāni kathayiṣyanti te' vyayām*
saṁbhāvitasya cākīrtir maraṇād atiricyate

अकीर्तिम् — dishonour, च — and, अपि — also, भूतानि — beings, कथयिष्यन्ति — tell, ते — thy, अव्ययाम् — everlasting, संभावितस्य — of the honoured, च — and, अकीर्तिः— dishonour, मरणात् — than death, अतिरिच्यते — exceed.

34. *People too will recount your everlasting dishonour; and to one who has been honoured, dishonour is more than death.*

That to a hero of fame dishonour is worse than death, is the other argument that Krishna brings to persuade his friend to give up his hesitation in fighting the great war. It is interesting to note how, seeing that his earlier thrusts from the common man's viewpoint, have been effective, Krishna sledgehammers his friend with more and more ideas of the same type. The vanity of Arjuna is obviously tickled when he is told that the 'whole world shall sing thy everlasting infamy'. In this section, the general import is that if Arjuna were to abandon the fight, he could do so only because of his cowardice, since the cause of the war is already known to be righteous. Certainly, there is an undercurrent of sympathy in Krishna's words; he realises that however great a hero Arjuna may be, even he can be weakened by wrong emotionalism.

"*Moreover*" :

भयाद्रणादुपरतं मंस्यन्ते त्वां महारथाः ।
येषां च त्वं बहुमतो भूत्वा यास्यसि लाघवम् ॥ ३५ ॥

35. *bhayād raṇād uparatam mamsyante tvam mahārathāḥ*
yeṣāṁ ca tvaṁ bahu-mato bhūtvā yāsyasi lāghavam

भयात् — from fear, रणात् — from the battle, उपरतम् — withdrawn, मस्यन्ते — will think, त्वाम् — thee, महारथाः — the great commanders, येषाम् — of whom, च — and, त्वम् — thou, बहुमतः — much thought of, भूत्वा — having been, यास्यसि — will receive, लाघवम् — lightness.

35. *The great battalion commanders will think that you have withdrawn from the battle through fear : and you will be lightly held by them who have thought much of you and your heroism in the past.*

Continuing his common man's point of view arguments, Krishna here says that not only the world shall blame him and history shall recount his infamy, but also immediately the great warriors and battalion commanders *(maharathas)* in the enemy lines will start ridiculing him. They will laugh and say the great archer Arjuna ran away from the battlefront because of sheer cowardice. They will interpret his conscientious objections against the fratricidal war as an act of cowardice from a hero during a weak moment in his life. No soldier can stand such a dishonour especially when it comes from one's own equals among enemy lines.

"Moreover" :

अवाच्यवादांश्च बहून्वदिष्यन्ति तवाहिताः ।
निन्दन्तस्तव सामर्थ्यं ततो दुःखतरं नु किम् ॥ ३६ ॥

36. *avācyavādāṁś cabahūn vadiṣyanti tavā 'hitāḥ*
nindantas tava sāmarthyaṁ tato duḥkataraṁ nu kim

अवाच्यवादान् — words that are improper to be spoken च — and, बहून् — many, वदिष्यन्ति — will say, तव — thy, अहिताः — enemies, निन्दतः — cavilling, तव — thy, सामर्थ्यं — power, ततः — than this, दुःखतरम् — more painful, नु — indeed, किम् — what.

36. *And many unspeakable words will your enemies speak cavilling your powers. What can there be more painful than this?*

Finding that Arjuna is conspicuously reacting well to these arguments, Krishna is driving home to him the folly in running away from the battlefront. It will be intolerance when his enemies scandalize his glorious name and chivalry in foul language too indecent even to repeat. Not only that history will immortalise his cowardly retreat, but even while he lives, he will be pointed out and laughed at as a hero who ran away from the battlefield.

"Now, when you fight with Karna and such other great heroes on the Kaurava lines" :

हतो वा प्राप्स्यसि स्वर्गं जित्वा वा भोक्ष्यसे महीम् ।
तस्मादुत्तिष्ठ कौन्तेय युद्धाय कृतनिश्चयः ॥ ३७ ॥

37. *hato vā prāpsyasi svargaṁ jitvā vā bhokṣyase mahīm*
tasmād uttiṣṭha kaunteya yuddhāya kṛtaniścayaḥ

हतः — slain, वा — or, प्राप्स्यसि — (you) will obtain, स्वर्गम् — heaven, जित्वा — having conquered, वा — or, भोक्ष्यसे (you) will enjoy, महीम् — the earth, तस्मात् — therefore, उत्तिष्ठ – stand up, कौन्तेय – O Kaunteya, युद्धाय — for fight, कृतनिश्चयः — resolved.

37. *Slain, you will obtain heaven; victorious, you will enjoy the earth; therefore, stand up, O son of Kunti, resolved to fight.*

In this great war, while fighting with the irresistible heroes like Karna and others, Arjuna is told by the Lord that he shall be the gainer whether he is victorious or vanquished. In either case, Arjuna has been reminded that he stands to gain. In case he has to give up his life on the warfront fighting for such a noble cause, he shall suddenly come to enter the 'Heavens of the Heroes' *(veeraswarga)* to stay and to enjoy there for aeons. In case he wins, he shall certainly come to rule over the kingdom and enjoy in the world and, thereafter, shall again go back to Heaven to enjoy there the status of a mighty hero who fought championing the cause of *dharma*. Either way he wins because he is on the side of the good, the war aims of the Pandavas being spotlessly righteous.

Therefore — meaning, for all the reasons so far enumerated* — "Arise, resolve to fight." Earlier, Arjuna, after expressing his desperations and feelings had sat down throwing his weapons, and became inert and motionless. Krishna asks his friend to get up from this moodiness and dejection 'determined to fight' the noble war.

The call to war is justified because of the particular situation in the *Mahabharata* where the Geeta happens to be given out. Generalising the call of Krishna, we may say that it is a divine call to man to discard his melancholy dejections at the face of life's challenges and to come forward to play out to his best 'the game of life' with a firm determination to strive and to win. In this, we have the true universality of the Geeta explicitly brought out, and those who understand it can find its vast application in the community of man.

"Now listen to the advice I offer you while you fight the battle" :

---

* Verses 30-37, apart from the philosophical arguments given from verse 11 onwards.

Refer Ch. I, verse 47, Ch. II, stanza 9.

सुखदुःखे समे कृत्वा लाभालाभौ जयाजयौ ।
ततो युद्धाय युज्यस्व नैवं पापमवाप्स्यसि ॥ ३८ ॥

38. *sukha-duḥkhe same kṛtvā lābhālābau jayājayau*
tato yuddhāya yujyasva naivaṁ pāpam avāpsyasi

सुखदुःखे — in pleasure and pain, समे — same, कृत्वा — having made, लाभालाभौ — gain and loss, जयाजयौ — victory and defeat, तत् — then, युद्धाय — for battle, युज्यस्व — engage thou, न — not, एवम् — thus, पापम् — sin, अवाप्स्यसि — shall incur.

38. *Having made pleasure and pain, gain and loss, victory and defeat, the same, you engage in battle for the sake of battle; thus you shall win and not incur sin.*

The Geeta is a textbook to be studied in itself since Vyasa's attempt in the Geeta is to present to the Hindus of his generation a re-statement of the entire Vedic theory and practice. As such, the very many popular terms and terminologies of Vedic flavour have been taken up to express a shade of meaning peculiar to the Geeta. Always we find in them a better sense of practical application and utility. One who is only a hasty student of the Upanishads may not fully come to realize all the implications of these words as used in the Geeta. No doubt, the Geeta talks the familiar language of the Vedas but implies a new meaning and indicates more practical ways of living the Vedas in a period when social living, communal tensions, lust for power and clash of cultural ideologies have come to stay.

In any textbook of science, there is a chapter discussing 'categories', which explains and defines the technical terms used in that science. The Geeta has its own lexicon, and Vyasa leaves its discovery to the diligent student's industry and self-application. We will find later on that *Karma Yoga* of the Vedas, wherein it meant only the self-purification gained through ritualistic sacrifices and mental concentration practices, has been re-employed here by Krishna to include and incorporate the activities of the world at all levels in everybody's day-to-day-existence.

The very word *Yoga* which perhaps frightened away the ordinary man by the time of the Puranic Age, is used here so liberally that we have got in the Geeta something like eight or ten different types of yogas advised : ***Bhakti Yoga, Buddhi Yoga, Anasakti Yoga,*** etc., besides ***Karma Yoga*** and ***Gnana Yoga***. And even Yoga has been described as 'dexterity in action'. This is, as it should be because at certain periods of history a generation comes to entertain a sentimental dread, along with an intellectual aversion, for the best in their own culture, and at all such moments a revival can take place only when this idle fear has been removed from the mind of the populace. And the easiest method of its removal is by bringing down the awe-inspiring words to cheaper usages — without spoiling the glow and fire of its pristine usage.

A child who is frightened of the domesticated cat soon grows to be an young cat-tyrant in the house, when it slowly gets familiarised with the animal. Similarly, in the case of the Vedic technique of Self-perfection which had become empty and hollow and even frightening to the Hindus of that period, Vyasa familiarised them with the tamer implication of the terms through the Bhagawad Geeta.

From this stanza onwards we have a slight hint upon the technique of *Karma Yoga* as explained in the Geeta. In the introduction we had already stated that the Second Chapter is almost a summary of the whole Geeta; later on, we shall see how the path of devotion also is in brief indicated in this very chapter. In this stanza we have Krishna's first direct statement on the technique of Self-Perfection and, as such, a very careful study of it must be extremely fruitful to all students of the Geeta.

The three pairs of opposites mentioned here fall distinctly as experiences at the three levels of our mortal existence. *Pain and pleasure* are the intellectual awareness of experiences unfavourable and favourable; *gain and loss* conceptions indicate the mental zone where we feel the joys of arrival and the sorrows of parting; and *conquest and defeat* indicate the physical fields wherein at the level of body we win ourselves or let others win over us. The advice that Krishna gives is that one must learn to keep oneself in equilibrium in all these different vicissitudes at the different levels of one's own existence.

If one were to enter the sea for a bath, one must know the art of sea-bathing or else the incessant waves will play rough on the person and may even take him off his feet and drag him into the bosom of a watery grave. But the one who knows the art of either saving himself — by ducking beneath the mighty waves or riding over the lesser ones — he alone can enjoy a sea-bath. To expect all the waves to end or to hope that the waves would not trouble one while he is in the sea is to order the sea to be something other than itself for one's convenience! This is exactly the folly man does in life. He expects his life to be without waves — and life is full of waves. Pain and pleasure, gain and loss, conquest and defeat must buffet the waters of life or else it is complete stagnation — it is death.

should be so, then we who have come to live life must know the art of living in it, unaffected by either the rising crests or the sinking troughs in it. To identify ourselves with any of them is to float on the surface and not to stand astride like a lighthouse on the bedrock of the very sea. Here Krishna advises Arjuna, while inviting him to fight, that he should enter the contest and keep himself unaffected by the usual dissipating mental tendencies that come to everyone while in activity. This equanimity of the mind alone can bring the beam of inspiration and give to your achievement the glow of real success.

It is very wellknown that in all activities inspired work gathers to itself a texture of divine perfection which cannot be imitated or oft-repeated. Be he a poet, or an artist, a doctor, or a speaker, irrespective of his profession, whenever an individual is at his best, his masterpiece is always accepted by all as a work of inspiration. When we thus work with the thrilled ecstasy of an unknown mood called 'inspiration', the idea, thought and activity that come out of us have a ringing beauty of their own which cannot be mechanically repeated by the very Creator. Thus Da Vinci could not repeat for a second time and copy on a different piece of canvas the enigmatic smile of his Mona Lisa; Keats' pen would no more recapture for a second time the song of the Nightingale in its flight; Beethoven could never again beat out of his faithful piano a second Moonlight Sonata; The Lord himself, when again after the war was requested by Arjuna to repeat the Geeta, admitted his inability to do so.

To the Western mind and understanding, inspiration is an accidental and mysterious happening over which the mortal has no control at all, while to the eastern Rishis inspired living is the real godly destiny of man when he lives in perfect unison with the Self in him. A balanced life wherein we live as an unaffected witness of even our own mind and intellect is the realm of self-forgetfulness where, instead of becoming inefficient, our profession gathers a scintillating glow of a new dawn. This extra aura in any achievement is that which raises an ordinary success to an inspired achievement.

The Yogis of the ancient Hindu lore discovered a technique whereby the mind and intellect can be thus unconsciously brought to a steadiness and poise, and this technique is called Yoga. The Hindus of the Vedic period knew it, practised it and lived to provide their country with their incomparable achievements, the golden era of the Hindus. The same idea is now reinterpreted here by Vyasa through Krishna's Song Divine, sung to his generation addressing a representative man of the time, the chivalrous Arjuna, the honoured prince of archers.

The philosophy of a country like India in the Vedic period must necessarily be Theistic, but it has its applications in all walks of life. If it fails in its all round application, it cannot be a philosophy. A theory of life which has no universal application can only be appreciated as a noble opinion of an individual which may have its own limited application, but it can never be accepted as a philosophy.

In the entire scheme of Bhagawan's arguments so far* he has provided Arjuna with all the necessary arguments which a healthy intellect should discover for itself before it can come to a reliable and a dependable judgement upon the outer happenings. A mere spiritual consideration is not the last word in evaluating the material situations. Every challenge is

* Chapter II, Verses 11-36.

to be estimated from the spiritual standpoint, from the intellectual stand point or reason, from the emotional level of ethics and morality, and from the physical level of tradition and custom. If all these considerations without any contradiction in themselves indicate a solitary truth, it is surely then the divine path of judgement that one should at all costs take up.

Arjuna came to this delusory miscalculation of the situation because he evaluated the war only from the level of his sentiments. The opposing forces were beaming with his own relations, and to kill and exterminate one's own cousins and uncles was indeed against the ethical point of view. But this emotionalism over-powered him and he could not discover any other data to check himself with, at this moment of his total inward chaos. He surrendered to Krishna as a mind should to the inner discriminative capacity. Therefore, the Lord, having accepted to guide Arjuna, provides him with all the available data gathered from the different points of view. Throughout the Geeta, Krishna plays the part of discriminative intellect in an individual — a true charioteer in the Upanishadic-sense of the term.

After placing thus for Arjuna's consideration all the possible points of view upon the problem — the spiritual, the intellectual, the ethical and the traditional — Krishna concluded in the earlier stanza that Arjuna must fight. In the stanza under review Krishna is trying to explain how he should fight the war with perfect detachment from all anxieties which generally come to an individual when he identifies himself with the non-Self *(anatma)* — at the level of his intellect with the concept of pain and pleasure, at the level of his mind with the fears of gain and loss, and at his body level with the restlessness of conquest and defeat.

Equanimity in all such mental challenges is a factor that ensures true success in life. Earlier we had already explained how the human mind is to be kept open, while at work in its given field of life, so that while living in the midst of life's battle it will get an exhaustion of the *vasanas* that are already there in it.* This purgation — catharsis of the soul — is the compelling purpose for which every living creature has arrived on the platform of manifested life. Viewed thus, each individual living creature — plant, animal or man — is but a bundle of *vasanas*.

Equanimity in the face of all situations, advised here, is the secret method of keeping the mind ever open for this outflow. When it gets clouded by the ego-sense and egoistic desires, then the outflow is choked, and new tendencies start flooding in. The ego is declared when an individual starts getting upset at all these pairs of opposites *(dwandwas)*, such as, joy and sorrow, etc. The attempt to keep equanimous is to act detached from the ego. Thus mental purification — *vasanas* — catharsis — is the benign result of real living and right action; and this is Yoga. This is explained later on in the Geeta in all detail as *Karma Yoga*.

The philosophical theory of Truth had been described already in the very opening of the Lord's message and, in order to drive home those conclusions into the practical mind of Arjuna, Lord Krishna gave the standpoint of the common man. Ultimately, he concluded that Arjuna must fight and he explained in what attitude he should fight. The practical side of religion is in living the philosophy one has understood.

---

* See Chapter I, General Introduction.

Hereafter, the scheme of the Geeta in this Chapter is to explain the techniques of living ultimately the Vedantic philosophy in and through Karma Yoga. Hence says the Lord :

एषा तेऽभिहिता सांख्ये बुद्धिर्योगे त्विमां श्रृणु ।
बुद्ध्या युक्तो यया पार्थ कर्मबन्धं प्रहास्यसि ॥ ३९ ॥

39. *eṣā te 'bhihitā sāṁkhye*
buddhir yoge tv imaṁ śṛṇu
buddhyā yukto yayā pārtha
karma-bandhaṁ prahāsyasi

एषा — this, ते — to thee, अभिहिता — (is) declared, सांख्ये— in Sankhya, बुद्धि — wisdom, योगे — in the Yoga, तु — indeed, इमाम् — this, श्रृणु — hear, बुद्ध्या — with wisdom, युक्तः — having known, यया — which, पार्थ — O Partha, कर्मबन्धम् — bondage of Karma, प्रहास्यसि— (you) shall cast off.

39. *This, which has been taught to thee, is wisdom concerning Sankhya. Now listen to the wisdom concerning Yoga, having known which, O Partha, you shall cast off the bonds of action.*

What have been taught so far constitute the wisdom *(buddhi)* concerning *Sankhya,* meaning, 'the logic of reasoning by which the true nature of Absolute Reality is comprehended'', which ends all sorrows rising from grief, attachment and the like. Here Bhagavan says that what had been so far told by him belongs to the Sankhya philosophy because it is human nature that no new idea given out on life will be accepted by another unless the recipient of the idea has got infinite faith in the giver of it. To Arjuna, Krishna was a cowherd boy, related to him through his wife. Familiarity breeds, if not contempt, at least a careless disregard, and in this mental attitude no declaration of Truth can go home to the faithless: Krishna, understanding this nature of man, here quotes his authority in declaring the philosophy of life in the above verses.

What has so far been said constitutes the philosophical theory and, Krishna promises that hereafter he will try to explain the technique of attaining the wisdom which is otherwise called Yoga — devotion through work. Naturally, a doubt here arises in the mind of Arjuna why he should after all practise this Yoga; for all practical, worldly-minded persons are indeed profit-seekers. In order to encourage Arjuna to listen to the technique of Self-perfection through right work and encourage him to live it, Bhagavan enumerates here the benefits that will accure to one who practises this 'Way of Life'.

In indicating the benefits of *Karma Yoga,* Bhagavan shrewdly estimates the immediate demands of Arjuna and points out to him that he will have all those particular demands satisfied. The problem in Arjuna's mind was that he would be incurring a great sin if he were to wage this was wherein he would be causing the death of so many of his kith and kin, teachers and patrons. Krishna says that he who practises this Yoga will get relieved from all bondages of *karma,* which is exactly that for which Arjuna's mind was thirsting.

Fruits of action *(karma-phala)* — The law of karma which is often misunderstood as the law of destiny, forms a very cardinal creed of the Hindus and a right understanding of it* is absolutely unavoidable to all students of the Hindu way of life. If I am justly punished for a crime committed by Sri Ramana Rao in Madras last year, then certainly there must be something common between the criminal Ramana Rao *then* in Madras and the saintly Chinmaya *now* in Delhi. The irrevocable law of the country must have slowly crept from Madras to Delhi discovering the identity of Ramana Rao in Chinmaya and must have ultimately booked the Swami for the crime of Rao.

Similarly, nature's justice is always perfect, and, therefore, if the Hindu philosophers accept that each of us individually suffers because of our crimes committed in another form and in a different locality at a different period of time in the past, certainly there must be some identity between the *sinner in the past* and the *sufferer in the present.* The identity, the Sastra says, is the mind-and-intellect equipment in each one of us.

Each act wilfully performed, according to the texture of motive entertained, leaves an impression upon the mind of the actor. In order to work out and remove these impressions — *vasanan*-catharsis — each individual arrives at his specific field of activity in life. Sin impressions in the mind can be wiped away only with the water of tears acting upon the mind in an atmosphere of sobs and sighs. Thus, every one gets his quota of chances to weep which, in many cases, come to be discovered later on as not so sorrowful after all. A mind which has thus been purified completely fails to see a situation worth weeping for. Weeping, in fact, is not ordered by the circumstances as much as demanded by the '*papa* tendencies' in the mind of the miserable.

---

* Refer Swamiji's *Discourses on Kathopanishad.*

Arjuna's fear was that by killing his elders and cousins he would be incurring such "impressions in his mind, for the removal of which he will have to enter fields of sorrow and sighs."* Krishna is here hinting at a truth that actions in themselves are neither good nor bad. This classification of merit and sin can come only with reference to the qualities of the motive and the mental attitude of the doer. In the earlier stanza Bhagavan advised Arjuna on what should be the mental attitude in fighting the battle of his life; keeping himself in perfect equipoise in all mental experiences, physical circumstances and intellectual agitations, fight on, was the instruction. To act in the field of the ture achievement is to act in such a way that no evil result can rise from them.

Merely because there is a gramophone record in my box, I will have no music. Even when it is placed on its disc and revolved with the required speed, the moving plate with the music record on it will not and cannot sing. Music can come out of it only when the needle is in contact with it. The unmanifested music in the plate can be brought to expression only through the sound box. Similarly, here the mental impressions cannot in themselves bring either disaster or reward unless they are connected with the external world through the needlepoint of our egocentric self-assertion.

One who lives, as we found in the earlier verse, in perfect equanimity in all conditions must necessarily come to live in a realm of his own, away from the pleasure and pain of the *intellect,* the fears of loss and gain of the *mind* and the sobs of success and failure of the *flesh.* To the degree an individual gets himself detached from the flesh, mind and intellect, to

* Note how often Arjuna had used the term sin *(papam),* Chapter I, Verses 36-45 and implied the very same idea in other verses throughout.

that degree the ego is dead, and, therefore, there cannot be any 'fruits of action' to be suffered since the sufferer is not available. Man Singh could not be brought to court, judged and punished with long-term imprisonment even if he deserved it because he was not available for cross-examinations and consequent punishment; he was dead in the encounter which ended in the police capturing his body.

Rightly understood, we shall realise during our discussions on this chapter how this theory of Krishna has not the novelty of an original idea. The more intimately we understand it, the more we shall realise that Krishna has but given a new vesture to an ancient idea. But due to this re-statement of a cardinal truth in ancient Hinduism in the Geeta, a religion that was dying revived itself. And from its days of origin, five thousand years before Christ was born, to even today, two thousand years after the Nazarene's death it has been beckoning us.

"Moreover" :

नेहाभिक्रमनाशोऽस्ति प्रत्यवायो न विद्यते ।
स्वल्पमप्यस्य धर्मस्य त्रायते महतो भयात् ॥ ४० ॥

40. *nehā 'bhikrama-nāśo' sti pratyavāyo na vidyate*
svalpam apy asya dharmasya trāyate mahato bhayāt

न — not, इह — in this, अभिक्रमनाशः — loss of the effort, अस्ति — is, प्रत्यवायः — production of contrary results, न — not, विद्यते — is, स्वल्पम् — very little, अपि — even, अस्य — of this, धर्मस्य — duty, त्रायते — protects, महतः — (from) great, भयात् — fear.

40. *In this there is no loss of effort, nor is there any harm*

(production of contrary results). Even a little of this knowledge, even a little practice of this Yoga, protects one from great fear.

Krishna is his own publicist. All his life nobody made him so great as he himself did. That gift for self-expression is abundantly clear here in the Geeta also. In driving home to Arjuna the Krishna-creed, the Lord uses subtle methods of emphasis much more deftly than any modern publicity consultant can ever plan for anyone. In the earlier stanza, He said that what He was going to say would release Arjuna from the bondage of his *karma* : in itself this is a sufficiently attractive bait for any seeker to jump at. Now, in this stanza, He is unveiling more and more alluring glories of his philosophy of action which He is to discourse upon.

In the Vedic period, *karma* (work) had only a limited meaning and comprised only the 'ritualistic action'. Vyasa here is trying to expand the Vedic implication to include in its purview every kindly act that a man may come to perform in this world. Students who are soaked in the Vedic tradition are very familiar with the dangers of Vedic ritualism. Unfinished ritualistic acts shall yield no fruit, just as ploughing is not fulfilled if the sequence of actions, such as ploughing, watering, sowing, weeding, guarding, harvesting, etc., is not kept. Similarly, some ritualistic acts, when not performed faithfully following all the strict injunctions, the chances are that the very same meritorious acts may result in sins, accrued through the non-performance of acts that are enjoyed or due to imperfect performance of enjoyed acts. This sin is called in the language of ritualistic literature a '*pratyavaya*'. In the material world also, we can find corresponding instances wherein a medicine misused may bring about a calamitous end to the patient.

These two are the dangers in the field of activities by which we are cheated of our expected results. Krishna here, as a pucca publicist of his own philosophy, vigorously asserts that his 'Path of Action' *Karma Yoga,* guarantees safety from these two main dangers in the life of action.

"The wisdom concerning Sankhya and Yoga thus far described is of the following nature":

व्यवसायात्मिका बुद्धिरेकेह कुरुनन्दन ।
बहुशाखा ह्यनन्ताश्च बुद्धयोऽव्यवसायिनाम् ॥ ४१ ॥

41. *vyavasāyātmikā buddhir ekeha kurunandana*
bahuśākhā hy anantāś ca buddhayo 'vyavasāyinām

व्यवसायात्मिका — one pointed, बुद्धिः — determination, एका — single, इह — here, कुरुनन्दन — O joy of the Kurus, बहुशाखा — many branched, हि — indeed, अनन्ताः — endless, च — and, बुद्धयः — thoughts, अव्यवसायिनाम् — of the irresolute.

41. *Here, O Joy of Kurus, there is a but a singel one-pointed determination; many-branched and endless are the thoughts of the irresolute.*

In *Karma Yoga,* which the Lord is now going to explain, even the highest achievement of Self-realisation is possible because then the man works with one resolute determination with a single-pointed mind. Those who perform actions labouring under endless desires for results get their inner personality disintegrated and, with a shattered, thousand pronged mind, they are not able to consistently apply themselves to any line of action; therefore, their endeavours invariably end in disastrous failure.

In this stanza lies the secret of Hindu success — hinted at briefly in hasty words. With a single pointed mind, if an individual can entertain any one resolute determination and act consistenly towards its success, certainly achievement must result. But invariably, man, victimised by his ego, entertains hundreds of desires, often self-contradictory and, therefore, comes to play upon these fields with an impoverished and exhausted mental strength : psychologically, what we call self-cancellation of thoughts. When this comes to plague the mental zone, it exhausts all the man's potentialities and loots away all his chances of success.* As a contrast to those who have a resolute purpose, Bhagavan places those who are always under the persecutions of unending desires.

The term *Karma Yoga* was very familiar to Arjuna as it was to his generation, and at that time by *Karma Yoga* was meant only the *Karma Kanda* of the Vedas which advised the various ritualistic performances. In order to show Arjuna that Krishna's intentions were not to expound the path of *karma* as adumbrated in the *Brahmana* portion of the Vedas, he is making a definite contrast between the *Purva-Mimamsakas* who believed in ritualism as the only path, and the true *Karma Yogis,* as the author of the Geeta conceives them to be. In the following stanzas we shall listen to the Lord's bitter criticism of the Vedic ritualism.

Krishna's *Karma Yoga,* as explained in the Geeta, is a path in which the seeker comes to entertain one single-pointed resolute idea and strives hard with all in him for its achievement, while in the *Karma Kanda,* the pursuer is ever riddled with unending desires for the fulfilment of which, as instructed in the Vedas, he performs the rituals. In each

* Refer Swamiji's *Discourses on Kathopanishad.*

particular ritual, they meditate upon the prescribed *Devata* — a special God's power — and they get more and more inwardly agitated even when they struggle hard in the field of their self-application. This idea is elaborately brought out in the following stanzas.

"As regards those who have no conviction of a resolute nature" :

यामिमां पुष्पितां वाचं प्रवदन्त्यविपश्चितः ।
वेदवादरताः पार्थ नान्यदस्तीति वादिनः ॥ ४२ ॥

42. *yām imam puspitām vācam pravadanty avipaścitaḥ*
veda-vāda-ratāh pārtha nānyadastiti vādinaḥ

याम् — which, इमाम् — this, पुष्पिताम् — flowery, वाचम् — speech, प्रवदन्ति — utter, अविपश्चित — the unwise, वेदवादरताः — taking pleasure in the eulogising words of the Vedas, पार्थ — O Partha, न — not, अन्यत् — other, अस्ति — is, इति — thus, वादिनः — saying.

42. *Flowery speech is uttered by the unwise, taking pleasure in the eulogising words of the Vedas, O Partha, saying, "There is nothing else".*

कामात्मानः स्वर्गपरा जन्मकर्मफलप्रदाम् ।
क्रियाविशेषबहुलां भोगैश्वर्यगतिं प्रति ॥ ४३ ॥

43. *kāmātmānaḥ svarga-parā janma-karma-phala-pradām*
kriya-visesa-bahulam bhagaisvaryā-gatim prati

कामात्मानः — full of desires, स्वर्गपराः — with heaven as their highest goal, जन्मकर्मफलप्रदाम् — leading to new births as a result of their works, क्रियाविशेषबहुलाम् — exuberant with various specific actions, भोगैश्वर्यगतिं प्रति — for the attainment of pleasure and Lordship.

43. *Full of desires, having heaven as their goal, they utter flowery words which promise new birth as the reward of their actions, and prescribe various specific actions for the attainment of pleasure and Lordship.*

भोगेश्वर्यप्रसक्तानां तयापहृतचेतसाम् ।
व्यवसायात्मिका बुद्धिः समाधौ न विधीयते ॥ ४४ ॥

44. *bhogaiśvarya-prasaktānāṁ tayāpahṛta-cetasām*
vyavasāyātmikā buddhiḥ samādhau na vidhiyate

भोगैश्चर्यप्रसक्तानाम् — of the people who cling to pleasure and Lordship, तया — by that, अपहृत चेतसाम् — whose minds are drawn away, व्यवसायात्मिका — determinate, बुद्धिः — reason, समाधौ — in Samadhi, न — not, विधीयते — is fixed.

44. *For, those who cling to joy and Lordship, whose minds are drawn away by such teaching, are neither determinate and resolute nor are they fit for study meditation and* Samadhi.

Vyasa was one of the first daring revolutionaries in Hinduism who ever came up to win back the Hindu culture from the forces of decadence into which it had fallen in his time. The Bible of the Revolution* that he created was the Geeta. Naturally, therefore, in the Geeta we find at places

* See Chapter 1, Verse 36.
See Swamiji's Introduction, *Discources on Aitareyopanishad.*
Refer Swamiji's *Discourses on Kathopanishad.*

direct attacks on the then existing vulgarities and misconceptions. Here, in these three stanzas, we find a daring, almost outrageous satire and open criticism of the extravagant indulgence in elaborate ritualism which had become, at the time of the *Mahabharata,* all show and no spirituality.

In the long unending history of Hinduism, we read repeatedly of great masters who had come to whip their generations out of the formalistic aspect of their religion to come on to an intelligent pursuit of an essentially unchanging technique of self-perfection. A few centuries ago, the Buddha came to cry down excessive ritualism and later on Sankara appeared to break the philosophy of mere ritualists. When Jewish ritualism became extremely formalistic and costly, a vast majority of the poor people could not be served by the same religion and, therefore, at that time we find the advent of Christ who openly declared that meek surrender through sincere love is more acceptable to the Father in Heaven than the elaborate rituals of the Pharisees. Indeed, only the son of Parasara, with the dexterity of a fisherwoman thrown into his composition, could have the self-confidence of his Self-Knowledge and the daring to express it against the national faith of the country in pure ritualism.

Vedic Culture falls into three distinct stages of development. And to serve the different layers of people, we have, in the very literature, three distinct types of texts, which fall under the titles, the *Mantras,* the *Brahmanas* and the *Upanishads*. Here the criticism is against the *Brahmanas* and it must be noticed that it is not an outright condemnation of the *Brahmana*-portion, but is only the condemnation of those who conceive this noble means as the very goal. In the *Brahmanas* we have innumerable descriptions of a variety of ritualism each one invoking one special power of the Lord, and elaborate promises are made for the performer as rewards for his actions. Thus, all those who have any special kind of wish for some particular kind of material gain or for some suprasensuous enjoyment can find the exact sacrifice that they are to perform so that they may be assured of its complete fulfilment.

Thus, the ritualistic portions of the Vedas address those who are deeply attached to pleasure and power and whose discriminative power — which in man explains to him the Real as distinguished from the un-Real — is stolen away by that portion of the Veda which explains the reward gained by the performer. The vigorous criticism felt by Vyasa is reflected in the words of Krishna when he characterises this portion of the Vedas as 'the flowery words of the unwise'. We have to mentally live the orthodox atmosphere of that age to understand the daring with which Vyasa must have come forward to put up this criticism so plainly.

These *karmas,* which promise for the performer a post-mortem heavenly existence with supra-sensuous carnal pleasures, are to be undertaken and laboriously pursued. In all these activities, man's inner personality has no time or chance to get integrated and evolved, and, therefore, from the spiritual standpoint of Vyasa, they are impotent methods of religion; naturally Krishna voices the author's own ideas.

Historically viewed, Veda Vyasa was the godfather of Vedanta. He introduced the Vedanta theory *(Uttara Mimamsa)* to the children of the Aryans who had by then forgotten the wondrous culture of knowledge *(gyana)* and God-realisation *(Iswara Darsan)* which the Rishis had recorded for the guidance of their followers. The *Brahma Sutra* is the great work of the son of Parasara wherein he liquidated all the seeming contradictions in the Upanishadic declarations, and established the theory of Self-realisation through right understanding and full intuitive apprehension of the Self.

Thus, as an expounder of the Transcendental and the Infinite, he is here laughing at those who mistake the means for the goal; the ritualistic portion if the means and Vedantic realisation through meditation is the end. The elaborate rituals *Karma kanda* prepare the mind to single-pointedness when they are pursued without specific desires *(niskama)* and such a prepared mind is fit for steady contemplation on the Upanishadic declarations.

The passage is concluded with the declaration that such persons tossed by their desires shall never discover any experience of tranquillity in their inner life.

"The Lord now speaks of the result accruing to those lustful persons who are thus wanting in discrimination" :

त्रैगुण्यविषया वेदा निस्त्रैगुण्यो भवार्जुन ।
निर्द्वन्द्वो नित्यसत्त्वस्थो निर्योगक्षेम आत्मवान् ॥ ४५ ॥

45. *traiguṇya-viṣayā vedā nistraiguṇyo bhavārjuna*
nirdvāndvo nitya-sattva-stho niryoga-kṣema ātmavān

त्रैगुण्यविषयाः — deal with the three attributes, वेदाः— the Vedas, निस्त्रैगुण्यः— without these three attributes, भव — be, अर्जुन — O Arjuna, निर्द्वन्द्वः– free from the pairs of opposites, नित्यसत्त्वस्थः— ever remaining in the *sattva* (goodness), निर्योगक्षेमः— free from (the thought of) acquisition and preservation, आत्मवान् — established in the Self.

45. *The Vedas deal with the three attributes; be you above these three attributes* (gunas). *O Arjuna, free yourself, from the pairs of opposites, and ever remain in the* sattva *(goodness), freed from all thoughts of acquisition and preservation and be established in the Self.*

Here, in this stanza, by the term Veda we must understand it to mean only the *Brahmana* portion of the Vedas no doubt, even the *Upanishad* portion explains but the finite realm of the three *gunas,* but passages in the Upanishads pant to indicate to the sincere students the Eternal that lies beyond the finite. After indicating the impotency of a mere blind obedience to the *Karma kanda* in the previous passages, Lord Krishna here is advising Arjuna — a representative of the 'evolvers' in the community of man — to transcend himself the triad of the *gunas.**

The three inseparable *gunas* always remain in the inner constitution of every living creature in varying proportions. The mind and intellect are constituted of this stuff. To go beyond these three temperaments is to literally go beyond the mind. If there is an alloy constituted of copper, zinc and tin, and a pot is made of that alloy, then to remove all tin, zinc and copper from the pot is to destroy the pot completely. Tea is made of hot water, tea leaves, sugar and milk; and from a cup of tea if you are asked to remove these four aspects of it, it amounts to saying : empty the cup. In the direct language of the Upanishads, man has been advised to transcend the mind and intellect, and they promise that individual shall thereby rediscover himself to be God. This direct explanation came to frighten away the Hindu folk out of the Aryan fold; and, here,

* See Swamiji's *Discourses on Kenopanishad* Introduction : 'Fall and Rise of Man'.

the Call of the Renaissance also means the same but puts it in different words when it says : 'Arjuna, transcend the *gunas*'.

If a doctor were to prescribe a medicine which is nowhere in the catalogue of any pharmaceutical company in the world and naturally, therefore, not available in any bazaar round the globe, that prescription is certainly useless. Similarly, it may be a prescription for Self-perfection when the Lord advises : "Be free from the triad of the *gunas*." If the student is practical minded and adventurous enough to try to live this advice, certainly he must be instructed on how he can go beyond these instinctive temperaments in man : unactivity *(sattwa)*, activity *(rajas)*, and inactivity *(tamas)*.

The second line in the stanza gives us a very practical and direct method of transporting ourselves luxuriously from the realm of imperfection to the boundless regions of bliss and beatitude. Earlier Krishna had indicated how Arjuna should enter the field and wage the war. The same mental equanimity is being advised here in a different language.

Pairs-of-opposites are the experiences in our life of joy and sorrow, health and disease, success and failure, heat and cold, etc. Each one of them can be experienced and known only with reference to, and as a contrast with, its opposite. Therefore, the term pairs-of-opposites *(dwandwas)* envisages in its all-comprehensive meaning all the experiences of man in life. Krishna advises Arjuna to be free from all pairs-of-opposites.

'*Nitya-sattwa-stha*' — Ever pure. The purity, the subtlest of the three *gunas*, often becomes impure by its contact with attachments and consequent agitations *(rajas)*, and the delusion and grief that attack the intellect and veil it from the right cognition of the real nature of things *(tamas)*. To be established in purity *(sattwa)* would naturally, therefore, mean to keep ourselves least agitated and, therefore, least deluded in our perceptions of things and beings, and in our estimation of their true nature.

Yoga and *Kshema* in their meaning include all the activities of every living being on the face of the universe. These are the two urges which goad every one in all their activities. *Yoga* means 'to acquire' for purposes of possessing them; and '*Kshema*' means all efforts at preserving the acquired'. Thus the two terms *Yoga* and *Kshema* indicate all our ego-centric activities motivated by selfish desires to acquire and, compelled by equally selfish wishes, to hoard and preserve what have been acquired. To renounce these two temperaments is to immediately get away from the two main fields that yield the poisonous harvest of extreme restlessness and sorrow in life.

These ideas should not be misunderstood and misinterpreted to mean that we as Hindus should not strive to better our conditions and diligently guard our national wealth, both secular and spiritual. Misreading our scriptures, we have ourselves perpetrated many a sad crime against our own national responsibilities and social duties. A superficial study of this stanza may give us a delusory concept that Hinduism, 'a religion of the coward for the coward, given out by a coward'! But historically, it is clear that this assumption is a big lie. For, as I said earlier, the Geeta is to be read against the background of its first chapter. If these terms in this chapter, called *Sankhya Yoga* are to be understood properly, we must not forget that these were given out as an advice to — Arjuna a great hero, on the battlefield, in order to redeem his potentialities from the muddy morass of dejection and despair into which they had fallen and sunk.

It may be easy for a spiritual master to advise an aspirant to be "free from the pairs-of-opposites, ever pure and free from the natural appetites for acquisition and greed for preservation". But the philosophy can be practical only when the seeker is advised how he can do so. This 'how' of it all has been indicated by the last word in the stanza : *Atmavan* — 'be established in the Self. The persecutions of the pairs-of-opposites, the instinct to be impure, the desire to possess and the anxiety to preserve, all belong to the ego-centre which is born when the Self identifies with the not-Self. Identifying with the body, mind and intellect the ego suffers the above explained pangs, anxieties, pains and sorrows.

To get ourselves detached from these by keeping a constant sense of awareness of our pure, divine nature is the path shown in the Geeta. Established in the Self, the individual ego finds itself beyond the experiences of the world, ever pure and free from all anxieties. Necessarily, he will be trans-*gunas*. One who is beyond the *gunas* has no more use for the Veda books — he is the master thereafter to amend the Vedas or to add to it; he is the master who shall give the Divine sanction to the very Vedic declarations.

Perhaps there was — and it was but natural — a look of staggering surprise in Arjuna's face. How dare Krishna thus make a Shivian statement upon the sacred Vedas, the eternal Sacred Book of the Hindus? Can the Lord justify his statement? Or is it only a bluff? Who is there who can go beyond the divine text of the Vedas?

"If all those endless profits which are said to result from the Vedic rituals are not to be sought after, to what end are they to be performed and dedicated to Iswara — Listen to what follows" :

यावानर्थ उदपाने सर्वतः संप्लुतोदके ।
तावान्सर्वेषु वेदेषु ब्राह्मणस्य विजानतः ॥ ४६ ॥

46. *yāvān artha udapāne sarvataḥ samplutodake*
tāvān sarveṣu vedeṣu brāhmaṇasya vijānataḥ

यावान् — as much, अर्थ — use, उदपाने — in a reservoir, सर्वतः — everywhere, संप्लुतोदके — being flooded, तावान् — so much (use), सर्वेषु — in all, वेदेषु — in the Vedas, ब्राह्मणस्य — of the Brahmana, विजानतः — of the knowing.

46. *To the Brahmana who has known the Self, all the Vedas are of as much use as is a reservoir of water in a place where there is flood everywhere.*

The meaning of this verse is obscure, and it is much disputed over, as the Sanskrit prose order, when translated, reads as a very incomplete sentence. A literal translation, in the sequence of the prose order, reads as : "Everywhere being flooded in a reservoir as much use of the knowing *Brahmana* in all the Vedas so much". It is evidently clear, therefore, that we have to complete it with words supplied; and each commentator has his own way of explaining it.

Of them the most acceptable seems to be Sankara's interpretation which says : "For the truly enlightened *Brahmana,** the utility of the Vedic ritual is comprehended in the right knowledge *(Gyana)* just as the utility of the tank is comprehended in that of the all-spreading flood of water." It is a wonderful simile that is used here, fully applicable in the context in which it is used. So long as there is no flood, every one from the vicinity will have to reach the well to collect

* Read Swamiji's *Talks on Vivekachudamani,* Verses 6 and 7.

drinking water, although everywhere there is a vein of water running but separated from us by the crust of the earth. Similarly, for the ordinary seeker, Veda is the only source of True knowledge, and every one necessarily must go to the Sacred Book for knowledge. But when the area is flooded, the wells and the tanks have disappeared in the spread of the flood and drowned yards deep below the surface, at that time the reservoir of water which used to be of service becomes comprehended in the span of water that lies spread all round.

Similarly, the Vedas, meaning here the ritualistic portion which promises fulfilment of all our various desires, can be useful only so long as the individual is riddled with delusory desires for sensuous satisfactions. However, in the case of a sincere student and seeker *(Brahmana),* when he 'comes to experience the Self' *(vijanatah),* to him these ritualistic portions of the Vedas become useless inasmuch as the benefits that they can give are comprehended in the perfection that he has come to live.

After all, the *Karma kanda* prescribes rituals for the satisfaction of desires whereby the individual can gain some finite joy, may be here or in the hereafter. Thus, on discovering the Self in oneself, the seeker comes to experience the infinite bliss of the Divine and all the pleasures derived from the performance of work enjoined in the Vedas are comprehended in the bliss which the realized soul discovers as the very essence of his own Self. Everyone must admit that all those limited satisfactions — experiences — are comprehended in the Infinite bliss of Self-experience.

This does not mean that Vyasa is ignoring or ridiculing the *Karma kanda* of the Vedas as such. The whip of the Cowherd Boy is descending upon the bare backs of the unintelligent who have mistaken the means for the goal and consider that through ritualism the Supreme and the Infinite can be gained.* *Karma,* when undertaken with no anxiety for the results, integrates the personality. When a heart is thus purified, a clearer discriminative power comes to play through it, and in its light Truth becomes clearly self-evident. Once having realised the Infinite Self spreading out all round without dimension or frontiers, thereafter the limited satisfaction promised by ritualism has no more chance to the man of Knowledge, the Self-realized.

The knowledge Veda indicates is comprehended in Pure Knowledge, which is the nature of the Self. So long as the ego exists it craves for the blessings, of the Vedas; when the ego has ended, the Self in Its Infinite divinity is capable of blessing even the Veda. A student of mathematics, having successfully passed his post-graduate course, need not read the arithmetic table since his present knowledge comprehends this elementary study.

"And as for you" :

कर्मण्येवाधिकारस्ते मा फलेषु कदाचन ।
मा कर्मफलहेतुर्भूर्मा ते सङ्गोऽस्त्वकर्मणि ॥ ४७ ॥

47. *karmany evādhikāras te mā phaleṣu kadācana*
mā karma-phala-hetur bhūr mā te sango 'stv akarmaṇi

कर्मणि — in work, एव — only, अधिकारः — right, ते — they, मा — not, फलेषु — in the fruits, कदाचन — at any time,

---

* Read Swamiji's *Talks on Vivekachudamani,* Verse 11.
Read Swamiji's *Talks on Vivekachudamani,* Verse 56.
Read Swamiji's *Talks on Vivekachudamani,* Verse 59.

मा — not, कर्मफलहेतुर्भूः— let not the fruits of action be thy motive. मा — not, ते — thy, सङ्गः — attachment, अस्तु— let (there) be, अकर्मणि — in inaction.

47. *Thy right is to work only; but never to its fruits; let not the fruit of action be thy motive, nor let thy attachment be to inaction.*

In the last two stanzas Bhagavan showed his great friend the Goal that is to be reached which lies beyond the arena of the Vedas. In and through *karma,* intelligently pursued, a man is to grow and fulfil his evolution and identify himself with his own real nature — the Self. But the charioteer of Arjuna knew him very well, and, therefore, the Lord now explains the path by which the Supreme Goal can be reached by the Pandavas.

The traditional belief of Hinduism — the theory that single pointed *karma* without desire for the fruits shall bring about inner purification, which is a necessary condition precedent to the spiritual awakening — has not yet been shaken at all by the Geeta. The Geeta only expands this idea to incorporate in it all activities in social and personal life; while in the Vedas, *karma* meant only the religious and the ritualistic activities.

Philosophy is not a theme that can be rightly understood by hasty students. The stanza now under review, when not properly understood, would seem to indicate an impossible method. At best it would look as religious sanction for the poor to continue to be poor and a sacred permission for the rich to continue tyrannising over the poor. To do our duties in life without any expectation of results would seem to be almost impossible to the one who is trying to understand the stanza through his imagination. But when the same individual, after his studies, walks out into the open fields of his life and there tries to practise them, he shall discover that this is the very secret of real achievement.

Earlier we had indicated how Krishna, through his *Karma Yoga,* was showing the art of living and acting in an ordered spirit of divine inspiration. Here also we shall find, as we tussle with this idea in our attempt to digest this, that Krishna is advising Arjuna upon the secret art of living an inspired life.

Wrong imagination is the bane of life and all failures in life can be directly traced to have risen from an impoverished mental equanimity generally created by the unintelligent entertainment of expected fears for the possible failures. Almost all of us refuse to undertake great activities fearing failures that might happen, and even those who dare to undertake noble endeavours invariably become nervous ere they finish it, again due to their inward dissipation. Avoid such wasteful expenditure of mental energy, work with the best that is in us, all dedicated to the noble cause of the work undertaken, is the secret prescription for work in high inspiration; and such work must always end in brilliant success. That is the eternal law of activity in the world.

The future is carved out in the present moment : tomorrow's harvest depends upon today's ploughing and sowing. But, in the fear of possible dangers to the crops, if a farmer wastes his present chances of ploughing sufficiently and sowing at right time, it is guaranteed that he shall not have any harvest at all to gather in the end. The present moments are to be invested intelligently and well so that we may reap better times in the future. The past is dead; the future is not yet born.

If one becomes unhealthy and inefficient in the present, certainly he has no reason to hope for a greater future.

This fundamental truth, very well known and easily comprehended by all, is applied here and, in the language of the Geeta, "If success you seek, then never strive with a mind dissipated with anxieties and fears for the fruits." In this connection it is very interesting to dissect carefully and discover exactly what the Sastra means when it says 'fruits of action'. In fact, the reward of an action, when we understand it properly, is not anything different from the action itself. An action of the *present* when conditioned by a future time, appears itself as the fruit of the action. In fact, the action ends or fulfils itself only in its reaction, and the reaction is not anything different from the action; an action of the present defined in terms of a future moment is its reaction. Therefore, to worry over and get ourselves preoccupied with the anxieties for the rewards of actions is to escape ourselves from the present and to live in a future that is not yet born.

We have already found that achievements are carved out in the present; to get ourselves, therefore, agitated over the 'fruits of the actions' is to escape the present and to live ourselves in the dream-land of the future which is yet unborn! In short, the Lord's advice here is a call to man not to waste his present moments in fruitless dreams and fears, but to bring his best — all the best in him — to the present and live vitally every moment. And the promise is that the future shall take care of itself and provide the *Karma Yogi* with the achievement divine and accomplishment supreme. When this scientific truth is put in the language of the Geeta we have the verse now we are trying to explain. Arjuna is advised that all that is given to you is to act and having known the cause of action to be a noble intention, bring into the activity all that is best in you and forget yourself in the activity. Such inspired action is sure to bear fruit and immediately it is its own reward.

The stanza gives the four injunction guiding us to a true worker. A real *Karma Yogi* is one who understands *(a)* that his concern is with action alone; *(b)* that he has no concern with results; *(c)* that he should not entertain the motive of gaining a fixed fruit for a given action and *(d)* that the above said ideas do not mean that he should sit back courting inaction. In short, the advice is to make the worker release himself from all his mental preoccupations and, through work, make him live in the joy and ecstasy of a divine self-forgetfulness. The work itself is his reward : he gets himself drunk with the joy and satisfaction of a noble work done.

By acting thus readily to all external challenges one can find peace easily, and a bosom thus purged of its existing *vasana*-bondages is, to that extent, considered better purified for the purposes of meditation and the final Vedantic realisation of the Infinite glory of the Self.

"If a man should not perform work urged by desires for their result, how then is it to be performed? The reply follows" :

योगस्थः कुरु कर्माणि सङ्गं त्यक्त्वा धनंजय ।
सिद्ध्यसिद्ध्योः समो भूत्वा समत्वं योग उच्यते ॥ ४८ ॥

48. *yoga-sthaḥ kuru karmaṇi saṅgaṁ tyaktvā dhanaṁjaya*
siddhy-asiddhayoḥ samo bhūtvā samatvaṁ yoga ucyate

योगस्थः — steadfast in Yoga, कुरु — perform, कर्माणि — action, सङ्ग — attachment, त्यक्त्वा — having abandoned, धनंजय — O Dhananjaya, सिद्ध्यसिद्ध्योः — in success and failure,

समः — the same, भूत्वा — having become, समत्वम् — evenness of mind, योगः — Yoga, उच्यते — is called.

48. *Perform action, O Dhananjaya, being steadfast in Yoga, abandoning attachment and balanced in success and failure. Evenness of mind is called Yoga.*

From this stanza onwards we shall have an exhaustive discussion of the technique of *Karma Yoga* as conceived by Krishna in his Doctrine of Action and expounded by Vyasa's Geeta. A complete technique of how one can live the life of a true inspired worker is explained here, and to any careful student who understands all the implications of the terms, it must be clear that a complete effacement of individuality and its vanities is to be achieved in this path for success; and this is gained also by practising the equipoise mentioned in the previous stanzas.

In this stanza, for the first time, the term *Yoga* has been used in the context of the evenness of mind through work, and in the very same stanza, before it concludes, we get an exhaustive definition too of the term *Yoga* as used here. 'Evenness of mind', tranquillity or mental composure in all paris-of-opposites*, is defined here as *Yoga.* Defined thus, the term *Yoga,* as used here, indicates a special condition of the mind in which it comes to a neutral equilibrium in all the ebb and flow of life's tides. The instructions in the stanza advise us that desireless action can be performed only when one gets completely established in *Yoga,* where the term means, precisely what Vyasa defines it to mean here.

Not only is it sufficient that a true workers should act in

* As indicated in Verse 38.

the world established in equipoise and equanimity, but he should also reinforce this poise amidst the changes of the world through a renunciation of his attachment *(asangh)*. Innumerable commentators hastily enter this stanza and leave this portion almost unexplained. They leave the idea raw to the reader and their commentary on this 'non-attachment' remains ever incomplete for a seeker. We shall try to enquire into the attachment mentioned here which a seeker should renounce so that he may become more efficient in performing inspired activities. To all sincere students who have so far followed the Lord's words, it should be clear that the non-attachment advised here is exactly the same as that against which Krishna had already warned in the earlier stanzas and insisted that we must renounce them : wrong imaginations, false expectations, daydreams about the fruits of actions, anxieties for the results, and fears for the future calamities that have not yet appeared to threaten our life. When it is put thus as a list of mistakes to be avoided, any ture *Karma Yogi* striving upon the path of *Yoga* should find it impossible to practise it. But when we analyse this further with our understanding of the Upanishads, we shall easily solvc the riddle.

All the above nerve-racking mistakes belong to the delusory ego-centre. When we analysc closely the stuff with which the ego is made, we can easily find that it is a bundle of memories of the past and hopes and expectations for the future. The past are dead moments that are no more to be ours; the future is yet unborn and does not yet belong to us now. To live in the ego and expect fruits of future is to live either on the burial grounds of dead moments or in the womb of time where the unborn future today rests. In all these preoccupations we are losing the immediate moments given to us to act, to strive, to earn and to achieve. It is this unintelligent squandering of the wealth of the present chances through our broodings and imaginations that is hinted at here by the genius of Vyasa when he said, "Act, established in equanimity abandoning attachment."

Thus, incomplete self-forgetfulness to get ourselves intoxicated with the activities undertaken in the present, is to live the immediate moments vitally, fully and entirely with all best that is in us. To dissolve ourselves thus — our past, our future, our hopes, our fears — into the fiery contents of the *present* is to work in inspiration. And inspired work ever guarantees the greatest returns.

An Artist who is at work, forgetting himself in the very joyous ecstasy of his work, is an example of what we have said above. One need not even be a great artist. And an artist, working interestedly with all his mind and intellect on a piece of work, will not be able to recognise immediately any chance intruder and will not be able to answer even the visitor's enquiries about his personal identity or his beloved belongings in life. It would take time for the artist to come down from the realms of his joyous mood and to the crystallisation of an ego in him to recognise the intruder, understand his enquiry, and give him an intelligent answer. In all inspired activity, the worker forgets himself in the work that he is doing.

In all such activities, when the worker has gained almost a self-forgetfulness, he will not care for the success or failure of his activity because to worry for the results is to worry for the future moment, and to live in the future is not to live in the present. Inspiration is the joyous content of thrilled ecstasy of each immediate moment. It is said that the content of a moment in itself is the entire Infinite Bliss.

Established thus in equanimity, renouncing all egocentric attachments, forgetting to worry over the results of success or failure in the activities, act on, says Krishna to Arjuna. And he adds that the great *Yoga* is to work thus with equipoise in all situations.

"In comparison with action thus performed with evenness of mind" :

दूरेण ह्यवरं कर्म बुद्धियोगाद्धनंजय ।
बुद्धौ शरणमन्विच्छ कृपणाः फलहेतवः ॥ ४९ ॥

49. *dūreṇa hy avaraṁ karma buddhi-yogād dhanaṁjaya*
buddhau saraṇam anviccha kṛpaṇaḥ phala-hetavaḥ

दूरेण — by far, हि — indeed, अवरम् — inferior, कर्म — action of work, बुद्धियोगात् — than the Yoga of wisdom, धनंजय - O Dhananjaya, बुद्धौ — in wisdom, शरणम् — refuge, अन्विच्छ - seek, कृपणाः — wretched, फलहेतवः — seekers after fruits.

49. *Far lower than the Yoga of wisdom is action O Dhananjaya. Seek thou refuge in wisdom; wretched are they whose motive is the fruit.*

Work done with a mind undisturbed by the anxieties for the results is indeed superior to the work done by a dissipated mind ever worrying over the results. Here the term used, *'Buddhi Yoga'* has tickled some commentators to discover in it a specific *Yoga* advised by the Geeta. I personally think that it is too much of a laboured theory. *Buddhi,* as defined in the Upanishad, is a determining factor in the inner equipment. *Nischayatmika* is intellect; *samsayatmika* is mind. Thus, when thoughts are in a state of flux and agitated, it is called the mind; and when it is single pointed, calm and serene in its own determination, it is the intellect. Thus *Buddhi Yoga* becomes 'established in the devotion to intellect.' Steady in your conviction, your mind perfectly under the control of your better discriminative intellect, to live a master of your inner and outer work is called *Buddhi Yoga.* Earlier we had mentioned how Vyasa is trying to remove the sense of strange unfamiliarity with the Vedic concept term of Yoga from the bosom of the people. Here he is contributing a new term : *Buddhi Yoga.*

Analysing the meaning of the stanza in terms of what we have already seen regarding the split personality and its cure through *vasana*-purgation* we may interpret *Buddhi Yoga* as an individual's attempt to live and act from the zone of the intellect which controls freely and steadily receives faithful obedience from the mind. The attempt of the mind to work in unison with the intellect, *i.e.,* the objective mind working under control and order of the subjective mind, is called *Buddhi Yoga.* By so doing, instead of incurring more and more liabilities of new *vasana*-bondages, the individual gains a release from the existing mental congestion created by the existing *vasanas.* Thus, when an individual ego surrenders itself completely, it is called 'established in Buddhi Yoga'. Hence it is said : 'Seek refuge in Buddhi' : let your mind be perfectly under the control and direction of the intellect.

There is a solid reason why we should live under the control of the intellect because those who are living in the mental zone tossed by the mind's agitations are those who get themselves perturbed by fears for the fruits of action. Such people are termed here as 'wretched'. It is a powerful statement in which Vyasa condemns such thoughtless, unintelligent crowd : "Wretched are they who act for the results." Understood properly, this is a wonderful guidance for us

---

* See Chapter I, General Introduction, Diagrams A and B.

following which we can totally eliminate all failures in life. Efficient activity in the present shall order true results.

They are 'wretched' because they will be, in their desire prompted activities, incurring new *vasanas* and thus thicken the veil of ignorance of their own glorious divinity. Unselfish work performed in a spirit of dedication and egoless surrender is the secret method of exhausting our *vasana*-store. Such a mind alone, purged clean, reflect the Self clearly and come to discover the eternal Godhood.

"Now learn as to what result he attains who performs his own duty with evenness of mind" :

बुद्धियुक्तो जहातीह उभे सुकृतदुष्कृते ।
तस्माद्योगाय युज्यस्व योगः कर्मसु कौशलम् ॥ ५० ॥

50. *buddhi-yukto jahātiha ubhe sukrta-duṣkṛte*
tasmād yogāya yujyasva yogaḥ karmasu kauśalam

बुद्धियुक्तो — endowed with wisdom, जहाति — casts off, इह — in this life, उभे — both, सुकृतदुष्कृते — good and evil deeds, तस्मात् — therefore, योगाय — to Yoga, युज्यस्व — devote thyself, योगः — Yoga, कर्मसु — in actions, कौशलम् — skill.

50. *Endowed with wisdom, evenness of mind, one casts off in this life both good deeds and evil deeds; therefore, devote thyself to Yoga; Yoga is skill in action.*

One who is established in evenness of temper — through his perfect withdrawal from the realm of sentiments and emotions — and who is established in his resolute intellect, gets himself transported from the arena of both good and bad, merit and demerit. The conception of good and bad is essentially of the mind, and the reactions of merit and demerit are left on the mental composition in the form of *vasanas* or *samskaras*. One who is not identifying with the stormy area of the mind is not thrown up or sunk down in the ruts of *vasanas*. This idea is explained here by the term *Buddhi yuktah*.

The Geeta, throughout this section, is sincerely making a call to man not to live on the outskirts of his personality which are constituted by the words of sense-objects, the physical body and the mind, but to enter into the realm of the intellect from there to assert his natural manliness. Man is the supreme-most creature in the kingdom of the living because of his rational capacities in his discriminative intellect. So long as man does not assert this special equipment in him, he has not, in his personality, come to claim his heritage as man.

Arjuna was asked by Krishna not to be a vain hysterical person as he exhibited himself, but to be a man and, therefore, ever a master in all external situations. The great hero, Arjuna, became so frail and weak because he started living in a delusory identification with the individual personalities manning the opposing army, with his own physical security and with his emotional attachments. Such men are not marked out for any great achievement in life. One who lives constantly asserting his full evolutionary status as a man becomes free from the chains and bondages of past impressions which he must have gathered in his pilgrimage through his different embodiments.

"Therefore, apply yourself," advises Krishna, "to the devotion of action, *Yoga*". In this context, again Vyasa is giving a definition of *Yoga* as he means it here. Earlier he had already explained* that "Evenness of mind is *Yoga*." Now he

* See Verse 48.

rewrites the same definition more comprehensively and says : "*Yoga* is dexterity in action."

In a science book, if in every chapter the very same term is defined differently, it would bring about confusion in its understanding. Then how is it that in the science of religion we find different definitions of the same term ? This riddle gets itself solved as soon as we try to understand the definition intimately. The earlier definition is being incorporated in the latter one, for the true dexterity of *Yoga* may be misunderstood as a more 'evenness of mind' producing inaction and slothfulness. Here, in this definition, that misunderstanding is pointedly removed, and thus *Karma Yoga,* as indicated in the all-comprehensive meaning implied herein, is that art of working with perfect mental equilibrium in all the different conditions indicated by the term 'pairs-of-opposites' *(dwandwas).*

After dissecting this stanza thus, we come to understand what exactly is the Lord's intention. When *Yoga* 'the art of working without desire,' is pursued, the *Karma Yogi* becomes detached from all the existing *vasanas* in himself, both good and bad. It is the *vasana*-pressure in the individual that causes the restlessness within. The inner equipment that has thereby become peaceful and serene is called the pure *antah karana* which is an unavoidable prerequisite for consistent discriminative self-application in meditation.

Evidently, we have here yet another example of Vyasa using the frightening word *Yoga* in a tamer context in order to make the society feel at ease with it.

"Why should we cultivate this evenness of mind and the consequent dexterity in action" :

कर्मजं बुद्धियुक्ता हि फलं त्यक्त्वा मनीषिणः ।
जन्मबन्धविनिर्मुक्ताः पदं गच्छन्त्यनामयम् ॥ ५१ ॥

51. *karma-jaṁ buddhi-yuktā hi*
phalam tyaktvā manīṣiṇaḥ
janma-bandha-vinirmuktāḥ
padaṁ gacchanty anāmayam

कर्मजम् — action born, बुद्धियुक्ताः — possessed of knowledge, हि — indeed, फलम् — the fruit, त्यक्त्वा — having abandoned, मनीषिणः — the wise, जन्मबन्धविनिर्मुक्ताः — freed from the fetters of birth, पदम् — the abode, गच्छन्ति — go, अनामयम् — beyond evil.

51. *The wise, possessed of knowledge, having abandoned the fruits of their actions and freed from the fetters of birth, go to the state which is beyond all evil.*

Being a man of action, extremely intelligent — and having not yet developed any blind faith in Lord Krishna's divine potentialities — Arjuna still questions mentally, and the Lord, anticipating his doubt, explains here why a true man of devotion to work should act, and with perfect evenness of mind strive to achieve. The wise, meaning, those who know the art of true living, undertake all work, maintaining in themselves the full evenness of the mind, and thus abandon all anxieties for the fruits of their actions. These two conditions under which the wise work bring out fully the picture of an entity who acts renouncing both ego and ego-motivated desires.

Identifying with the agitations of the mind, the ego is born, and the ego so born gets riddled with desires as it gets anxious over the fruits of its actions. When one works thus with neither ego nor desires, one gets one's *vasana*-purgation. It is the mental-impressions in us that shoot the subtle body from one embodiment to another, and when the existing *vasanas* have ended *i.e.*, when we get completely relieved from both the ego and the ego-prompted desires, that entity can no longer have any occasion to take to another embodiment.

An individual minus his ego is the Self and, therefore, rid of the ego, the *Karma Yogi,* it is hoped, may reach, theoretically at least, that state beyond all sorrows. But it has been made clear by Sankara in all his works that mere *karma,* however noble and perfect it may be, cannot give us the Eternal and Immortal*. But here, in a spirit of forecast, it is said : "A *Karma Yogi* will go to that state which is beyond all evils." In sequence, selfless actions purify the mind and prepare the individual for higher meditations through which ultimately he discovers himself to be the Self 'which lies beyond all evil'.

"When is that conviction attained, which arises as soon as the mind is purified by Karma Yoga or devotion to work? The answer follows" :

यदा ते मोहकलिलं बुद्धिर्व्यतितरिष्यति ।
तदा गन्तासि निर्वेदं श्रोतव्यस्य श्रुतस्य च ॥ ५२ ॥

52. *yadā te moha-kalilaṁ buddhir vyatitariṣyati*
tadā gantasi nirvedaṁ śrotavyasya śrutasya ca

यदा — when, ते — thy, मोहकलिलम् — mire of delusion, बुद्धिः — intellect, व्यतितरिष्यति — crosses beyond, तदा —

* See Swamiji's *Talks on Vivekachudamani,* Verses 6, 7, 11, etc.

then, गन्तासि — you shall attain, निर्वेदम् — to indifference, श्रोतव्यस्य — of what has to be heard, श्रुतस्य — what has been heard, च — and.

52. *When your intellect crosses beyond the mire of delusion, then you shall attain to indifference as to what has been heard and what has yet to be heard.*

When the intellect crosses over the morass of delusion, when the intellect sloghs off its delusions, the stanza here assures Arjuna that his intellect shall develop a disgust "for all that are actually heard and that are yet to be heard." Here the term 'what is yet to be heard' must be understood as a representative word standing for all sense-organ experiences that are yet to be experienced. Naturally therefore, when the intellect becomes purer, it should then lose all its present charms for the sense-experiences — what it had before, and what it may gain in the future.

Essentially godly and divine, spiritual consciousness seems to fall under a self-delusion which, when analysed, becomes perfectly evident as to its effects. This cause of delusion is conceived of as the indescribable power called *maya*. Like unmanifest electricity, *maya* as such is not perceptible except in its different manifestations; it is a quality that can be fully estimated and accounted for only through its varied expressions.

Observing and analysing the effects of *maya* within the constitution of all individualised and embodied souls, the Vedantic masters have beautifully concluded that it comes to play in two distinct modes of expressions at two different layers of the human personality. Thus at the intellectual level it expresses itself as a film of doubt and hesitation in its understanding or experiencing of the Self in us. This expression, *maya,* is termed by the masters as the Veiling Power.* Due to this mist of ignorance that envelops the intellect when it is not conscious of the spiritual reality behind it, the mind starts projecting forth the world of the not-Self and superimposes upon it two firm ideas that 'it is true' *(satyattwa),* and the sense that 'I am nothing other than the projected world' *(atmabuddhi)***

In this stanza it is said that once the intellect in us is purified through the art of steady work, called 'devotion through work,' it becomes possible for it to peep over the veil of ignorance that separates it from the splendour of the spiritual entity. When the intellect sloughs off its delusions, it goes beyond its attachment to the charms of the sensuous world. At present the intellect, ignorant of its spiritual destiny, pants to fulfil itself and surge forward seeking satisfaction among the world of finite sense-objects. Each passing joy in the sense-world only sharpens its appetite for the Infinite Bliss which is its real nature. But when the intellect discovers in itself a capacity to pierce through the dreary veil of ignorance, it comes to live its own real nature of bliss Infinite. To the extent the clouds have moved and the sun has emerged out, to that extent the one warming at the fireside moves away from the fireplace to walk into the open and bask in the all-enveloping warmth of the bursting sun. Similarly, to the extent the illusion of ignorance melts itself off in an integrated intellect, to that extent its wanderings in the sensuous world are curtailed.

---

* Read Swamiji's *Discourses on Kenopanishad,* Introduction : 'Fall and Rise of Man.'

* Refer Swamiji's *Talks on Vivekachudamani,* Verse 137.

The sense-world is beautifully indicated by a representative term : "what has been heard *(srutam)*, and what is yet to be heard *(srotavyam)*. We must include in it and read in our understanding the seen and the unseen, the smelt and the unsmelt, the tasted and the not-tasted, the touched and not-yet-touched. In short the intellect of such a purified *Karma Yogi* comes to forget itself to relive in its memory the sensuous joys it had lived in the past and also comes to overlook to remember that it has to experience more joys through its sense-organs in the world of sense-objects.

In case we take the word-meaning of these terms literally we get the usual interpretation of the commentator : "When the seeker's mind is not fluctuated by the seemingly different and often opposing conclusions of philosophers, do not upset him any more than he is established in inward purity."

Sankara connects this stanza with the following : *"You may now ask, 'When shall I attain true conviction of the Self after crossing beyond the veil of ignorance and obtain wisdom through the discrimination of the Self and the non-Self?' Listen" :*

श्रुतिविप्रतिपन्ना ते यदा स्थास्यति निश्चला ।
समाधावचला बुद्धिस्तदा योगमवाप्स्यसि ॥ ५३ ॥

53. *śruti-vipratipannā te yadā sthāsyati niścalā*
samādhāv acalā buddhis tadā yogam avāpsyasi

श्रुतिविप्रतिपन्ना — perplexed by what you have heard, ते — your, यदा — when, स्थास्यति — shall stand, निश्चला — immovable, समाधौ — in the Self, अचला — steady, बुद्धिः — intellect, तदा — then, योगम् — Self-realisation, अवाप्स्यसि — you shall attain.

53. *When your intellect, though perplexed by what you have heard, shall stand immovable and steady in the Self, then you shall attain Self-realisation.*

When one's intellect comes to have a steady equipoise, undisturbed by any of the experiences that reach its subtle body through the five great archways of knowledge, then the individual is considered as having attained *Yoga.**

Some commentators take the word *srutam* 'the heard' literally and come to interpret it as 'what you have heard about the multifarious means and ends in life'. This interpretation clips the word to some extent of its wings and does not allow it to fly over the entire stretch of our experiences in life. Instead, as in the earlier stanza, if we take the word as a representative expression standing for all the sense-experiences, then the stanza would ring truer of its universal application.

The mind gets agitated mainly due to the impulses created at the reception of its ever new stimuli from the outer world. Sense-organs are the inlets through which the world's antennae creep in to enter and disturb the mental pool. One is considered as having attained *Yoga* only when one, even in the midst of sensuousness and even while the sense-organs are letting in a flood of stimuli, does not at all get disturbed in his inner serenity and equipoise. This idea is better developed and exhaustively dealt with later in the chapter where Krishna enumerates the visible qualities and the perceptible signs of one's establishments in Knowledge *(Sthitapragna)*.

This discussion so far explained makes Arjuna so much

---

* 'Evenness of mind is Yoga'.

interested that he lives no more under the influence of his hysteria. He has come to forget his dejection and sorrow, and has come to take an active interest in Krishna's exposition. He could not control himself from expressing his sincere doubt as to what exactly is the nature of such a perfected one who is beyond the storms of sensuousness. The question evidently shows that though the intellect in Arjuna says that the theory of Krishna is true, something in him is not quite ready to accept the theory fully.

He measures himself from his present mental condition and realises the distance he has to cover to reach the goal of perfection pointed out. And the hero despairs. Therefore, he wants to enjoy the enchanting bosom of such a Perfected One at least through the words of Krishna. This is the natural instinct in all of us when we hear of a friend's experiences in a distant land in strange circumstances. We would certainly question him to tap more and more information from him so that we may at least vicariously live the personal experience of our friend through his words.

Sanakra says, while linking up this stanza with the next "*Anxious to know the characteristic feature of one whose intellect has come to an equipoise, he asks this question as soon as he gets a chance to interrogate*" :

अर्जुन उवाच

स्थितप्रज्ञस्य का भाषा समाधिस्थस्य केशव ।
स्थितधीः किं प्रभाषेत किमासीत व्रजेत किम् ॥ ५४ ॥

Arjuna uväca

54. *sthita-prajnasya ka bhāṣā samādhi-sthasya keśava*
stihita-dhiḥ kiṁ prabhaṣeta kim āsita vrajeta kim

स्थितप्रज्ञस्य — of the sage of steady wisdom, का — what, भाषा — description, समाधिस्थस्य — of the (man) merged in the superconscious state, केशव — O Kesava, स्थितधीः — the sage of steady wisdom, किम् — what (how), प्रभाषेत — talks, किम् – what (how), आसीत — sits, व्रजेत — walks, किम् — what (how).

Arjuna said

54. *What, O Kesava, is the description of him who has steady wisdom, who is merged in the Super-conscious state? How. does one of steady wisdom speak, how does he sit, how does he walk?*

In the last two stanzas the discussion naturally turned towards the Ultimate Goal which a *Karma Yogi* reaches when he has, with evenness of mind, practised for sufficiently long the perfect art of healthy work.

The idea seems to be quite appealing and the theory indeed logical. There is a ring of conviction added to it when the theory comes from the mouth of Lord Krishna. Arjuna has such a mental constitution that *Karma Yoga* appealed to him the most. The despondent of the first chapter has forgotten his own hysteria and has come to take an active interest in the discussion, and here, in the stanza, we find Arjuna asking some necessary questions to clear his doubts and gain a better understanding. As a practical man, he is rather afraid that after gaining this great Goal of life through the *Buddhi Yoga* he may not be able to live afterwards as vigorously as now in the world outside.

In the Vedic usage of the term, one is apt to misunderstand that the perfected *Yogin*, who has come to rediscover the Self, lives exclusively in a world of his own. The description of the Upanishads can give a raw student the notion that a perfected sage is ill-fitted to live in the world. Arjuna, as a child of that age of hatred and diplomacy, was curious to know fully the condition of the perfected master before he actually accepted the theory and tried to live it.

The anxiety in him to know the entire Truth is clearly shown here in his very questions upon the non-essentials, such as, 'how does he speak,' 'how will he sit,' 'how will he talk,' etc. These questions must be considered as quite appropriate and dramatic when they come from one who had been till recently a patient of hysteria. Again the first half of the stanza demands a description of a man of steady wisdom while in *samadhi,* meaning, with regard to his inner life, and the second half is asking for a description of how such a master will act in the world outside if given the chance. Arjuna is asking a double-forked question : *(a)* a description of the state of mind in a man of realisation merged in the Self experience; and *(b)* a demand for an explanation of how that experience will influence his actions in the outer world when he has emerged out of the transcendental experience.

The following verses describe the 'man of steady wisdom' *(Sthitaprajna)*, meaning, one who has through a direct realization come to experience and live his godly Selfhood.

"The Lord now paints out those characteristic attitudes in a realised saint which, since attainable by all through right effort, constitute the means as such" :

श्रीभगवानुवाच

प्रजहाति यदा कामान्सर्वान्पार्थ मनोगतान् ।
आत्मन्येवात्मना तुष्टः स्थितप्रज्ञस्तदोच्यते ॥ ५५ ॥

Sri Bhagavān uvāca

55. *prajahāti yadā kāmān sarvān pārtha mano-gatān*
ātmany evātmanā tuṣṭaḥ sthita-prajñas tadocyate

प्रजहाति — casts off, यदा — when, कामान् — desires, सर्वान् — all, पार्थ — O Partha, मनोगतान् — of the mind, आत्मनि — in the Self, एव — only, आत्मना — by the Self, तुष्टः— satisfied, स्थितप्रज्ञः — of steady wisdom, तदा — then, उच्यते — (he) is called.

The Blessed Lord said

55. *When a man completely casts off, O Partha, all the desires of the mind and is satisfied in the Self by the Self, then he is said to be one of steady wisdom.*

From this verse onwards till the end of the chapter, we have a complete and exhaustive exposition of the inner experience and the outer conduct of a 'man of steady wisdom'. By narrating thus the inner and outer life of the 'man of Self-realisation,' Geeta helps us to detect for ourselves the right type of masters from the counterfeit wretches that try to wear the goatskin and enter the fold of the faithful. Apart from this, these passages have a direct appeal to all sincere *sadhaks* inasmuch as this section gives them an easy rule of thumb as to what types of values and mental attitudes they should develop during their practice in order that they may come to realise the ever-effulgent divinity in them : the Pure Awareness.

This very opening stanza of the section in the chapter is a brilliant summary of all that we should know of the mental condition of the Perfect. The words used in this stanza can be understood fully only when we can remember the significant fragrance of these words as they stand dancing among the hosts of other blossoms in the garden of the Upanishads. One is considered a man of wisdom only when he has completely cast away all the desires in his mind. Reading this stanza in conjunction with what Krishna has so far said, we can distinctly come to enjoy the Upanishadic fragrance in these inspired words of Vyasa.

It has already been said that the intellect is ordinarily enveloped in a mist of ignorance, and when it crosses over the layers of its own ignorance, and peeps beyond, it shall come to rediscover the glory of the Self. A man of steady wisdom is one who has accomplished this feat and experienced the Self. Therefore, a man of steady wisdom is one who has reached beyond the veil of ignorance and, as such, not even traces of ignorance can be in his intellect.

An intellect contaminated by ignorance becomes the breeding-ground for desires and one who has relieved himself of this ignorance through right knowledge gained in perception, naturally becomes one who is 'desireless'. By explaining here the absence of the *effects,* the Lord is negating the existence of the *cause* : where desires are not found there ignorance has ended, and the Knowledge had already come to shine forth.

If this alone is a deciding factor of a man with steady wisdom, then any modern man would have condemned the Hindu man of wisdom as a rank lunatic; the Hindu wise man becomes one who has not the initiative even to desire ! Desire means at least a capacity of the mind to see ahead of itself a scheme or a pattern in which the one who desires can probably be more happy than he is at present. "The wise man seems to lose even this capacity as he goes beyond his intellect and experiences the Self," is a criticism that is generally heard from the materialists.

The stanza under review cannot be condemned with this criticism since it adds in its second line that the Perfect One is blissful in his own experience of the Self. A perfect man is therefore, defined here, not only as one who has no desire, but also as one who has positively come to enjoy the bliss of the Self.

When one is an infant, he has got his own playmates, and as he grows from childhood to boyhood, he leaves his own toys and runs after a new set of things. As the boy grows to youthfulness, he again loses his desires for the things of boyhood and craves for a yet newer set of things. Again, in old age the same entity casts away all objects that were till then great joys for him and comes to demand totally different sets of objects. This is an observed phenomenon. As we grow, our demands also grow. With reference to the new scheme of things demanded, the old sets of ideas come to be cast away.

In the egocentric concept of the ignorant, he has burning desires for the sense-objects, a binding attachment to emotions, and a jealous preference for his own pet ideas. But when the ego is transcended, when the ignorance, like a mist, has lifted itself, and the finite ego stands face to face with the divine Reality in him, it melts to become one with the Infinite. In the Self, the man of steady wisdom, 'self-satisfied in the Self', can no more entertain any desire or appetite for the paltry objects of the body, mind, or intellect; he has come to live the very source of all bliss.

Such an one is defined here by Vyasa as the 'man of steady wisdom' *(Sthitaprajna)*, and as it comes from the mouth of Krishna it gathers the divine ring of a Truth incontrovertible.

Moreover :

दुःखेष्वनुद्विग्नमनाः सुखेषु विगतस्पृहः ।
वीतरागभयक्रोधः स्थितधीर्मुनिरुच्यते ॥ ५६ ॥

56. *duḥkeṣv anudvigna-manāḥ sukheṣu vigata-spṛhaḥ*
vīta-rāga-bhaya-krodhaḥ sthita-dhīr munir ucyate

दुःखेषु — adversity, अनुद्विग्नमनाः — of unshaken mind, सुखेषु — in pleasure, विगतस्पृहः— without hankering, वीतराग-भयक्रोधः— free from attachment, fear and anger, स्थितधीः — of steady wisdom, मुनिः— sage, उच्यते— (he) is called.

56. *He whose mind is not shaken by adversity, who does not hanker after pleasures, who is free from attachment, fear and anger, is called a sage of steady wisdom.*

In describing the characteristic attributes of a perfect sage, having explained that he is one who has come to sacrifice all his petty desires in his self-discovered Self-satisfaction in the Self, here, in the stanza, Krishna explains that the next characteristic feature by which we can note a sage is from his 'equanimity in pleasure and pain'. If in the last stanza Krishna considered the man as an *actor*, herein he is considering him as a *bearer of body-afflictions.*

One who is a stable being. whose heart is undisturbed in sorrow or in joy, unattached, fearless, and sans anger* is described here as a *muni* — a silent sage. Of the emotions that must be absent in an individual who is a master in all situations, we have been emphatically told here of only these three : attachments *(raga)*, fear *(bhaya)* and anger *(krodha)*.

In fact, when we observe through the reported bio-

* Read Swamiji's *Discourses on Mandukyopanishad*, Chapter II, Mantra 35.

graphies of the perfected ones in the entire history of man, we find in almost all of them an antithesis of an ordinary man A hundred emotions that are common to the ordinary one are not seen at all in a Perfect One, and in fact, we feel, surprised when we think that the absence of only these three qualities is asserted so emphatically here. Naturally, a careful student gets suspicious. Has Vyasa overlooked all other features? Can this be a complete statement? But a closer study shall reveal that in the discussion here he has not committed "the crime of inappropriate emphasis upon the non-essentials", as critics have been tempted to point out.

In the earlier stanza, the theme was that the Perfect is one who has forsaken all cravings that bubble up in his mind, and this stanza asserts the mental stability of such an entity. In the world outside, in our intercourse with the sense-objects, we can very easily realise for ourselves that our attachments to things create in us the pains of the perplexing fear phobia. When an individual develops a desire strong enough to be a deep attachment, instinctively he starts entertaining a sense of fear for the non-winning of the object so deeply desired for, and once it has been secured, then again for the security of the same acquired object.

Similarly, when an object has charmed one to a point of deep attachment, and when fear itself has started coming up in waves to disturb the individual, then such an individual's attitude against those that come between himself and his object of attachment is called *anger*. Anger is thus nothing but 'an attachment for an object' when expressed towards an obstacle between ourselves and our object of attachment; the anger thus risen up in a bosom is directly proportional to the fear one entertains on the score that the obstacle may hold him back from winning his object of love. Anger, therefore, is only the *raga* for an object expressed at an obstacle that has interfered with our love, threatening to rob us of the object of our desire.

Sankara says that a 'man of steady wisdom' is not distressed by calamities *(a)* such as those that may arise from the disorders of the body *(adhyatmika)*; *(b)* those arising from external objects, such as tiger, etc. *(adhibhautika)*; and *(c)* those arising from unseen causes such as the cosmic forces causing rains, storms, etc., *(adhidaivika)*. Fire increases when fuel is added, but the 'fire of desire' in a Perfect one does not increase when more pleasures are attained. Such an one is called 'a man of steady knowledge', a silent sage.

Moreover :

यः सर्वत्रानभिस्नेहस्तत्तत्प्राप्य शुभाशुभम् ।
नाभिनन्दति न द्वेष्टि तस्य प्रज्ञा प्रतिष्ठिता ॥ ५७ ॥

57. *yaḥ sarvatrānabhisnehas tat tat prāpya śubhāśubham*
nābhinandati na dveṣṭi tāsya prajñā pratiṣṭhitā

यः — he who, सर्वत्र — everywhere, अनभिस्नेहः — without attachment, तत् — that, प्राप्य — having obtained, शुभाशुभम् — good and evil, न — not, अभिनन्दति — rejoices, न — not, द्वेष्टि — hates, तस्य — of him, प्रज्ञा — wisdom, प्रतिष्ठिता — is fixed.

57. *He who is everywhere without attachment, on meeting with anything good or bad, who neither rejoices nor hates, his Wisdom is fixed.*

An inspired artist, trying to express his mental idea on the canvas in his language of colour, would off and on stand back from his easel, and, would again, with growing tenderness and love, approach the child of his art to place a few more strokes with his brush. Here Krishna, inspired by his own theme, is again and again choosing right words to add more light and shade to the picture of the Perfect One which he was painting upon the heartslab of his listener : Arjuna.

He who without attachment squarely meets life with all equanimity and poise is one who is established in wisdom. Here also we have to understand the stanza as a whole or else there will be the danger of misinterpreting its true meaning. A mere detachment from things of live is not a sign of perfection or true discriminative understanding. But many unintelligent enthusiasts actually desert their duties in life and run away hoping that in the quietitude of the jungle they will gain their Goal, since they have developed perfect detachment from the sensuous world. Arjuna himself had expressed earlier that he would renounce the call of duty and the field of activity and by thus retiring into quietitude the Pandava hero hoped to reach 'perfection and peace*'. To persuade Arjuna away from this calamitous mistake, Krishna started his discourse very seriously in the second chapter.

Detachment from suicidal affections and unintelligent tenderness in itself cannot take man to the higher realms of divinity. The detachment from the world outside must be equally accompanied by a growing balance in ourselves to face all challenges in life — auspicious *(subha)* and inauspicious *(asubha)* — in perfect equipoise without either any uncontrolled rejoicing at the *subha* or any aversion for the *asubha* experiences.

* Verse 5.

A mere detachment in itself is not the way of the perfect life, inasmuch as it is only a negative existence of constantly escaping from life. To live in *attachment* is again, living in slavery all through our life to the things to which we are attached. But the Perfect One is he who, with a divine freedom, lives in the world dangerously meeting both the joys and sorrows which life provides for him. To be, in winter, out in the sun and lie basking in its rays is to enjoy its warmth and at the same time to suffer its glare. To complain of the glare is to bring sorrow into the very enjoyment of the warmth. One who is intelligent will either try to ignore the glare and enjoy the warmth fully, or shade off the glare and bask in the enjoyable warmth. Similarly, life by its very nature is a mixture of both good and bad, and to live ever adjusting ourselves — avoiding the bad and striving to linger in the experience of the good — is to live unintelligently. The Perfect One experiences the best and the worst in life with equal detachment because he is ever established in the True and Eternal which is the very Self.

In Arjuna's question, he had enquired of Krishna how a perfect master would speak. This stanza may be considered as an answer to it. Since the perfect Man of Wisdom neither feels any aversion for the sorrows nor rejoices at the joys of life, he neither compliments anything in the world, nor does he condemn anything. To him everything is wonderful. He sees things as they are, uncoloured by his own mental moods. Such a Perfect One is beyond all the known principles of behaviourism of Western psychology.

Moreover :

यदा संहरते चायं कूर्मोऽङ्गानीव सर्वशः ।
इन्द्रियाणीन्द्रियार्थेभ्यस्तस्य प्रज्ञा प्रतिष्ठिता ॥ ५८ ॥

58. *yadā samharate cāyaṁ kūrmo 'ngāniva sarvaśaḥ*
indriyāṇīndriyārthebhyas tasya prajñā pratiṣṭhitā

यदा — when, संहरते — withdraws, च — and, अयम् — this (Yogi), कूर्मः — tortoise, अङ्गानि — limbs, इव — like, सर्वशः — everywhere, इन्द्रियाणि — the senses, इन्द्रियार्थेभ्यः — from the sense-objects, तस्य — of him, प्रज्ञा — wisdom, प्रतिष्ठिता — is steadied.

58. *When like the tortoise which withdraws on all sides its limbs, he withdraws his sense from the sense-objects, then his wisdom becomes steady.*

After explaining that a Perfect One is *(a)* ever satisfied in the Self, *(b)* that he lives in perfect equanimity in pleasure and pain, and *(c)* that there is in him a complete absence of attachment to rejoicing and aversion, here it is mentioned that a 'man of steady wisdom', has the special knack of withdrawing his senses from all the disturbing 'fields of objects'. The simile used here is very effective. Just as a tortoise can instinctively withdraw all its limbs into itself even at the most distant suggestions of danger and feels safe within itself, so too, a 'man of steady wisdom' is capable of withdrawing all his conscious antennae that peep out through the five arches of knowledge called the sense-organs.

In the theory of perception* in Vedanta, the mind, bearing Consciousness, goes through the sense-organs to the sense-objects and there it takes, as it were, the shape of the sense-objects, and then the individual mind comes to have the knowledge of the object perceived. This idea is very figura-

* See Verse 14.
Read Swamiji's *Discourses on Prasna*, Chapter II. (Section IV).

tively put in the Upanishad that the Light of Consciousness, as it were, beams out through the seven holes in the cranium, each special 'beam' illuminating only one specific type of object. Thus, the light that passes through the eyes is capable of illuminating only the forms and colours, while that which emerges through the ears illumines sound. In the material world we can take the example of the electric light that comes through an ordinary bulb illuminating the objects in the room, while the light emerging from the X-ray penetrates through the form and illumines things that are ordinarily not visible to the naked eye.

Thus, in each individual, five distinct beams of the same awareness flow out like antennae and they give us the complete knowledge of the external world. These five avenues of knowledge, bring to us the innumerable stimuli from the outer world which, reaching the mind, provide all the disturbances that man feels in his life of contacts with the outer world. If I am blind, the beauty that is passing by cannot disturb my mind; if I am deaf, I cannot overhear criticism against me and, naturally, it cannot reach me to agitate my bosom! The untasted or the unsmelt or the unfelt sense-objects can never bring any pang or sorrow into the bosom. Here Krishna reassures Arjuna that a man of steady wisdom is he who has the ready capacity to fold back his senses from any or all the fields of their activity. This capacity in an individual to withdraw his senses at will from the fields of objects is called in the *Yoga Sastra* as *pratyahara* which the *Yogi* accomplishes through control of breath *(pranayama)*. To a devotee this comes automatically because he is all eyes and ears only for the form and stories of his beloved Lord. To a Vedantin, again this *uparati* comes out of his well-developed and sharpened discriminative faculty with which his intellect makes his mind understand the futility of its licking the joy and happiness crumbs in the wayside ditches of sensuousness, while it, in its real nature, is the lord of the community's food-store of Bliss Infinite.

Sankara considers the following stanza as an answer which the Lord gives to a possible doubt in Arjuna's mind.

"Now, even the senses of a man who is ill, and consequently not able to partake of the sensuous objects, are seemingly under control but the taste for them does not thereby cease to exit. How does even the taste for sense-objects end finally?" Listen :

विषया विनिवर्तन्ते निराहारस्य देहिनः ।
रसवर्जं रसोऽप्यस्य परं दृष्ट्वा निवर्तते ॥ ५९ ॥

59. *viṣayā vinivartante nirāhārasya dehinaḥ*
rasa-varjaṁ raso 'py asya paraṁ dṛṣṭvā nivartate

विषयाः — the objects of senses, विनिवर्तन्ते — turn away, निराहारस्य — abstinent, देहिनः — of the man, रसवर्जम् — leaving the longing, रसः — longing, (taste), अपि — even, अस्य — of his, परम् — the supreme, दृष्ट्वा — having seen, निवर्तते — turn away.

59. *The objects of the senses turn away from the abstinent man leaving the longing (behind); but his longing also turns away on seeing the Supreme.*

Without *pratyahara* or *uparati* we can observe cases wherein an individual comes to maintain sense-withdrawal from the sense-objects due to some physical incapacity or due to some special mental mood of temporary sorrow or misery.

In all those cases, though the sense-organs come to feel an aversion to the respective objects, their inclinations for these objects are lying somewhere dormant for the time being. Similarly, Arjuna doubts that even in a *Yogi* the capacity to withdraw from the sense-world is also temporary and that under favourable or sufficiently tempting circumstances, they may again raise their hoods to hiss and to poison. His doubt is answered here.

From an abstinent person, the sense-objects get repelled no doubt. If you observe the flight of the objects of sensuousness from the shops to their customers, you can understand this point very clearly. They always reach only those who are courting them and are panting to posses them. The wine cellars get emptied when they walk out to replenish the sideboards of the drunkards. Ploughs made by the smithy are not purchased by artists and poets, doctors and advocates, but they must necessarily reach the homes of the farmers. Similarly, all sense-objects ultimately reach to serve those who are courting them with burning desires. From one who is completely abstinent, sense-objects must necessarily get repelled.

But even though the sense-objects may temporarily seem to turn away from one who is abstinent, the deep taste for these sense-objects ingrained in the mind of the seeker is very difficult to be completely erased. Here Krishna in his supreme wisdom assures the seeker that all those mental impressions of sensuous lives lived in the past by the ego from the beginning of the creation to date will be totally erased or atleast made ineffective — as roasted seeds — when the seeker transcends the ego and comes to experience the Self.

And this is not very difficult to understand since we know that the objects of sorrow and occasions of tragedy in one plane of consciousness are not available in another plane of awareness. The kingship that I enjoy in my dream does not add even a jot to my dignity when I wake up to realise my insignificant existence, so too, my meagre existence in the waking state will not debar me from the full kingly glory in my dream kingdom! Similarly; the ego, existing now through the waking, dream and deep-sleep states, has gathered to itself a dung-heap of impressions, all of them purely sensuous. But these cannot be effective when the same ego, transcending these three planes, comes to experience the plane of God-consciousness.

"He who would acquire steadiness of Right Knowledge (prajna) should bring the senses under control. For, if not controlled, they will do harm. So, the Lord says :"

यततो ह्यपि कौन्तेय पुरुषस्य विपश्चितः ।
इन्द्रियाणि प्रमाथीनि हरन्ति प्रसभं मनः ॥ ६० ॥

60. *yatato hy api kaunteya puruṣasya vipaścitaḥ*
indriyāṇi pramāthīni haranti prasabhaṁ manaḥ

यततः — of the striving, हि — indeed, अपि — even, कौन्तेय — O Kaunteya, पुरुषस्य — of man, विपश्चितः — (of the) wise, इन्द्रियाणि — the senses, प्रमाथीनि — turbulent, हरन्ति — carry away, प्रसभम् — violently, मनः — the mind.

60. *The turbulent senses, O son of Kunti, do violently carry away the mind of a wise man though he be striving to control them.*

In his discourse so far, the Lord has emphasised that a Perfect Master is one who has a complete control over his sense-appetites. In India a mere philosophical idea in itself is not considered anything more than a poetic ideology, and it is not accepted as a spiritual thesis unless it is followed by a complete technique by which the seeker can come to *live* that philosophy in his own subjective experience. True to this traditional Aryan faith, here, in the Geeta, the Lord is indicating to Arjuna the practical methods by which he should struggle hard in order to reach the eminence of perfection in all men of "steady wisdom".

The ignorance of the spiritual reality functions in an individual in three distinct aspects : unactivity *(sattwa),* activity *(rajas);* and inactivity *(tamas).* When the *sattwa*-aspect in us is molested by the veiling in the intellect *(avarana)* and the lack of tranquility *(viksepa),* then the individual comes to feel the sorrows caused by their endless roamings through the sense-organs. Unless these are well-controlled, they will drag the mind to the field of the sense-objects and thus create a chaotic condition within, which is experienced as sorrow.

"This happens even to a higher evolved seeker," is a statement of the Lord in this stanza. With this assertion he is warning the seeker in Arjuna that he should not, on any score, let his objective mind take hold of and enslave his subjective intellectual personality. This warning is quite appropriate and timely in the scheme of thought in this chapter.

Invariably, among those who are practising religion, the common cause by which very many true seekers fall off from the path is the same all over the world. After a few years of practice they, no doubt, come to live a certain inexplicable inward joy and, over-confident and often vainful of their progress, relax in their *tapas*. Once they come back to the fields of the senses, "the turbulent senses* do violently snatch away the mind" from the poise of its perfect meditation.

तानि सर्वाणि संयम्य युक्त आसीत मत्परः ।
वशे हि यस्येन्द्रियाणि तस्य प्रज्ञा प्रतिष्ठिता ॥ ६१ ॥

61. *tāni sarvāṇi saṁyamya yukta āsīta mat-paraḥ*
vaśe hi yasyendriyāṇi tasya prajñā pratisthitā

तानि — them, सर्वाणि — all, संयम्य — having restrained, युक्तः — joined, आसीत — should sit, मत्परः — intent on Me, वशे — under control, हि — indeed, यस्य — whose, इन्द्रियाणि — senses, तस्य — his, प्रज्ञा — wisdom, प्रतिष्ठिता — (is) settled.

61. *Having restrained them all, he should sit steadfast, intent on Me; his wisdom is steady whose senses are under control.*

Since the sense-organs are thus the saboteurs in the kingdom of the spirit who bring the disastrous downfall of the empire of the soul, Arjuna is warned here that as a seeker of Self-perfection he should constantly struggle to control all his sense-organs and their mad lustful wanderings in their respective fields. Modern psychology certainly would look down with a protruding squint eye upon this Geeta theory because, according to Frued and others, sensuousness is instinctive in man and to curb it is to suppress the sensuousness in man.

According to the West, to *control* is to suppress, and no science of mental life can accept that suppression is psychologically healthy. But the Vedic theory is not pointing to any mental suppression at all they are only advising an inward blossoming, an inner growth and development, by which its earlier fields of enjoyments through the senses drop out of the

* Read Swamiji's *Discourses on Kathopanishad*, Chapter 2, Section IV, Mantra 1.

fuller grown man who has come to the perception of a newer field of ampler joys and more satisfying bliss.

The idea is very well brought out here in the stanza when Lord Krishna, as though in the very same breath, repeats both the negative and the positive aspects of the technique of self-development. He advises not only a withdrawal from the unhealthy gutters of sensuousness but also gives the healthy method of doing so by explaining to us the positive technique in Self-perfection. Through a constant attempt at focussing our attention "On Me, the Supreme," he advises the disciples to sit steady.

In this simple-looking statement of half-a-stanza, Geeta explains the entire technique of Self-development. Immoral impulses and unethical instincts that bring down a man to the level of a mere brute are the result of endless lives spent among sensuous objects during the infinite number of different manifestations through which the embodied soul — the ego — in each one of us had previously passed. The thick coating of mental impressions that we gathered thus in our pilgrimage is humanly impossible for one solitary individual to erase or transcend in one's own little lifetime. Naturally, this is the despair of all the promoters of ethics, the teachers of morality and the masters of spirituality. The rishis of old, in vivid experience, have discovered for themselves a technique by which all these mental tendencies can be eradicated. To expose the mind to the quite atmosphere of meditation upon the All-perfect Being is to heal the mind of its ulcers. By this process, he who has come to gain a complete mastery over his sense-organs is called the one who is 'steadfast in wisdom'.

The concealed suggestion in the stanza is quite obvious : nobody who with excessive force controls his *indriyas* by the sheer strength of his will and sense of abstinence has any chance of flowering himself into full-blown spiritual beauty. When the sense-organs have, of their own accord, come back tamely to lie surrendered at the feet of one who has come to rediscover the Infinite Perfection in himself, he is called 'a Man of Perfection'. Neither has he ruined his instruments of cognition nor has he closed down the arches of knowledge in him. A Perfect One is he whose sway over the animal in him is so complete that the inner Satan has become, for the sage in him, a tame cannibal to run errands and serve him faithfully.

"Now the Lord proceeds to point out the source of all evils in the case of the unsuccessful" :

ध्यायतो विषयान्पुंसः सङ्गस्तेषूपजायते ।
सङ्गात्संजायते कामः कामात्क्रोधोऽभिजायते ॥ ६२ ॥

62. *dhyāyato visayān pumsah sangas tesūpajāyate*
sangāt samjāyate kāmah kāmāt krodho bhijāyate

ध्यायतः — thinking, विषयान् — on objects of the senses, पुंसः — of a man, संगः — attachment, तेषु — in them, उपजायते — arises, संगात्— from attachment, संजायते – is born, कामः — desire, कामात् — from desire, क्रोधः – anger, अभिजायते - arises.

62. *When a man thinks of objects, attachment for them arises; from attachment desire is born; from desire arises anger.*

क्रोधाद्भवति संमोहः संमोहात्स्मृतिविभ्रमः ।
स्मृतिभ्रंशाद् बुद्धिनाशो बुद्धिनाशात्प्रणश्यति ॥ ६३ ॥

63. *krodhād bhavati sammohaḥ*
saṁmohāt smṛti-vibhramaḥ
smṛti-bhraṁśād buddhi-nāśo
buddhi-nāśāt praṇaśyati

क्रोधात् — from anger, भवति — comes, संमोहः— delusion, संमोहात् — from delusion, स्मृतिविभ्रम — loss of memory, स्मृतिभ्रंशात् — from loss of memory, बुद्धिनाशः— the destruction of discrimination, बुद्धिनाशात् — from the destruction of discrimination, प्रणश्यति — (he) perishes.

63. *From anger comes delusion; from delusion loss of memory; from loss of memory the destruction of discrimination; from destruction of discrimination he perishes.*

From this verse onwards, Lord Krishna explains in five noble stanzas the Indian psychological theory on the fall of man from goodhood. This section of five stanzas expounds the theory only to bring home to Arjuna later on* that he, the mighty-armed, must try to annihilate and totally win over all his *indriyas* from all sides, and such a man, concludes Krishna, is 'a Man of Perfection' as conceived and contemplated, as lived and enjoyed, as explained and glorified in the scriptural times of the Hindus.

This section also gives us a clear story which, in its pattern, gives us the autobiography of all seekers who have, after long periods of practice, come to wreck themselves upon the rocks of failure and disappointment. To a true seeker in Vedanta no fall is ever possible. Instances of unsuccessful seekers are not few and in all of them the mistake that we

---

* Read Swamiji's *Discourses on Kathopanishad,* Introduction : 'Fall and Rise of Man.'

notice is that they ultimately fall back to be a victim in the sense-entanglements. And in all those cases we also notice that the fallen one goes to the very dregs of it; there is no half-way for such victims : for them a slip means destruction!

The ladder of fall is very beautifully described here. The path of destruction in a seeker is so elaborately detailed in these stanzas that, fallen as we are, we shall know how to get back to our pristine glory and inward perfection.

The source of all evil, like a tree from a seed, starts from our own wrong thinking or false imaginations. Thought is creative; it can make us or unmake us. If rightly used, it can serve constructive purposes; if misused, it can totally destroy us. When we constantly think of the sense-objects, the *consistency of thought* creates in us an *attachment* for the object of our thought, and when more and more thoughts flow towards an object of attachment, they get hardened to form a *burning desire* for the possession and enjoyment of the object of attachment. The same motive force of the emotion, when directed towards, obstacles that threaten the non-fulfilment of our desires, is called anger *(krodha)*.

An intellect fumed with anger *(krodha)* comes to experience *delusion* and the deluded discrimination comes to lose all *memories of the past*. Anyone excited with anger in capable of doing acts during which the poor victim seems to have totally forgotten himself and his relationship with all others. Sri Sankaracharya says in this connection that a deluded fool in this mental condition may even fight with his own teachers or parents forgetting his indebtedness to these revered men.

When thus an individual, through his own wrong channel of thinking, gains an attachment to an object which matures itself into a burning desire, and when that object of desire shoots him up into a fit of anger, the mental disturbance caused by the emotion deludes the intellect and makes it forget its own sense of proportion and the sense of relationship with things and beings around it. When thus a deluded intellect forgets its own dignity of culture, it comes to lose its discriminative capacity, which is often called in common parlance as conscience *(buddhi)*. Conscience is that differentiating knowledge of the good and the right, which often forms a standard in ourselves, and whenever it can, it warns the mind in us against its lustful sensuousness and animalism. Once this 'conscience' is dulled, the man becomes a two-legged animal with no sense of proportion or with no ears to hear any subtler call in him than the hungers of the flesh. Thereby, he is guaranteeing for himself a complete destruction inasmuch as, such a bosom cannot come to perceive or strive for the higher, the nobler and the diviner.

"The contemplation of sense-objects has been described as the source of all evils. Now the means of deliverance (moksha) is described as follows" :

रागद्वेषवियुक्तैस्तु विषयानिन्द्रियैश्चरन् ।
आत्मवश्यैर्विधेयात्मा प्रसादमधिगच्छति ॥ ६४ ॥

64. *rāga-dveṣa-vimuktais tu viṣayān indriyaiś caran*
ātma-vaśyair vidheyātmā prasādam adhigacchati

रागद्वेषवियुक्तैः — free from attraction and repulsion, तु — but, विषयान् — objects, इन्द्रियैः— with senses, चरन् — moving (amongst), आत्मवष्यैः— self-restrained, विधेयात्मा — the self controlled, प्रसादम् — to peace, अधिगच्छति— attains.

64. *But the self-controlled man, moving among objects*

with his sense under restraint and free from ***both attraction and*** *repulsion,* ***attains*** *peace.*

He alone, who with perfect self-control goes through life among the infinite number of sense-objects, each impinging upon him and trying to bind him with its charm, and approaches them with neither love nor hatred, comes to enjoy peace. By running away from the sense-objects, nobody can assure himself an internal peace because the inner disturbance depends not upon the presence or the absence of the sense-objects in the outer world, but essentially upon the mind's agitations for procuring the desirable object or for getting rid of the undesirable objects.

But a master of wisdom, with perfect self-control; moves among the objects of the world with neither any love for nor any particular aversion against them, and on such a man the ineffectual sense-objects try but vainly to smile or grin at. Wherever I go, my shadow must play all round me according to the position of the light; but the shadow can neither entangle me in love nor destroy me in my hatred! The outer world of objects is able to whip man because man himself lends the power to the objects to beat him down!

Supposing there is a lunatic who is whipping himself and weeps in pain, his sorrows can be ended only when he is persuaded not to take the whip in his hand! He can be advised, even if he keeps the whip in his hand, not to swing his arms in the fashion in which he is doing at present! Similarly, here the mind wields the objects and gets itself beaten. It is told as an advise that an individual who lives in self-control will no longer lend his own life's dynamism to the objects to persecute him through his own sentimental aversion to or love for these objects.

When the lunatic is taught not to weild the whip and strike himself, he is immediately saved from the sorrows of the whip. Similarly here, when a mind is trained in these two aspects, *(a)* to live in self-control, and *(b)* to move among the sense-objects with neither attachment for nor aversion to them, the disturbances and agitations in the mind caused by the sense-enchantments are all immediately brought under control. This condition of the mind is called tranquillity or peace *(prasada)*. This is symbolically represented in the sweets distribution after every *puja* in all religions, which is also called among the Hindus as *prasad* or *bhog,* meaning, one who has during the ritual practised perfect self-control and God-contemplation comes to enjoy as a result of his action a tranquillity in the mind which is termed spiritual grace, or divine peace *(Iswara prasada)*.*

Here, as far as a Vedantin is concerned, *prasada* is the mental purification because that mind is considered as pure which has felt in it the least sense-disturbances. One who has learnt to live on the principle of self-control and has also trained himself to live among the sense-objects in a spirit of least attachment with or aversion for them, has the least disturbance because of the ineffectiveness of the sense-objects upon him. Thereby his mind automatically becomes more and more calm and tranquil, and is considered as pure *(prasada)* for purposes of spiritual life.

"What will happen when peace is attained? Listen."

प्रसादे सर्वदुःखानां हानिरस्योपजायते ।
प्रसन्नचेतसो ह्याशु बुद्धिः पर्यवतिष्ठते ॥ ६५ ॥

---

* Read Swamiji's *Discourses on Kathopanishad,* Chapter I, Section II, Mantra 20.

65. *prasāde sarva-duhkhānāṁ hanir asyopajāyate*
prasanna-cetaso hy āśu bhuddhiḥ paryavatiṣṭhate

प्रसादे — in peace, सर्वदुःखानाम् — (of) all pains, हानिः — destruction, अस्य — of him, उपजायते — arises (or happens), प्रसन्नचेतसः — of the tranquil-minded, हि — because, आशु — soon, बुद्धिः — intellect (or reason), पर्यवतिष्ठते — becomes steady.

65. *In that peace all pains are destroyed; for the intellect of the tranquil-minded soon becomes steady.*

It is natural for an Arjuna-mentality of uncompromising intellectualism to ask Krishna, "Then what?" And as an answer, the Lord explains why he should develop and maintain tranquillity of the mind in himself : "In tranquillity all sorrows are destroyed." This sentence is obviously commented upon as a definition of happiness. Peaceful mind is a significant condition of happiness; peace is happiness, happiness is peace. The least agitated mind is itself proof against all sorrows inasmuch as the sorrow-condition is nothing but the state of agitation in the mind.

This commentary does not satisfy us completely since Krishna's assertion is that 'sorrow will be destroyed' *(hani)*. In order to bring out clearly the meaning implied in the phrase 'destruction of sorrows', we will have to understand it as 'elimination of *vasanas*'. Earlier, in the Introduction we have said that the *vasana*-granules giving a thick coating for the subjective mind is the cause for its delusion which creates all sorrows for the imperfect, while the Perfect is one who has transcended the *vasanas* through *Buddhi Yoga* explained earlier.

It is very well known that all the *vasanas* existing in an individual who is facing life constantly cannot be fully eradicated by him. The secret of doing so has been explained here by the Lord. Keeping the mind exposed to an atmosphere of tranquillity *(prasada)* consciously brought about through an intelligent life of self-control is the secret whereby all the *vasanas* can get themselves eliminated.

This interpretation of ours has been very well supported by the second line of the verse wherein Krishna says that "In a tranquil mind the intellect soon gets established in firmness." A purified mind guarantees a sharpened, singlepointed, subtlized-intellect.

"This tranquillity is extolled here by Lord Krishna" :

नास्ति बुद्धिरयुक्तस्य न चायुक्तस्य भावना ।
न चाभावयतः शान्तिरशान्तस्य कुतः सुखम् ॥ ६६ ॥

66. *nāsti buddhir ayuktasya na cāyuktasya bhāvanā*
na cābhāvayataḥ śantir aśāntasya kutaḥ sukham

न — not, आस्ति — is, बुद्धिः — knowledge (of the Self), अयुक्तस्य — of the unsteady, न — not, च — and, अयुक्तस्य — of the unsteady, भावना — meditation, न — not, च — and, अभावयतः — of the unmeditated, शान्तिः — peace, अशान्तस्य — of the peaceless, कुतः — whence, सुखम् — happiness.

66. *There is no knowledge (of the Self) to the unsteady, and to the unsteady no meditation and to the unmeditated no peace; to the peaceless, how can there be happiness?*

Here is an explanation why the quietude of the mind is so often and so insistently emphasized in the literature explaining the Hindu technique of Self-perfection. Unless the mind is quiet, the individual will not have the intellectual leisure for cultural self-development nor the internal energy needed for development which man yearns for unconsciously. Unless there is tranquillity, there cannot be steadiness of intellectual application to the problems of life, and without this self-evaluation of life and true observation with a clear discriminative analysis, we cannot have in us a devotion of Self-knowledge *(bhavana)*. Without such a glorious goal in front of us constantly beckoning us unto itself like a pole star our life shall be a lost ship in the bosom of an ocean, going now here, reaching nowhere, and ultimately getting itself floundered upon some treacherous rock.

One who has no philosophical goal of life to strive and yearn for will not know what peace is in the mind, and to one who is thus restless, "where is happiness?" In short, to live in balance and sail safely upon the uncertain waves of the ocean of life, across both its smiling weather and stormy days, we must have a constant perception of the Real. Without a drummer, the dancer's footwork cannot be rhythmic and cannot keep perfect time.

"Why is there no knowledge for the unsteady? — Listen" :

इन्द्रियाणां हि चरतां यन्मनोऽनुविधीयते ।
तदस्य हरति प्रज्ञां वायुर्नावमिवाम्भसि ॥ ६७ ॥

67. *indriyāṇāṁ hi caratāṁ yan mano 'nuvidhīyate*
tad asya harati prajñāṁ vāyur nāvam ivāmbhasi

इन्द्रियाणाम् — senses, हि – for, चरताम् — wandering, यत् — which, मनः — mind, अनुविधीयते— follows, तद् — that, अस्य —

his, हरति— carries away, प्रज्ञाम् — discrimination, वायुः— the wind, नावम्— boat, इव — like, अंभसि— in the water.

67. *For the mind, which follows in the wake of the wandering senses, carries away his discrimination as the wind carries away a boat on the waters.*

As a ship with sails up and its helmsman dead would be completely at the mercy of the fitful storms and reckless waves, and cannot reach any definite harbour, but would get destroyed by the very tossings of the waves, so too, life gets capsized and the individual drowned by the uncertain buffets of passionate sense-storms. Therefore, the senses are to be controlled if man is to live a better and more purposeful life, designed and planned for enduring success.

"Having explained the proposition enunciated earlier, the Lord concludes by reaffirming the same topic" :*

तस्माद्यस्य महाबाहो निगृहीतानि सर्वशः ।
इन्द्रियाणीन्द्रियार्थेभ्यस्तस्य प्रज्ञा प्रतिष्ठिता ॥ ६८ ॥

68. *tasmād yasya mahābāho nigṛhitāni sarvaśaḥ*
indriyāṇīndriyārthebhyas tasya prajñā pratiṣṭhitā

तस्मात् — therefore, यस्य — whose, महाबाहो — O mighty-armed, निगृहीतानि — restrained, सर्वशः — completely, इन्द्रियाणि— the senses, इन्द्रियार्थेभ्यः— from the sense-objects, तस्य — his, प्रज्ञा — knowledge, प्रतिष्ठिता— (is) steady.

68. *Therefore, O Mighty-armed, his knowledge is steady whose senses are completely restrained from sense-objects.*

---

* Verses 61, 62.

It is natural in our conversations with our friends that we do not give directly our wise conclusions upon the do's and dont's without giving them earlier a definite logic of our thoughts leading to the conclusions to be asserted. Without preparing our friend's mind to perceive the logic of these conclusions, we dare not declare to him any truth, however divinely acceptable the declarations be. This principle is most faithfully followed, especially when we want our friend to follow exactly our advice. Arjuna has been told earlier all the necessary arguments, and here, in the stanza, Krishna reasserts the same proposition which he had enunciated earlier, 'Life in self-control alone is life worth living, if we demand from life anything more enduring than tears, sobs, sighs, and groanings.'

He is a man of wisdom, rooted in joy and bliss, who has restrained completely all his senses from thier wild roamings all round among their sense-objects. Here, Arjuna is addressed as 'mighty-armed', which in itself includes a suggestion that however great a hero he might be in the outer battle with arms against the heroic kings and chieftains of his age, he cannot be considered a real hero until he is able to fight against all his enemies within and win for himself a perfect mastery over the mind. He is a hero, 'mighty-armed', and therefore the suggestion is that he can and must try to win over his inner enemies who plunder his wealth of joy and success in the kingdom of Heaven within.

"By destroying the sense-organs roaming in the sense-objects" — it does not mean that a man of self-development should destroy his capacities for perception of the world outside, nor does it mean that he is one who has been rendered incapable of enjoying life as any man would. Sense debility is no sign of better knowledge. It is only meant here that the

sense-objects filtering through the five archways of knowledge will not, in a Perfect man, flood the mind to bring chaos and destruction to his established inner peace and tranquillity.

The ordinary individual in his egocentric existence becomes victimized by the sense-organs while he who has conquered the ego and has transcended his matter-identifications comes to live in freedom and perfect control over the tyrannical sense-organs.

"In order to make it clear, the Lord proceeds" :

या निशा सर्वभूतानां तस्यां जागर्ति संयमी ।
यस्यां जाग्रति भूतानि सा निशा पश्यतो मुनेः ॥ ६९ ॥

69. *yā niśā sarva-bhūtānāṁ tasyāṁ jāgarti saṁyami*
yasyāṁ jāgrati bhūtāni sā niśā paśyato muneḥ

या — which, निशा — night, सर्वभूतानाम् — of all beings, तस्याम् — in that, जागर्ति — wakes, संयमी — the self controlled, यस्याम् — in which, जाग्रति — wake, भूतानि — all beings, सा — that, निशा — night, पश्यतः — (of the) seeing, मुनेः — of the Muni.

69. *That which is night to all beings, in that the self-controlled man wakes; where all beings are awake, that is the night for the sage* (muni) *who sees.*

In order to bring home to Arjuna the idea that the world as experienced by an individual through the goggles of the mind-intellect-body, is different from what is perceived through the open windows of spirituality, this stanza is given. The metaphorical language in this verse is so complete in detail that a datamongering modern intellect is not capable of entering into its poetic beauty. Of all the peoples of the world, the Aryans alone are capable of bringing a combination of poetry and science, and when the greatest poet-philosopher of the world takes his *writing-rod* to pour out his art of perfection on to the ancient palmyra leaves to express the bliss of Perfection, in the ecstasy of his poetry he could not have used a better medium than the Geeta, to pour himself out.

Here the two points of view of the ignorant and the wise are contrasted. The ignorant never perceives the world as it is; he always throws his own mental colour on the objects and understands the imperfections in his mind to be part and parcel of the objects themselves. When a child is looking out on to the world through the coloured panes of the bedroom window, through each glass he sees the world coloured in the colour of the glass through which he is looking. But the world as such can be seen only when the panel of the window is open; then with a naked eye the naked world is seen.

The Consciousness in us is today capable of recognising the world only through the media of the body, mind and intellect. Naturally, we see the world imperfect not because the world is ugly but because of ugliness in the media through which we perceive.

When an electrical engineer comes to a city, and when at the lighting time the whole city smiles forth with its lights on, he immediately enquires, "Is it A.C. or D.C. current?" While the same vision to an illiterate villager is a wondrous sight and he only exclaims, "I have seen the lights that need no wick or oil." From the standpoint of the villager, there is no electricity and no problem of A.C. or D.C. currents. The world the engineer sees among the very same bulbs is not realized or known by the unperceiving intellect of the villager. Nor is the engineer awake to the world of strange wonderment which the villager enjoys.

A master mind is he who, rooted in his wisdom, opens up the panes of his perception and looks on at the world with his eye of wisdom.

Here, in the stanza, we are told that the egocentric finite-mortal is asleep to the world of perception enjoyed and lived by the Man of Steady Wisdom; and the Perfect One cannot see and feel the thrills and sobs which the ego gets in its selfish life of finite experience.

"The Lord proceeds to teach by an illustration that a wise devotee alone, who has abandoned desires and whose wisdom is steady, can attain moksha and not he who without renouncing cherishes desires" :

आपूर्यमाणमचलप्रतिष्ठं
समुद्रमापः प्रविशन्ति यद्वत् ।
तद्वत्कामा यं प्रविशन्ति सर्वे
स शान्तिमाप्नोति न कामकामी ॥ ७० ॥

70. *āpūryamāṇam acala-pratiṣṭhaṁ*
samudram apaḥ praviśanti yadvat
tadvat kāmā yaṁ praviśānti sarve
sa śāntim āpnoti na kāmā-kāmī

आपूर्यमाणम् — filled from all sides, अचलप्रतिष्ठम् — based in stillness, समुद्रम् — ocean, आपः — water, प्रविशन्ति — enter, यद्वत् — as, तद्वत् — so, कामाः — desires, यम् — whom, प्रविशन्ति — enter, सर्वे — all, सः — he, शान्तिम् — peace, आप्नोति — attains, न — not, कामकामी — desirer of desires.

70. *He attains Peace into whom all desires enter as waters enter the ocean which, filled from all sides, remains unmoved; but not the 'desirer of desires'.*

It is a very well-known example that although gallons of waters reach the ocean through the various rivers, yet the level of water in the ocean does not change even by a fraction. Similarly, even though through the five sense-channels the infinite number of sense-objects may pour in their stimuli, they no doubt reach the mental zone of the Perfect Man, and yet they do not create any commotion or flux in his bosom. Such an individual, who is ever finding his own level in spite of the fact that he is living amidst the sense-objects with his sense-organs naturally in contact with the objects, is called a Man of Perfection — a true saint. And Krishna asserts that such an individual alone can truely discover peace and happiness in himself. The Lord of the Geeta, not satisfied with this negative assertion, positively denies any true peace or joy to those who are 'desirers of desires'.

This idea is totally in opposition to the modern belief in the material world. The materialists believe that by fanning up desires and satisfying as many of them as possible, one is helepd to live a life of joy and happinesss. The modern civilisation based upon industrialisation is attempting to whip up desires, and this attempt has now succeeded so much that an average man has a million times more desires today than his forefathers ever entertained a century ago. The financiers and the indutrialists, with the aid of the modern scientific knowledge, struggle hard to satisfy the new desires, and to the extent an individual has come to fulfil his newly created desires, he is taught by the civilisation that he is happy.

On the other hand the great thinkers of the past in India,

perhaps, through their experience or through their more careful and exhaustive thinking, discovered that the joy created through satisfaction of desires can never be complete. They discovered that joy or happiness at any given time is a quotient when the 'number of desires fulfilled' is divided by the 'total number of desires entertained' by the same individual at that time. This mathematical truth has been accepted by the modern preachers of secularism also; but in their practical application the old rishis and the modern politician seem to differ to a large extent.

In the modern world the attempt is to increase the numerator, which is represented by the 'number of the desires fulfilled.' The scriptural masters of India also were living in a world peopled by a society of men, and their philosophical contemplations were upon man as a social being and their aim too was to bring more happiness to society. Unlike the present prophets of profits, these rishis of religion did not conceive that an attempt to increase the *nominator* without a corresponding attention to the rate of increase of the *denominator* could produce any palpable increase in joy. On the other hand, today, we are struggling hard to increase the 'number of desires fulfilled', but, at the same time, we are not trying to control the 'number of desires entertained'. That this state of affairs cannot produce any palpable increase in the *quotient of happiness* is the scriptural verdict which seems to be a perfectly realizable scientific truth.

The Geeta herein is only repeating what the Upanishadic rishis are never tired of emphasising in the scriptures of India. The 'desirer of desires' can never come to perfect peace *(Santi)*. Only one who has in his spirit of detachment gained a complete control over his mind so that the sense-objects of the outer world cannot create in him an infinite number of yearnings of desires, he alone is the man of peace and joy. The objects in the outer world cannot themselves tease a man by their existence or by their non-existence. The outer world can borrow its capacity to ill-treat man only when the individual exposes himself unguarded, and thus he gets wounded and crushed by his own attachments to a wrong valuation of the sense-objects.

In this stanza Bhagavan is only giving a more elaborate and complete commentary upon the opening line of this section wherein he started the description of a Man of Steady Wisdom. He there explained that "When a man completely casts off all the desires in his mind, he is then said to be one of steady knowledge."

"Because it is so, therefore"

विहाय कामान्यः सर्वान्पुमांश्चरति निःस्पृहः ।
निर्ममो निरहंकारः स शान्तिमधिगच्छति ॥ ७१ ॥

71. *vihāya kāmān yaḥ sarvān pumāṃś carati niḥspṛhaḥ*
nirmamo nirahaṃkāraḥ sa śāntim adhigacchati

विहाय — abandoning, कामान् – desires, यः— that, सर्वान्– all, पुमान् — man, चरति — moves about, निस्पृहः– free from longing, निर्ममः — devoid of mine-ness, निरहंकारः — without egoism, सः — he, शान्तिम्– to peace, अधिगच्छति – attains.

71. *The man attains peace who, abandoning all desires, moves about without longing, without the sense of 'I-ness' and 'my-ness'.*

There are commentators who believe that this and the following stanza are explaining the path of renunciation which is, in fact not altogether ignored in the text of the Geeta. Since, as we said earlier, the second chapter is almost a summary of the entire Divine Song, it has to indicate even this *Sannyasa Yoga* which will be later on explained at length and hinted at different places during the entire length of the Geeta.

The stanza under discussion now seems to ring clear the significant advice given earlier by Krishna almost at the very opening of his philosophical discussions in this chapter. He had advised therein : "That having conquered the mental agitations created by the pairs-of-opposites, fight the battle of life." The same idea seems to be resounding here at the close of the chapter.

The first line of the stanza explains the mental condition of one who comes to discover real peace in himself. Such an individual, it says, should renounce all desires and must be without attachments or longings. The second line describes the condition of such an individual's intellect and it asserts that it is without any sense of 'I-ness' or 'my-ness'. The ego is the cause of all sense-attachments and longings. Where the ego is not perceptible, as in sleep, there are no longings or desires in the individual. Thus if the first line of the stanza is describing a negation of the effects of ignorance, the second line asserts the absence of the very cause from which desires and the agitations arise.

Earlier, in the Introduction, we explained that the split in the personality of Arjuna was caused by the intervention of the sense of his ego and his egoistic desires which broke up his subjective and objective minds into two independent islands with a vast ocean of surging waves of desires between them. With a soft suggestion, after explaining all the logic of thought, Krishna is carefully placing his finger on the very ulcer of the Pandava's mental disease.

The stanza, in its sum total, advises us that all our suffering in the world is caused by our own egocentric misconception and consequent arrogance characterised by our ever-multiplying demands for wealth and our endless desires.

Sannyasa means sacrifice, and to live in a spirit of sacrifice after renouncing completely one's ego and its desires is true *sannyasa,* wherein an individual comes to be a *sannyasin* who has learnt the art of living is life of divinity. The general misunderstanding that to run away from life is *sannyasa* or to colour the cloth is to become a true monk, has brought about an irreparable slur on the philosophy of the Upanishads. Hinduism considers him to be a *sannyasin* who has learnt the art of living his life in constant inspiration which is gained through an intelligent renunciation of his egocentric misconceptions.

Sankara beautifully explains this point of view in his commentary on the stanza. I can do not better than quote the Acharya : "That man of renunciation who entirely abandoning all desires, goes through life contented with the bare necessities of life, who regards not as his, even those things which are needed for the mere bodily existence, who is not vain of his knowledge — such a man of steady knowledge, that man who knows Brahman, attains peace *(nirvana),* the end of all the misery of mundane existence *(samsara).* In short, he becomes the very Brahman."

"This Devotion to Knowledge is extolled as follows" :

एषा ब्राह्मी स्थितिः पार्थ नैनां प्राप्य विमुह्यति ।
स्थित्वास्यामन्तकालेऽपि ब्रह्मनिर्वाणमृच्छति ॥ ७२ ॥

72. *esā brāhmī sthitiḥ pārtha nainām prāpya vimuhyati*
sthitvāsyām anta-kāle 'pi brahma-nirvāṇam ṛcchati

एषा — this, ब्राह्मी — of Brahman, स्थितिः — state, पार्थ — O Partha, न — not, एनम् — this, प्राप्य — having obtained, विमुह्यति — is deluded, स्थित्वा — being established, अस्याम् — in this, अन्तकाले — in the end of life, अपि — even, ब्रह्मनिर्वाणम् — oneness with Brahman, ऋच्छति — attains.

72. *This is the* Brahmic *state, O Son of Pritha. Attaining this, none is deluded. Being established therein, even at the end of life, one attains to oneness with Brahman.*

To renounce all desires is to end completely the last ventures of one's ego. Renunciation of ego is not a state of dull, meaningless, emptiness. Where the delusory ego has ended, the state of Full-Knowledge or Selfhood has dawned. To realise the Self in one's own bosom is to realise at once the Self which is all-pervading and eternal *(Brahman)*. When the ego has ended, the Consciousness is not known by anybody other than the Eternal, and, as such, the knower of Truth in a brilliant experience of the Self becomes the Self, and, therefore, this state is called Selfhood *(Brahmisthitih)*.

A doubt may still arise that after this realisation we may again fall into the delusion of the ego and the ego's world of imperfections and sorrows. To deny this tragedy, we have been told how, having realised the Self once, no more can the individual fall back into his ancient delusions. This experience of the Self need not necessarily take place in the very youthful days of one's life. Even in old age — nay, even at the last moment of this embodiment — if a seeker can come to experience even for a moment this egoless state of tranquillity and poise, even a passing glimpse of Selfhood is sufficient to gain this *Brahmic* state pointed out in the Vedantic literature.

'Negation of the false and the assertion of the True' is the path that has been indicated in the Upanishads. The very same path, in its practical application, is denoted here in the Geeta in Vyasa's original contribution, the *Karma Yoga*. To work without attachment and desire, egoism and vanity, ever in perfect equilibrium at both success and failure, is to deny the ego its entire field of activity and, unconsciously, to assert the greater truth, the Self. Thus, in technique, Geeta's *Karma Yoga* is not at all different from the Vedantic technique of meditation. But Arjuna got confused and perplexed because he understood Krishna's words too literally and, therefore, in the following chapter, he expresses in the opening lines his mental confusion. The Lord explains the *Karma Yoga* exhaustively in the next chapter.

ॐ तत्सत् इति श्रीमद्भगवद्गीतासूपनिषत्सु ब्रह्मविद्यायां योगशास्त्रे
श्रीकृष्णार्जुन संवादे सांख्ययोगो नाम द्वितीयोध्यायः ।

Om Tat-Sat Iti śrimad bhagawadgitäsüpanisatsu
brahmavidyäyäm yogaśästre Śrikrsnärjunasamväde
sankhyayogo näma dwitiyo adhyäyah

Thus, in the Upanishads of the glorious Bhagawad Geeta in the Science of the Eternal, in the scripture of Yoga, in the dialogue between Sri Krishṇa and Arjuna, the second-discourse ends entilted : THE YOGA OF KNOWLEDGE

This chapter is named *Sankhya Yoga* not in the sense that it is the *Sankhya* philosophy here summarised or borrowed by Krishna. Here the word *Sankhya* is used only in its etymological sense as 'the sequence of logic in any line of correct thinking and the logical enumeration of the arguments based on which a certain intellectual conclusion has been derived.' It is in this sense that the highly philosophical Chapter II of the

Geeta is termed as *Sankhya Yoga* in its epilogue *(sankalpa vakya)**

It is true that in the original *Mahabharata,* the Geeta chapters do not carry this *sankalpa vakya* Commentators differ in attributing to any single individual its authorship. However, it has been accepted that some scholar or scholars analysed the contents of each chapter and gave a title to each. To all students of the Geeta it is indeed a great help. Sankara, however, does not comment upon this portion at all.

* For commentary refer to what has been said at the end on Chapter I.